How To Trade Stocks Using Options: The Dart-Throw Traders Kick A$$ Strategies To Throwing Darts – Picking Stocks – Making Money

WWW.DartThrowTrading.com

Jimmy Slagle

OUR COURSE(S), PRODUCTS AND SERVICES SHOULD BE USED AS LEARNING AIDS ONLY AND SHOULD NOT BE CONSTRUED AS INVESTMENT ADVICE. IF YOU DECIDE TO INVEST REAL MONEY, ALL TRADING DECISIONS ARE YOUR OWN RESPONSIBILITY. BY USING DARTTHROW TRADER INFORMATION ON A LIVE ACCOUNT WITH REAL MONEY THE USER AGREES TO NOT HOLD THE DEVELOPER LIABLE FOR ANY TRADING DECISIONS MADE BY THE USER.

THE DEVELOPER OF THE DART-THROW TRADER – JIMMY SLAGLE WILL NOT BE HELD LIABLE FOR ANY REAL MONEY LOSSES INCURRED THROUGH USE OF THE DART-THROW TRADER SYSTEM.

Additional products and services will be offered for sale.

I wrote this book to describe how I like to structure trades. No statement in this book should be construed as a recommendation to purchase or sell a security, or to provide investment advice. You should understand that I have a significantly different market outlook than most retail investors. You should always consider commissions and taxes prior to making any investment. Options involve risk and are not suitable for all investors. Prior to buying or selling an option, you should receive and read characteristics and risks of standardized options, a document written and provided by the options clearing Corporation (OCC). Copies of this document may also be obtained from your broker or from any exchange on which options are traded. If you choose, you can write to the options clearing Corporation at: 440 S. LaSalle St, Suite 2400 Chicago, IL 60605. You can also download pertinent information about options from their website: www.optionsclearing.com.

Legal Notice

While attempts have been made to verify the information contained within this publication, the author, publisher, and anyone associated with its creation, hereby assume absolutely no responsibility as it pertains to its contents and subject matter; nor with regards to it's usage by the public or in any matters concerning potentially erroneous and/or contradictory information put forth.

Furthermore, the reader agrees to assume all accountability for the usage of any information obtained from it; and therefore, completely absolves Jimmy Slagle, the publishers and any associates involved, of any liability for it whatsoever.

Disclaimer

I WANT TO BE PERFECTLY CLEAR ABOUT ONE IMPORTANT FACT; NOT ONE OF THE 52 TRADES DESCRIBED IN THIS BOOK WERE EVER EXECUTED IN A LIVE ACCOUNT. EACH TRADE WAS COMMENTED ON AND HYPOTHETICALLY SIMULATED UNDER REAL MARKET CONDITIONS AND ACTUAL SECURTIES PRICES WERE USED IN THE FORMULATION OF THE OUTCOMES. SINCE THE TRADES HAVE NOT BEEN EXECUTED, THE RESULTS MAY HAVE UNDER OR OVER COMPENSATED FOR THE IMPACT, IF ANY, OF CERTAIN MARKET FACTORS, SUCH AS LACK OF LIQUIDITY. SIMULATED TRADING PROGRAMS IN GENERAL ARE ALSO SUBJECT TO THE FACT THAT THEY ARE DESIGNED WITH THE BENEFIT OF HINDSIGHT. NO REPRESENTATION IS BEING MADE THAT ANY ACCOUNT WILL OR IS LIKELY TO ACHIEVE PROFIT OR LOSSES SIMILAR TO THOSE SHOWN.

The information presented within this ebook solely and fully represents the views of the author as of the date of publication. Any slight to, or potential misrepresentation of, any peoples or companies are entirely unintentional. As a result of changing information, conditions or contexts, this author reserves the right to alter content or option with impunity. This book is for informational purposes only and the author does not accept any responsibility for any liability resulting from the use of this information. While every attempt has been made to verify the information contained herein, the author and his resellers and affiliates cannot assume any responsibility for errors, inaccuracies, or omissions.

U.S. GOVERNMENT REQUIRED DISCLAIMER

OPTION TRADING CAN OFFER LARGE POTENTIAL REWARDS; BUT ALSO LARGE POTENTIAL RISK. YOU MUST BE AWARE OF THE RISKS AND BE WILLING TO ACCEPT THEM IN ORDER TO TRADE OR INVEST IN OPTIONS. NEVER TRADE WITH MONEY YOU CAN'T AFFORD TO LOSE. THIS IS NEITHER A SOLICITATION NOR AN OFFER TO BUY OR SELL CURRENCIES, FUTURES, STOCKS OR OPTIONS. NO REPRESENTATION IS BEING MADE THAT ANY ACCOUNT WILL OR IS LIKELY TO ACHIEVE PROFITS OR LOSSES SIMILAR TO THOSE DISCUSSED IN THIS MATERIAL. PAST PERFORMANCE OF ANY TRADING SYSTEM OR METHODOLOGY IS NOT NECESSARILY INDICATIVE OF FUTURE RESULTS.

CFTC RULE 4.41 – HYPOTHETICAL OR SIMULATED PERFORMANCE RESULTS HAVE CERTAIN LIMITATIONS. UNLIKE AN ACTUAL PERFORMANCE RECORD, SIMULATED RESULTS DO NOT REPRESENT ACTUAL TRADING. ALSO, SINCE THE TRADES HAVE NOT BEEN EXECUTED, THE RESULTS MAY HAVE UNDER OR OVER COMPENSATED FOR THE IMPACT, IF ANY, OF CERTAIN MARKET FACTORS, SUCH AS LACK OF LIQUIDITY. SIMULATED TRADING PROGRAMS IN GENERAL ARE ALSO SUBJECT TO THE FACT THAT THEY ARE DESIGNED WITH THE BENEFIT OF HINDSIGHT. NO REPRESENTATION IS BEING MADE THAT ANY ACCOUNT WILL OR IS LIKELY TO ACHIEVE PROFIT OR LOSSES SIMILAR TO THOSE SHOWN.

Dedicated with gratitude:

To my amazing wife Nancy, without whom this book could never have been written; it was her courage, love, support and words that enabled me to take a concept and bring it to life. It has been said that behind every successful man is a good woman; I would suggest that ***beside*** every successful man is a strong, patient, loving supportive, tolerant woman (rolling her eyes). I love you honey.

To my cherished daughters who are my inspiration, the reason I get out of bed every morning and do the things that I sometimes do not want to do. All three are gifts from God and I am grateful that He chose me to be their father.

To my parents for showing me that it doesn't matter what you do, just do it with all your heart. For teaching me, by example, that family is one of the most powerful forces in the universe. For teaching me that you should always give more than is asked of you, even when you think you can't.

To my sister for answering the phone late one night so many years ago, just to listen to a brother who had lost his way. For never giving up on me, even when it seemed that was the easiest thing to do.

To Rance who saw something in me that even I didn't see. For giving me a shot even though I was untrained and untested. For supporting me when things looked bleak and for looking the other way when he had to.

To every person I have had the opportunity to stand in front of and share my vision.

To everyone who ever said "no" to me or didn't believe.

To God my Heavenly Father, who has given me a vision so great it was doomed for failure without Him in it; the courage to step up when I was all alone and the faith to see it through.

"At the end of the day, week, month or year a stock is either going to go up in price, down in price or stay the same... it can't do anything else."

- Jimmy Slagle, The Dart-Throw Trader

Preface.

This book, if you can call it a book, is actually a year-long journal of sorts, chronicling a challenge that I had given myself in 2004. In reality, it took me two years to step up to the challenge, and commit to doing the work involved.

This book is really about journey of self-discovery. It's about taking an idea and running with it. It's about having an argument and proving my point. It's about being right.

I didn't write this book to teach you how to make $1 million dollars in a week or to day-trade your way to riches. I wrote this book to prove a point and to prove that whatever we choose to do--whether it is investing, trading, or any other major career decision-- we must educate ourselves first.

Education is an ongoing process; true learners share a commitment to life-long learning, a desire to continually grow in knowledge and expertise within their chosen fields.

The most fascinating thing about the markets that I discovered is that they continue to evolve. Stocks hit new highs, stocks hit new lows, new products are introduced new methods are theorized; at times the markets can become overwhelming. Other times, many investors just merely want to close their eyes and have somebody else do it for them.

What I would suggest is that you take this book, this year-long behavioral analysis of the financial markets, and use it as a foundation for your continuing education into this amazing field of study.

My hope is that somewhere in the pages of this book, you will find that "one thing": the kernel of truth in which you can latch onto, dig deeper into, and create a home for yourself.

Maybe it's one core strategy, maybe its one core idea, maybe it's just one different way of looking at the markets than you have in the past which will ultimately help you to become a better trader, a better investor, and maybe even a better person.

My wish for you is that you will get something out of this book, something that will enable you to become more secure in your own approach to the financial markets. I wish for you the best of success. I wish that all of your trades will be winners. I wish that you, during this educational journey, will make a commitment to helping one other person become a better investor as well.

As you read through the trades, and the commentary that accompanies each one, I want you to remember something very important about what you read: the trade commentary was lifted from my journal, verbatim.

This means some of the sentences will run together, punctuation may be non-existent or even wrong. There will be incomplete sentences and a number of other disturbing things if you are a student of grammar and punctuation.

I lifted the commentary from my trade journal and, like most traders, I sometimes think in incomplete sentences. I lifted the notes exactly as they were written 90% of the time because this was a discovery journal and not a doctoral thesis.

Most of the commentary is as it was written at the time of the trade. I did leave some things out either because they were not relevant to the trade or not relevant to the idea. That is why you will sometimes run across sentences that abruptly change direction.

To rewrite the commentary and try to "clean it up" would have stolen from the honesty of the moment and the thought process at the time of evaluation.

I promise that as you read through the trade commentary it will make sense in the moment, in spite of the punctuation and grammatical errors.

Oh, and one more thing. If you take anything I talk about in this book out of context and attempt to apply it to your own personal trades without adequate financial guidance, there is certainly a possibility that you will lose money, so my very best advice is to

1. **Never invest with money you can't afford to lose.**
2. **If you are confused… see number 1.**

Jimmy Slagle
The Dart-Throw Trader

**"We Must Respond...
When Others React."**

- Jimmy Slagle, The Dart-Throw Trader

Contents

"A blindfolded monkey throwing darts at a newspaper's financial pages could select a portfolio that would do just as well as one carefully selected by experts."

- Burton G. Malkiel

Section 1 – What The *&%$#@ Is a Dart-Throw Trader?

"And what I am interested in is investing in people"

- Arthur Rock

Who is Jimmy Slagle? (www.jimmyslagle.com)

My first experience in financial markets occurred in 1986; at the time I thought it was just another class. In hindsight, it was one of the best decisions I ever made.

After graduating high school and moving out from under my parents' watchful eyes, I went to college to become a pilot. I attended a small college in the great state of Arkansas. (I tell you this to prove a point: even with my "Arkansas" education I was able to become a successful investor.)

In my pursuit of a pilot's license, I was fortunate enough to attend a school that had just started its flight program. This meant that there were few students involved, which pretty much gave me unlimited access to planes and flight time.

To make a long story short, I was able to get all of my flight requirements completed in just over 2 years. The upshot is that I'd satisfied all the flight requisites for a degree in aviation, yet hadn't made a dent in my "core curriculum" required to get a degree (things like English, history and other basics.) My junior year I was preparing for registration and I decided that I would take some filler courses (read: easy A's) so I could improve my GPA and get on to the friendly skies.

As I was browsing through the available courses at the registrar's office, I ran across one that I thought would be a no-brainer, based on my family history and "extensive financial market knowledge". It was titled "Personal Investing". I was thinking Easy "A", so I registered for it.
I will never forget the first day of class. I remember it so well because it was on Tuesday morning at 10:00 A.M. And the reason I remember that was because my last two years of college I only took Tuesday/Thursday classes (I didn't want to cut into my weekend time). That morning's class is still so vivid in my mind because it was the day I found my true calling.

I remember sitting in that classroom with about 35 other students waiting for our instructor to arrive. Most of my fellow classmates were fraternity brothers and we were having a good time speculating on the future outcome of this class. In the midst of our fun, our instructor arrived. I will never forget this man and the impression he made.

He walked into the room, an older gentleman probably late 50's early 60's. He carried a worn brown leather briefcase and carried himself with an air of confidence. As he began to settle in you could hear the buzz beginning around the room. Most of us were discussing, "How in the world could this man teach us about the markets and how to make money"? I mean, come on; this guy has probably been a teacher most of his adult life. What could he possibly have to share with us about the real world?

And then it began...

He opened his brown leather briefcase and pulled out a few papers and a worn, off-white textbook. This textbook had significance because I, and everyone else in the class, was in possession of the exact same book.

However, mine was white and still shrink-wrapped.

He stepped to the front of his desk and leaned back; in his left hand he was holding that off-white textbook. He began to flip through the pages of the book, grinning and surveying the room. He began to explain to us how this was a wonderful textbook written and edited by talented writers and editors. How it was filled with terms, definitions, examples and theory. Then he abruptly slammed the book shut and promptly through it into the trash.

At that moment I glanced down at my white, shrink-wrapped textbook and laughed. I was thinking to myself, "Great, I just spent $80.00 on this book and my professor just threw his into the trash". Best-case scenario: I can take my book back to the university bookstore and sell it back. However now it is a used book and the best I am going to get is maybe $40.00. Fifteen minutes into class and I have already lost 50% of the value of my investment. Things weren't looking too good in my "personal investing" class.

Then he explained to us why he did what he did. He told us that it was, in fact, an excellent book and that it was filled with marvelous theory. He stressed the point theory. He explained to us that theory was great to talk about and debate, but wasn't applicable to the real world. He explained to us that the markets didn't trade logically, most of the time they were driven by emotions, most prevalent of these being fear and greed.

From there he proceeded to explain how the class was to be conducted. Surprisingly, he wasn't a lifelong college professor.

He was a lifelong investor, and was teaching this course to share with impressionable young minds his 30+ years of being in the trenches.

He informed us that he was going to give all of us in the room $100,000.00 (play money, of course) to trade with. He was going to spend the next 3 months teaching us everything he knew about selecting stocks, analyzing them, balancing our portfolio based on our risk profiles, and putting in trigger points to exit on profits and losses. Basically he was going to teach us how to make money.

His grading system was right up my competitive alley. At the end of the term whoever had the most money got an "A" and the rest of the class would be graded on a curve. That was pretty much all I needed to hear. I was ready to begin.

Thus began my journey into the financial world, a journey that I am still on today.

Fast forward to May 1989...

I am now living in Atlanta, Georgia. (How I got here is another story for another time.) I am working at small, family oriented health club. I am a single 23-year-old male in the big city of Atlanta, desperately trying to find my place in this world.

Although health club membership sales paid well, I realized that this was not the career path that I was called to pursue for a lifetime.

Each day I scoured the want ads, my contacts, and the "network" for job leads that would ultimately shape my destiny... It was through a small ad in the newspaper that I met Scott.

Scott wasn't much older than I, yet he appeared to be extremely successful. Scott was a Vice-President at one of the country's oldest mutual fund companies and after two intense interviews he said the following words... "Jimmy, if you are serious about this opportunity, I want you to call me on Monday at precisely 1:30. If you call you will have an opportunity, if you don't... well, it was nice meeting you.

Scott took me under his wing and began to educate me on the inner-workings of the mutual fund industry. I was hooked. One day Scott invited me to lunch and laid an offer on the table. He asked me if I would be interested in coming to work with him. He told me that with his knowledge and experience combined with my enthusiasm, we could take over the world with the split being 60/40. How could I refuse an offer like that?

Thus began my career in the financial industry... October 1989.

A lot has happened since October 1989.

The firm I started with got sued by every state's attorneys general and my choices were to stay on with a sinking ship or leave the firm and look for opportunity elsewhere. I chose to start an independent financial advisory practice with an associate from the firm. We set up our private practice, moved our securities licenses with an independent broker-dealer, and began to offer our clients any investment vehicle they wanted. During our first year of private practice we attended our broker-dealer's annual conference. This is when I met Jeff.

Jeff had a reputation as the most successful, prestigious broker at the company, and it became my mission to get to know him at a personal level. Over the next several months, I logged countless hours (and dollars) on long-distance phone calls and plane tickets in my dogged pursuit of what I perceived to be Jeff's extensive knowledge of the markets. My motives, of course, were entirely self-serving: I was secretly planning my coup to replace Jeff as the company's Top Dog.

Meanwhile, my business partner back in Atlanta calls me at home one evening to inform me that he had just inherited a large sum of money (mid six figures) and no longer needed to work for a living. It was a surreal moment, and once again I was faced with a choice... do I continue with my investment advisory practice independently, or do I take my knowledge and client base and head for the corporate world?

Thus began the second phase of my financial industry career... March 1994.

At this point, I had about five years of stock market experience under my belt. I was bulletproof, invincible, and ripe for a fall, so I proceeded to make the second biggest mistake of my life: I decided to go back into the corporate arena. I don't know how many of you have ever been self employed and then went back to work for someone else... It was a nightmare. I could not wait to get out of that mess.

So I decided to do what any man would do: I'd go out and conquer the world on my own. I knew that my investment advisory practice was not going to pay the bills (I didn't have a clue of how to run a business). So I began to look for a way to make money. To that end, I began to attend every seminar I could find: real estate, 900 numbers, travel agencies, you name it. I went. I was looking for a way to make truckloads of money without having to work. Sounds great in theory, but it doesn't pay the bills. The good news is my wife was working as a teacher and pretty much supported us as I tried and failed to conquer the world.

Then, like an iceberg hitting the Titanic, I was struck with this thought: discover what you love to do and then find someone to pay you to do it. My next-door neighbor worked in the public school system as the director of adult education and offered to pay me to teach classes on debt elimination and investing. I jumped at the chance and began to teach others how to get out of debt and begin to invest. I thought: this is amazing! I will get paid to teach others, be viewed as an expert, and I can use this as a stepping-stone to rekindle my investment advisory practice. Brilliant.

For the next two years, I taught others how to take control of their financial lives and I was having a ball. In July of 1996 I met a man who I believed was going to propel me to financial freedom. A cab driver.

Now this was no ordinary cab driver, no sir, this was a man who had become a self-made millionaire by investing in real estate and the stock market and was apparently willing to teach me how to do the same. Just think: no boss, no 9-to-5, just back up the truck of cash and give me my free time to enjoy it. Who could ask for more?

So in July of 1996 I made yet another decision. I would do something very profound. I decided to take the money that we had and some borrowed funds from my family, go invest in the markets, and become a professional trader.

At the dawn of 1997 I quit my job and began to trade full time in the stock market. I had spent the previous six months studying at the feet of a cab driver. Using what I learned from him, this is what I was able to do: I took roughly seventeen thousand dollars... (I did pretty well; check this out.) I took seventeen thousand dollars all the way to zero in six months.

It was very hard to do that, even in a tepid economy. My results, then, are even more impressive considering we were in a very bullish market at that time. How in the world, as a former broker and investment advisor, could I possibly pull that off? Simple. As a broker I was never taught how to trade; I was taught how to sell. I was taught how to make cold calls. And then there's the obvious question: how many cab drivers do you know who are actually making any real money in the markets?

I took roughly seventeen thousand dollars to zero. That was a very frustrating experience for me as I am sure you can imagine. For you, maybe that kind of money is nothing or maybe it's a lot, for me it was everything. It was all I had. The bad side of this for me (as if losing money is not bad enough) was that my wife did not know that I had done this, she thought I was doing well (because that is what I had led her to believe).

I was in a mess here and I needed to find a way out fast. So once again I did what any man would do. I stepped up and found a way to make some money to pay the bills while I could figure a way out of this mess.

I took a job throwing newspapers. It didn't pay a lot of money and I was ashamed and embarrassed; however I did what I had to do. This job would allow me to pay the bills and still have time to study the markets to find a way out.

One morning, while running my newspaper route, I was startled out of my routine by the ringing of the market bell over the radio. When I heard that very distinctive sound I knew one of two things was taking place: I was either very late running my route or still home dreaming. As it would turn out neither was true; I was listening to an ad on the radio discussing a new way to trade in the financial markets.

I will always remember that radio ad.

It said, "Come to this free seminar and we will teach you how to make money in the market safely, stress free, with a low defined amount of risk, regardless of market direction". That appealed to me. When I arrived home that morning my first call was to register for the class that I had heard advertised.

One week later I was in a hotel room on a Wednesday night in July of 1997. I was sitting there waiting for the instructor to teach me how to make money in the market safely, regardless of market direction. I was sitting on the front row and this guy walks up to the front of the room, spun himself around and introduced himself as Rance Masheck.

For about the first hour of this three-hour seminar, the information Rance gave the class was nothing new to me, but the last two hours changed my life forever.

At the end of that three-hour seminar Rance gave everyone in the room a life-changing directive. He challenged everyone to continue their education in the markets and give him the opportunity to teach them all they could learn.

Three months later, I was in Boston attending a two-day, knowledge intensive, live market-action trading class with three of the most respected traders in the industry.

The day after I arrived home from Boston I began contacting my client base to explore the new opportunities in trading I had learned. Most of my clients rejected my newfound approach and brushed my suggestions aside. Determined to prove that my newly-acquired market knowledge was the answer to many of my clients' financial problems, I initiated a personal challenge to myself.

I opened a small trading account that I would only use for trading the new strategies I had been taught. My purpose was to share the results with my clients and then begin to move them into this newly-discovered style of trading. After just four months of trading, I comfortably quit my newspaper delivery gig. I had found the "Holy Grail". I had found what I had been searching for from the moment I bought my first share of stock way back in 1986.

I was now obsessed with finding the right combinations of trades and strategies that would enable me to reach a point where I could do what I wanted, when I wanted, without having to ask anyone else. To accomplish this task, I approached my original Boston instructors and asked for all the help they would be willing to offer... books, classes, tapes, conversations, anything they could suggest. Anything they offered or suggested, I took. As my knowledge began to increase my mistakes began to decline. I began to share my results and breakthroughs with those who had introduced me to this type of trading, and was consequently invited to share what I had learned with others.

Thus began the third phase of my financial industry career... January 1998.

In January of 1998 I taught my first trading class in Dallas, Texas and never looked back.

From January 1998 through July of 2006 I traveled the country teaching individual investors how to make better trading decisions based on logic (which stemmed from education) rather than on emotion.

In that 8-year span I taught over 400 live investment training programs to over 20,000 students in the United States and Canada. I enjoyed almost every minute (except for a few specific ones that I will reveal later) that I spent with students.

It is an amazing joy watching the face of an investor light up when the proverbial light-bulb comes on. I lived for those moments when the education and the student collided; when their new knowledge transitioned from theory to practical application.

Maybe one day I will write a book of those eight years, maybe not, but I will always treasure the people and personalities I met and the stories they told.

In June of 2006 I walked away from the teaching-and-training phase of my career, maybe because of travel burnout (living in a hotel room week to week gets old). Most importantly, my third daughter was due to be born and I promised myself, and my wife, that I would be fully present for the miracle that was coming.

Thus began the fourth phase of my financial career...

This is the phase that I am living now, the phase that allows me to be a full time husband to my wife and father to my three amazing girls.

This is the phase where I act upon a personal challenge that I issued in 2004 (but had neither the time nor the inclination to act upon). This is the phase where I discover more about who I am and how much I know (and don't know) about trading and investing.

This is the phase where I discover more about my students than I ever did when I was face-to-face with them in training rooms across the country.

This is the phase where I invite you to momentarily set aside most of what you know about the markets as I take you on an amazing journey of discovery: how accepting the truth of the markets will make you a better trader than listening to the talking heads on TV and radio as they suck the life and oxygen out of us all.

The Misunderstood History of Throwing Darts and Making Money

In 1965 (the year before I was born) an amazing financial scholar wrote his doctoral theses titled: The Behavior of Stock Market Prices. This oft quoted and much debated piece of work was the beginning (although indirectly) of America's and probably the world's fascination of Throwing Darts to Pick Stocks.

When Dr. Eugene Fama wrote this now famous document, I am sure (and I intend to ask) he had no idea the cultural phenomenon he was about to inspire.

With your permission, I would like to take you down a historical road of investing that will reveal many surprises around each significant corner.

Our journey begins in 1965 with the publishing of Dr. Fama's thesis in the Journal of Business Volume 38, No. 1 January 1965, page 34-105.

In his doctoral theses Fama proposed the following question: *"To what extent can the past history of the common stock price be used to make meaningful predictions concerning the future price of a stock?"*

According to Fama, at that particular moment in time, there were to prevailing answers:

1. Although there are many different chartist theories, they all make the same basic assumption. That is, they all assume that the past behavior of a security's price is rich in information concerning its future behavior. History repeats itself in that "patterns" of past price behavior will tend to recur in the future.

If, through careful analysis of price charts, one develops an understanding of these "patterns," this can be used to predict the future behavior of prices and, in this way, increase expected gains.

2. By contrast, the theory of random walks says that the future path of the price level of a security is no more predictable than the path of a series of cumulated random numbers.

In statistical terms, the theory says that successive price changes are independent, identically distributed random variables. Simply put, this implies that the series of price changes has no memory (that is, the past cannot be used to predict the future in any meaningful way).

In his 70-page Ph.D. Thesis, *The Behavior of Stock Market Prices*, Fama suggested that by utilizing the tremendous resources that a major brokerage firm can muster for researching industry trends, effects of interest rates, accounting data (and by talking to managers of firms, consulting economists and politicians), a security analyst should be able to consistently outperform a randomly selected portfolio of securities of the same general risk.

Since in any given situation, the analyst has a fifty percent chance of outperforming the random selection (even if his skills are negligible), Fama's conclusion was that the analysts do not consistently outperform a market.

Based on his work and the assumptions contained therein, Fama coined the famous phrase "Efficient Market" Theory.

The theory proposed that all investors (professional or not) have access to, and can act on, all relevant information around any given stock as it becomes available.

This theory suggests that whatever individual stock information is available to one investor is available to all investors (except, of course, insider information, but insider trading is illegal).

Since everyone has the same information about a stock, the price of a stock should reflect the knowledge and expectations of all investors.

The upshot is that an investor should not be able to beat the market since there is no way for him/her to know something about a stock that isn't already reflected in the stock's price. Proponents of this theory do not try to pick stocks that are going to be winners; instead, they simply try to match the market's performance.

In 1965, that theory makes some sense. In 2009, possibly even more, because of the abundance of information available.

However, I am not here to debate the merits of efficient market theory; I am only here to give the history of the proverbial stock market dartboard.

Because of the controversial content of Fama's book, it quickly began to circulate through the professional investment community.

The idea that every stock's current price was a reflection of the current fundamental value of the company (because all investors had access to "known" information) was unpalatable to those who claim that they could anticipate future price swings in an asset's price.

What professional investors and traders inferred from Fama's work was that they (professionals) could not beat the market, because any available information is already incorporated in the current price of any given asset.

Disdain for the book among Fama's detractors grew. At the 1968 Institutional Investor conference, one irate money manager insisted that what he and others did for investors had to be worth more than ***just throwing darts at the Wall Street Journal.***

Momentum for Fama's work continued at a steady pace. By 1973, five years after the irate money manager's outburst at the Institutional Investor conference, Burton G. Malkiel published his book, *A Random Walk Down Wall Street*, which clearly lays out several of the principles of the academic research described by Fama.

In the book, the Princeton Professor theorized that ***"a blindfolded monkey throwing darts at a newspaper's financial pages could select a portfolio that would do just as well as one carefully selected by experts."***

Fast-forward to October 04, 1988, when the Wall Street Journal began a contest that was inspired by Burton Malkiel's book.

The Journal set out to create an entertaining contest to test Malkiel's theory while simultaneously giving its readers some new investment ideas in the process.

With Wall Street Journal staff members assuming the role of the monkeys (the Journal listed liability insurance as one reason for not going all the way and actually using live monkeys), the contest quickly became a popular feature for the Journal and drew much interest and commentary from journalists, investors, and academics.

Initially the contest was to last a month, but recognizing that the publication of the contest was creating a "publicity effect" on the pro's stock picks, the Journal began measuring the results over a six-month period beginning in 1990.

The rules changed at various times during the contest, but were largely contained to the following format. Each month four "professionals" are given the opportunity to select one stock (long or short) for the following six months. The stocks must meet the following criteria.

1. Market capitalization must be at least $50 million.

2. Daily trading volume must be at least $100,000.
3. Price must be at least $2.
4. Stocks must be listed on the NYSE, AMEX, or NASDAQ and any foreign stocks must have an ADR.

The pro's stock picks competed against four stocks (usually chosen by Journal staffers) flinging darts at the Wall Street Journal stock tables pasted to a board. At the end of six months, the price appreciation for the pro's stocks and the dartboard stocks were compared (dividends are not included). The two best performing pros were invited back for the next contest and two new professionals were added.

On November 27, 1992 the television news show 20/20 decided to jump on the bandwagon and had John Stossel interview Professor Burton Malkiel, among others, during a segment about the stock-picking-dartboard phenomenon.

The transcript of that segment can be read below...

John Stossel Dart Throw on 20/20 transcript. Source... http://ifa.com/Library/Support/Articles/Popular/NewsShowTranscript.htm

November 27, 1992

ANNOUNCER: Cashing in on the stock market can be easier than you think. Experts offer all kinds of advice. Did you ever meet a hotshot analyst? Just look at what John Stossel discovered.

JOHN STOSSEL: The odds are you would be better picking stocks this way; throwing darts at the stock table.

ANNOUNCER: It's true. And tonight, John proves it. Watch this report, and you might say, Who Needs Experts? Those stories tonight, November 27, 1992 after this brief message.

HUGH DOWNS: For people who have never dabbled in it, the stock market can be very intimidating. So many companies to choose from, so much money to be made or lost. So if you want to try your luck, what is the soundest way to choose stocks? Many people, of course, turn to the most obvious sources of advice, the expert analysts, who work for stockbrokers or investment newsletters or mutual funds. But a while ago, John Stossel discovered that some of the experts may be selling hot air. As he reported back then, you may do just as well with a good set of darts.

JOHN STOSSEL: Want to make some money or just stay ahead of inflation? Most financial experts will tell you the single best investment you could make is putting your money in the stock market.

PROFESSOR BURTON MALKIEL, PRINCETON UNIVERSITY: Historically, the stock market is like a gambling casino with the odds in your favor. Over the long pull, stocks are given something like nine and a half to ten percent compounded per year. The banks have probably given you something in the order of four to five.

JOHN STOSSEL: And the ten percent beats inflation.

PROFESSOR MALKIEL: The ten percent beats inflation and beats it by a great deal.

JOHN STOSSEL: So, if the stock market is such a good investment, then it's logical that we should listen carefully to those experts, the men and women, mostly men, actually, who make their living studying stocks and sharing their wisdom with us. You see them on news programs and financial advice shows.

STOCK BROKER 1: Stick with Pepsico; it's a defensive type of stock with very good growth characteristics.

JOHN STOSSEL: They really sound like they know what they are talking about.

DENNIS KELLEY, JANNEY MONTGOMERY SCOTT: I like Schering Plough, a stock that came from 65 down to 60, and Georgia Pacific, I had great success with that.

JOHN STOSSEL: So it makes sense to go to these experts for advice.

PROFESSOR MALKIEL: No, it doesn't.

JOHN STOSSEL: Economist Burton Malkiel wrote, "A Random Walk Down Wall Street." In the book, he says, yes, Wall Street analysts call and visit individual companies. They study the balance sheets, new products, marketing techniques, but this gives them no advantage he says, because what they learn is information all the analysts have. What they don't have is knowledge of the other factor that moves the market; news events. But since news is unpredictable, so is the market. Therefore, he says, the advice produced by Wall Street experts has little value.

PROFESSOR MALKIEL: Most of this is just absolute nonsense. Most of it is really designed to get people to trade more than they should.

JOHN STOSSEL: Trading is how the brokerage firms make their money. Every time they buy and sell stock, they charge you a commission. A big part of that commission goes to pay for the so-called expert analyst, who visit the companies, study all the numbers and works full-time coming up with this impressive sounding recommendation.

STOCK BROKER 2: The cyclicals, the autos,...forget them. They won't perform and therefore any rallies I'd sell if I still had them.

JOHN STOSSEL: The big research departments help justify that image of wisdom the firms project in their commercials.

SHEARSON LEHMAN COMMERCIAL: We're number one in investment research. Talk with us.
PRUDENTIAL COMMERCIAL: So for peace of mind, investment advice, and your future on the Rock.

MERRILL LYNCH COMMERICAL: At Merrill Lynch we know that risk can be dealt with. It can be managed.

JOHN STOSSELL: Sounds impressive? But the surprising thing is that despite all of this complicated sounding research, despite these rooms filled with people in suits studying the numbers, the advice that comes out of most of these big brokerage firms is so consistently mediocre that odds are you would do better picking stocks this way, by throwing darts at the stock tables. It's hard to believe that this would be a better way to pick stocks. But the people who chart the brokerage firms recommendations say the numbers don't lie.

JOHN STOSSEL: Over the years, the 500 stocks that make up the Standard and Poor's average had done just as well as the stocks that brokers suggested we buy.

JOHN STOSSEL [throwing darts]: Oops, CBS. Oh, I also hit Munsing Wear. I've worn their underwear and Grumman, I ride their buses. This is known in the business as having a monkey throw darts at the stock tables and, remarkable as it is, this method often does better than following the experts recommendations.

JOHN STOSSEL: But the researcher really believes that he's right, doesn't he?

PROFESSOR MALKIEL: I believe they do, hope springs eternal.

JOHN STOSSEL: So all these experts are fooling themselves?

PROFESSOR MALKIEL: It's like giving up a belief in Santa Claus. Even though you know Santa Claus doesn't exist, you kind of cling to that belief. I'm not saying that is a scam. They generally believe they can do it. The evidence is, however, that they can't.

JOHN STOSSEL: Surprisingly, no one kept track of brokerage house recommendations until recently. Now it's all laid out in John Dorfman`s column in the Wall Street Journal. He started it five years ago.

JOHN DORFMAN: It's been amazing me for decades. Brokers have been giving people advice and no one ever measured what would happen to you if you took it.

JOHN STOSSEL: The journal paid Zack's Investment Research of Chicago to gather all those impressive sounding recommendations from 10 of the biggest brokerage firms and then calculate how they did compared to the market as a whole. Or more precisely, the stocks that make up the Standard and Poor's 500. Most of the brokerage firm's results were embarrassing. For the year ending June 30th, the Standard and Poor's was up seven percent, but seven out of the ten big firms did worse than that. We also asked Zacks to track 20/20's 20-stock dart throw.

BEN ZACKS: And then we'll measure the three months and 12 months performance and see how this compares to what the 20/20's portfolio did.

JOHN STOSSEL: Over the one-year period, our stocks did pretty well. We were up 17 percent. That beat the expert recommendations from nine out of the 10 big brokerage firms. All that money the experts spend, visiting companies, studying the numbers, led to advice in this case was less useful than tossing darts.

JOHN STOSSEL: So, are they stupid? Are they looking at the wrong things? Are they just spinning wheels?

JOHN DORFMAN: Well, let's just say that, they may not be stupid, but they may not be any brighter than you.

JOHN STOSSEL: The results over the years were different. Some years better, others worse, but most times since the Wall Street Journal started tracking the experts, the Standard and Poor's average did better than most of the famous firms.

JOHN STOSSEL: We wanted to ask the brokerage firms about this. Why should anyone listen to their important sounding advice, given their poor track record? That's what we wanted to ask them, but not one of the big New York brokerage firms would agree to talk to us about this. I guess I could understand why.

JOHN STOSSEL: We did talk to money manager, Robert Stovall, who used to run research departments EF Hutton and Dean Witter-Reynolds. He defended the experts.

ROBERT STOVALL: One third of the money managers tend to beat the market every year.

JOHN STOSSEL: Two thirds do worse.

ROBERT STOVALL: Two thirds do worse, but it's different ones each time.

JOHN STOSSEL: Why do these brokerage firms have these big research departments if they don't make money [for their clients]?

ROBERT STOVALL: Everybody has a boss. Professionals won't buy Coca-Cola or some other stock unless they have reports in the file produced by well-known analysts. So if something goes wrong with the stock they buy and they show their boss, hey, I've got a big file on this stock. All these analysts say it was a good one. Something went wrong. That's known as prudence.

JOHN STOSSEL: So even if the research is lousy, it protects them.

ROBERT STOVALL: That's right.

JOHN STOSSEL: So, where does this leave you, should you have some money to invest?
PROFESSOR MALKIEL: And I think everyone should probably have at least some of their assets in the stock market.

PROFESSOR MALKIEL: My philosophy is not to trade, not to listen to your broker who says sell this, buy that, but rather to buy-and-hold a diversified group of securities.

JOHN STOSSEL: The most practical way to do that is to buy what is called an index fund. Some of these own as many as four thousand different stocks. So by buying them, it's like buying the entire market; or, if you like gambling, try the dart technique. You could hit some bad stocks and lose money, but remember, the odds are that if you use a dart, you'll do at least as well as most of America's biggest and richest brokerage firms.

BARBARA WALTERS: Okay. So, how did the stocks do this year?

JOHN STOSSEL: For the first three quarters of this year, the market as a whole is up about three percent. Our dart portfolio is up 20 percent.

BARBARA WALTERS: That's very good. How did the brokers do?

JOHN STOSSEL: The brokers have done well, as well. They, on average, are up 10 percent.

BARBARA WALTERS: Not as good as the darts?

JOHN STOSSEL: No, but they have been hot, and of the big firms, only two of them worse than average.
BARBARA WALTERS: But there are some investment funds and newsletters and mutual funds?

JOHN STOSSEL: Yeah, none of the experts are very "expert". I didn't mean to single out the brokerage firms, but the mutual funds for example, the averages are up three percent. They lost money this year.
BARBARA WALTERS: But John, I am always reading about people who done so terrifically well. You know, you look at the names and...

JOHN STOSSEL: You read about them when they do well. That year, they're hot. You don't read about the other years.

BARBARA WALTERS: So the moral of the story is to diversify?

JOHN STOSSEL: Diversify, and hold on to it, don't trade.

BARBARA WALTERS: Or learn how to play darts, :-).

The Wall Street Journal Dart-Board Contest ran from 1988 – 2001. Sadly the contest was retired in 2001. The Wall Street Journal never really said why the contest was retired; they only hinted that maybe after 14 years it had simply run its course.

So now you know the history of the infamous Stock Picking Dart Board.

The Dart Board Time line.

Fama	IIC	Malkiel	Contest	20/20	Argument	Proven	Challenge
1965	1968	1973	1988	1992	2004	2006	2012

1965 – Eugene Fama writes "Behavior of Stock Market Prices" coins the term - "Efficient Market". He basically says that traders can't beat the market because news is already priced into the stock.

1968 – An irate money manager at the Institutional Investor Conference says: "That what he and other's did for investors had to be worth more than just throwing darts at the Wall Street Journal".

1973 – Burton Malkiel writes his book, A Random Walk Down Wall Street and is quoted from his book saying: "A blindfolded monkey throwing darts at a newspapers financial pages could select a portfolio that would do just as well as one carefully selected by experts".

1988 – October 4, Wall Street Journal Begins the Dart Board stock-picking column pairing pros against the dart board. It runs until 2001.

1992 – November 27, 20/20 does a segment about the dart board and interviews Burton Malkiel.

2002 – March 28, Wall Street Journal Dart Board Contest Ends after 14 years.

2004 – I have an argument with a student in New York and say "if you know what you are doing you can throw darts and make money".
2006 – I test the dartboard theory and do 52 trades (1/week) and produce a 222% ROR. Growing a $5,000 account to $16,110

2009 – The book is released to the public.

2012 – The $100,000.00 Dart-Throw Charity Challenge Begins. Visit www.DartThrowTrading.com for Details.

"While one person hesitates because he feels inferior, the other is busy making mistakes and becoming superior."

- Henry C. Link

How A Simple Argument Birthed The Dart-Throw Trader

The Dart-Throw Trader was born out of two very specific encounters that I had with two former students.

1. A trading student from Chicago, who took 10 years to achieve his goal of getting a financial education because he couldn't afford the cost of tuition.

2. An angry student in New York who claimed that the only way anyone could consistently make money in the markets was they had to be "Right" all the time.

These two events coming together sent me on a quest, beginning in July 2005, to discover, once and for all, what was missing in the financial education arena.

So I spent two years surveying more people than I thought I could, asking more questions than I probably should have, and picking more brains than a zombie from Night of the Living Dead.

One of the most enlightening discoveries made during this two year quest was that 71% of the people I surveyed shared with me that they had spent more money on education than the education, in turn, made for them.

I found this to be an amazingly lopsided statistic. Does that mean that the education was not good, or did it mean the student didn't apply what was taught?

More questions to uncover…

So I asked, and here is what I was told. The top three reasons why the education that many people have invested their hard earned money into did not produce the desired results was because

Inadequate training (#1)

Lack of focus (#2)

Lack of specific skill sets taught (#3)

What that really means, as I dug deeper, is this:

People just like you are investing in (what they believe to be) focused training, yet what they are getting is a set of inadequately-taught generic skills and strategies.

So I asked the following question...

If you could create the perfect trading system, what would it look like? What follows are the results that were shouted back to me:

1. 92% of people surveyed said they are tired of the "sales seminars".
2. 73% said they want a pay-as-you-go system.
3. 88% said they would like to choose from a list of strategies.
4. 79% said they would like to learn from multiple instructors.
5. 74% said they would like to learn 1-3 strategies per month.
6. 75% said they would like to get winning trades each month.
7. Only 14% of people surveyed said they would like someone to just do it for them.

So based on my encounter with a student from Chicago, an incredulous student from New York, and two years of asking questions...

The DartThrow Trader was born.

Before I go any further, I want to be on the record with a few things...

#1 – This challenge is not, nor will it ever be, for everyone.
#2 - The DartThrow Trader Challenge is a work in progress.

My goal was to create a trading system that actually met the needs of the disenfranchised investors I had spoken to from July 2005 – September 2007.

So let's get to the much-anticipated details of this challenge so you can discover exactly why it was called... ***"The most innovative and outrageously creative, on purpose, financial program ever attempted by mortal man".***

To understand that quote, let me share with you how the DartThrow Trader Concept was born.

This whole "Dart-Throw" concept was born out of an "argument" in 2004.

I have been a financial markets "insider" since 1989, and have been teaching others how to trade since 1994.

In 2004 I was teaching a class in New York City and had a student approach me, in an attempt to start an argument.

His position was based on an erroneous presumption that the only way anyone could make money in the financial markets was if they were "right" all the time.

"Are you serious?" I asked. (His red-faced expression indicated he was.) I began to laugh (out loud). And then the words came flying out of my mouth without the hint of regret.

Although I can't recall the conversation verbatim, I remember saying something to the effect of, "If you know what you are doing you can simply put the stock quotes on the wall, throw a dart, randomly select stocks and make money."

It's that frickin' simple.

Of course he didn't believe me. I shrugged my shoulders and simply said... "It's true!"
So there you go, somebody (gasp!) doubted me. I had to prove what I said was true, especially to myself.

That is how this all started. Could I really throw a dart, randomly pick a stock, and make money? Well, as they say, there is only one way to find out.

The Rules

The first thing I had to do was establish some rules. (Establishing your own rules is just one of the "perks" to Original Game Creation.) I didn't want to skew the opportunities; however, I believe there is more to trading than just going "long" or "short".

My first rule: the only stocks eligible for the dart board had to be optionable. According to the 2006 CBOE market statistics data, this would be a list of 2027 stocks to choose from, providing more than enough stocks to fill a wall full of targets.

My second rule: eligible stocks had to be trading above $20 per share at the beginning of the year.

My third rule (and this narrowed it down the most): the stocks not only had to be above $20 per share and be optionable, but they also had to be listed on One Chicago and have Single Stock Future Contracts available. This brought my overall list down to about 476 stocks.

Now I know what you are thinking: *If I only had to watch 476 stocks, I could also make money.* You know what? That's probably true. The problem, as I see it, is that most people are constantly looking for the hot stock of the day, the "can't-lose" pick, blah, blah, blah...

Most investors I've met over the years spend most of their time trying to pick the stock, the system, the newsletter, or the Guru that will win *every time*. The sad truth is you can't win all of the time. However, you can amazingly increase your odds of winning if you take the time to learn how to trade only in the *three market conditions* that can ever exist.

Do you know what they are? Of course you do... Bullish, Bearish and Stagnant (and I would suggest one more... the "I-don't-have-a-frickin-clue!" Yes, that is a market condition. Just ask any trader.)

The "I-don't-have-a-frickin-clue" market condition is the one that most stocks live in, but many investors are afraid to admit.

Think about it. Most investors have spent thousands of dollars (directly or indirectly) on education, software, newsletters, computers, and various other gadgets and trading widgets (anyone still use the magic 8-ball?).

What's the perceived "need" for all that stuff? It is because they "don't have a frickin clue" where a stock (or the market) is heading most of the time. I mean, let's just be honest with ourselves...

If we truly knew where a stock was heading, we wouldn't need all the peripheral accessories. I know the argument: "But Jimmy, all that stuff helps me determine which way my stock is heading".
Oh really? Why don't I believe you? Maybe it's because I bought into all the hype myself. In fact, I spent the better part of the last 10 years "selling" some of the hype.

Do we need education, software, newsletters, computers, gurus and magic 8-balls? In a word: yes. The purpose of these things is to *make our trading easier and more efficient,* not difficult and time consuming.

You Like Fish, Don't You?

The problem is most investors are looking for a "fish-feeding" system.

What?

Remember the old adage, "Give a man a fish, you feed him for a day; but teach a man to fish and you'll feed him for a lifetime"?

The reality is most people do not want to "learn how to fish"; they want someone to feed fish directly to them (preferably with an adult-size bib and a generous amount of drawn butter).

If you are looking for someone to feed you fish you will love The Dart-Throw Trader because, seriously, all you have to do is throw a dart. (Ah, sorry... you'll have to bring your own bib and butter. I'm watching my cholesterol.)

If you are looking for someone to teach you how to fish, you will love The Dart-Throw Trader because, by allowing us to feed you a "weekly" fish, you will learn "how to fish" in the process.

The Dart-Throw Trader is the best of both worlds. You get fed and educated all in the same place, at the same time. And you know what? It's painless...and fun!

So how did the challenge work, and (more importantly) what's in it for you?

Beginning in January 2006 I threw a dart each week at my 476-eligible-stocks dartboard, so that each stock I traded was picked at random.

According to Malkiel, any blindfolded monkey can throw a dart. I just got to be the "chosen monkey"! (I used to let my kids have a shot at it, but discontinued this practice when their limited dart-throwing skills led them to accidentally spear the dog.)

Once the stock had been selected, I would then evaluate the fundamentals, technical's, sentiment, and news around the stock to determine what type of trade would be most prudent for the stock's current exhibited behavior.

You remember the four behaviors we talked about earlier, right? Yeah, you know... bullish, bearish, stagnant and I-don't-have-a-frickin-clue (the last one is my favorite, also).

Once the stock's current behavior had been evaluated (to the best of my ability and understanding), then can I began to determine which of the 70 (give or take) different trading strategies will be best for my newly-predicted outlook.

There really are over 70 different things you can do around a stock these days; the good news is, most are overrated and useless.

Maybe I would explore the Bull Call Spread... maybe the Bullput Spread... the Condor could be a possibility, although I really like the Iron Condor... some like the Straddle, others the Strangle or the Strip... have you ever seen a Call Ratio Back-spread correctly structured?

Yes, I know, lots of interesting terms to consider. That is the beauty of having a toolbox full of strategies, instead of just being limited with the boring one-dimensional long or short trade.

Once a week I would throw a dart. I would evaluate the stock based on fundamentals, technical analysis, sentiment and news. I would determine a current behavior based on my analysis. From there I would choose a trading strategy relevant to the current behavior. I would then place a trade and watch it unfold, just to see if I could actually...

Put stock quotes on a wall,

Throw a dart,

Randomly pick a stock...

And make money.

Once the stock had been selected and evaluated and a strategy had been chosen, I begin to monitor the trade's performance for my pre-determined exit strategy.
Occasionally I would exit a trade before my pre-determined exit target. However, that only occurred in one of two possible scenarios: if the stock either made a strong move against me with no hope of recovery, or if it made a strong move in my favor and I wanted to lock-in those sweet profits.

I have often said and it's worth quoting... ***"You will never go broke taking profits, but you might if you leave them on the table!"*** - Jimmy Slagle, The Dart-Throw Trader

Here is A Step by Step Outline of what I did...

Step 1: On Monday (sometimes Tuesday) of each normal week at precisely 1:00 PM EST I threw the proverbial dart.

Step 2: Once the stock had been selected and the dart safely put away (for the benefit of the dog), I began the evaluation process.

Step 3: After the stock's evaluation was completed, I decided on the most prudent strategy based on my now-decided outlook.

Step 4: Once I had selected the strategy I felt would most profit from the expected behavior, I then structured a trade around the chosen stock.

Step 5: Once the trade had been placed and my exit targets had been identified, I monitored the trade on a daily basis, looking for an early exit if either 1) the stock moved against me without hope of return, or 2) if the stock moved rapidly in my favor and profits needed to be realized.

Step 6: If the need to exit the trade became apparent, I made that decision and the action was taken.

Step 7: Repeat Steps 1-7 the next week.

Obviously this type of "rebel-without-a-cause" approach doesn't appeal to everyone. The good news is I understand; the better news is I'm a rebel; and the best news is; I do have a cause.

My cause is to help you become a better, more consistent trader so that you can spend less time trading and more time doing the important things you wish you had more time to do (and to raise a lot of money for charity... more about that later).

So now you know how the DartThrow Trader Concept was born.

The "million dollar" question is: Why did I do this?

Up until October of 2006 I was under contract with a seminar company that asks (and gets) up to $30,000 for the types of skill sets and strategies that I traded week after week.

Most Stock and Mutual fund newsletters average cost is $120.00 to $200.00 per year; with some exceeding the $1,500.00 per year barrier. I don't have to tell you what you get with a newsletter service; I'm sure by now you have subscribed to a least one, so you know what to expect from a "service" that offers no service.

In fact in 2006, according to the most respected, unbiased newsletter ranking service in the country, that currently ranks over 180 different newsletters, the Number One rated newsletter for the 25-year period returned 19.5%, Number One for the 20 year period returned 15.4%, Number One for the 15 year period returned 25.5%, Number One for the 10 year period returned 17.8%, Number One for the 5 year period was an impressive 55.5%, although the last one is considered highly speculative and not for the faint of heart.

As you probably already know, most newsletters are great at feeding you investment and trading ideas, giving you all the reasons why you should invest in their recommendations, the research behind their picks, their price and time targets... yes, you are getting what you pay for.

My only problem with newsletters is: *they have to be right!* And there is a high probability you will not be able to take advantage of every recommendation they make, which means you will have to do your own research to determine which "picks" you actually put in your own portfolio.

Furthermore, if the one or two stocks you choose from their extensive list of recommendations turns out to be the one or two *losers* of the bunch, then you have lost... even though they could potentially claim an overall *win* for the year. We have seen it happen time after time.

So what's my point? It is simply this...

In 2006, I threw darts at a dartboard of 476 stocks. By doing this, I randomly selected 52 stocks throughout the year (each one is profiled in the following chapters of this book).

Using specialized trading skills gleaned from the "front lines" of the trading floors, I focused on what the stock *could* do, and not necessarily what it *was* doing.

By focusing on what the stock could do (go up, down or stay the same), I was able to select a strategy that would most profit from the expected behavior.

Now, remember my challenge goals...

1. Randomly select a stock by throwing darts.

2. Evaluate the randomly selected stock.

3. Select the most prudent strategy based on my outlook.

4. Position myself (using really powerful trading strategies) around the selected stock so that I could potentially profit regardless if the stock moved up, down, or sideways.

5. Monitor the trade on a daily basis, looking for exit points.

6. Exit the trade (hopefully at a profit).

7. Rinse and Repeat each week.

Now for those of you from Arkansas (like me), my goals are simply to...

1. **Throw Darts.**
2. **Pick Stocks.**
3. **Make Money.**

So my next objective is to walk you through the results.

So the results ("hypothetically" of course, because you didn't do any of the proposed trades for 2006) are as follows...

I started with a $5,000 balance (I thought this was a reasonable minimum amount someone should start with).

I tried to keep the cost of each trade around $500.00. This way I would never have more than 10% of my account at risk at any given time, yet still enabling me to (theoretically) have as many as five trades open simultaneously.

I did 52 trades (one per week). Each stock was randomly selected by literally throwing a dart (hence the name Dart-Throw Trader) and constructing a trade based on where the dart landed that week.

Of the 52 trades that were proposed, 12 trades lost money. The average loss was 39% or roughly $200.00 per loss.

However, of the 52 trades that were proposed, 40 trades made a profit. The average profit was 71% or roughly $355.00 per profit.
Simply stated, the results were better than even I expected. At the end of the year my $5,000 account had grown to $16,110.00 or, stated another way...

Throwing darts and randomly selecting stocks (plus a little bit of trading education thrown in) produced an...

$11,110.00 profit or a 222% Annual Return.

OUTSTANDING!

Outstanding, compared to what?

Well, the numbers are in; 2006 is history.

So I did what anyone would do. I went to Google and typed in "best performing mutual funds 2006".

And this is what I found:

According to Dustin Woodward (About.com), the best-performing mutual fund of 2006 was Dreyfus Premier Greater China A up 85.58%

I went to Kiplinger.com and couldn't find any 2006 mutual fund data.

I went to Morningstar.com and tried to search for that information on their site. I couldn't find it.

In fact, after 20 minutes I got tired of searching. Maybe you will have better luck if you try to find it.

So for now I will stick with Dustin Woodward's claim about the China fund, which was up 85.58%.

What about the overall markets? I checked on the Dow Jones Industrial average and the S&P 500 to see how they did. Here is what we found from Morningstar.com...

The S&P 500 was up 15.8% (amazing)

The Dow 30 was up 19.05% (wow)
The NASDAQ was up 9.52% (yawn)

The Russell 2000 was up 18.37% (nice)

But let's break it down to what this means to you.

If you had invested your $5,000.00 in the best performing mutual fund you would have made a potential profit of $4,275.00.

The Dow 30 could have made you $952.50; The Russell 2000 could have made you $918.50; The S&P 500 could have made you $790.00; and the NASDAQ could have netted you a whopping $476.00.

Did you get that?

Let me recap...

China fund... 85.58%... $4,275.00

Dow 30... 19.05%... $952.50

Russell 2k... 18.37%... $918.50

S&P 500... 15.8%... $790.00

NASDAQ... 9.52%... $476.00

Or you could have thrown darts with me, usually having less than $500.00 of your money at risk in any one trade. You'd have only made one trade per week and had someone else do the work (find, evaluate, structure, monitor and provide exit instructions). And at the end of the year your $5,000.00 account would have returned...

Dart-Throw... 222%... $11,110.00 profit.

(Hypothetically of course, because you didn't do it.)

Hmmmm... My plastic dime-store calculator says I beat the best performing mutual fund by 136.42%, or $6,835.00.

The Dow 30 by 202.95% or $10,157.50.
The Russell by 203.63% or $10,191.5.

The S&P 500 by 206.2% or $10,320.00.

And the NASDAQ by 212.48% or $10,634.00.

What does all of this mean? Simply this...

EDUCATION IS PRICELESS!

With that quote in mind, I am going to spend the remainder of this book walking you through each stock that was chosen and each trade I constructed. My hope is that by the end of this book you will want to become...

"If you know what you are doing you can simply place the stock page on a wall, throw a dart, randomly pick a stock and make money."

- Jimmy Slagle, The Dart-Throw Trader

Section 2: A DART-THROW TRADER – A Smart Trading Foundation...

"People with a sense of fulfillment think the world is good, while the frustrated blame the world for their failure."

- Eric Hoffer

The More Options You Have – The More Wealth You Can Create!

Most "un-educated" investors, traders and brokers will tell you that options are evil, nasty, scary, ugly, evil things. Did I mention EVIL? And truth be known, they are if you don't understand them. However, when options are used they way they were created and designed to be used they can be safer than the bank. In fact, when you understand their inherent behavior they can create wealth for you faster than the market can crash. I'll simplify this mystical world for you and bring you into an understanding of knowledge that will make Myron Scholes and Fischer Black proud. (Myron Scholes won a Nobel prize in 1997 for the creation of the option pricing model).

PUTS AND CALLS

Puts and calls generally have longer maturities than rights, though they are considerably shorter than those on warrants; their life span ranges from thirty days to nine months in duration, and occasionally to one or two years. They are much like warrants to the extent that they provide attractive speculative outlets, offer appealing leverage potential, and can act as a nice alternative to the direct investment in common stock. Although for years puts and calls were written almost exclusively on common stocks, dramatic changes occurred in this market in the autumn of 1981, when trading began in other kinds of options.

Today, investors can trade puts and calls on:

• Common stock• Debt instruments• Foreign currencies• Stock indexes• Commodities and financial futures. As we will see, although the underlying financial assets may vary, the basic features and behavioral characteristics of these securities are much the same.

Definitions and Characteristics

One of the phenomena of the market of the 1970s was the remarkable performance and investment popularity of stock options—puts and calls on common stock. By the early 1980s, the interest in options spilled over to other kinds of financial assets and was a major factor behind the development of interest rate, currency, index, and futures options. Not surprisingly, much of the popularity of the options market derived from the fact that individual investors can buy a lot of price action with a limited amount of capital, and yet nearly always enjoy limited risk exposure with puts and calls. For example, an investor can buy an option on $200,000 worth of Treasury bills for as little as $600.

A negotiable instrument

Puts and calls are negotiable instruments issued in bearer form that allow the holder to buy or sell a specified amount of a specified security at a specified price (as an example, puts and calls on common stocks cover 100 shares of stock in a specific company).

Negotiable instruments issued in bearer form that allow the holder to buy or sell a specified amount of a specified security at a specified price (as an example, puts and calls on common stocks cover 100 shares of stock in a specific company).

A put enables the holder to sell the underlying security at a specified price over a set period of time;

a call, in contrast, gives the holder the right to buy the securities at a stated price within a certain time period.

Puts and calls possess value to the extent that they allow the holder to participate in the price behavior of the underlying financial asset. As with any option, there is no interest or dividend income, no voting rights, and no privileges of ownership.

Puts and calls are traded on listed exchanges and, on a much smaller scale, in the over-the-counter market. They provide attractive leverage opportunities because they carry relatively low prices—at least relative to the market price of the underlying financial assets.

To illustrate, consider a call on a common stock that gives the holder the right to buy 100 shares of a $50 stock at a price of, say, $45 a share. The stock would be priced at $50, but the call would trade at an effective price of only $5 a share (or the difference between the market price of the common and the price it can be purchased at, as specified on the call). However, since a single stock option always involves 100 shares of stock, the actual market price of our $5 call would be $500—$5 x 100 shares = $500.

Maker versus purchaser

Puts and calls are a unique type of security since they are not issued by the corporations that issue the underlying stocks and bonds. Instead, puts and calls are created by investors.

It works like this: Suppose one individual wants to sell to another the right to buy 100 shares of common stock. This individual would write a call; the individual or institution writing the option is known as the option, maker or writer. The maker who writes (and sells) an option is entitled to receive the price paid for the put or call (less modest commissions and other transaction costs).

The put or call option is now a full-fledged financial asset and trades in the open market much like any other security. Puts and calls are both written and purchased through security brokers and dealers, and they can be actively bought and sold in the secondary market.

The writer stands behind the option at all times, regardless of how many times the security has been traded or who the current owners are, for it is the writer who must buy or deliver the stock or other financial asset according to the terms of the option.

Puts and calls are written for a variety of reasons, most of which we will explore below. At this point, however, suffice it to say that writing options can be a viable investment strategy and can be a profitable course of action since, more often than not, options expires unexercised. But when options do hit, they usually hit big. **BIG**.

As a result, individuals are also lured to the buy side of these securities by the profits they offer and the low-cost, speculative nature of the issue. In essence, the buyers of puts and calls are willing to invest their capital in return for the right to participate in the future price performance of the underlying security, and to do so at low unit cost and limited risk exposure.

How puts and calls work

Using the buyer's point of view, let us now briefly examine how puts and calls work and how they derive their value. To understand the mechanics of puts and calls, it is best to look at their profit-making potential.

For example, consider a stock ; currently priced at $50 a share; assume we can buy a call on the stock for $500, with the call enabling us to purchase 100 shares of the stock at a fixed price of $50 each. A rise in the price of the underlying security (in this case, common stock) is what the investor would hope for.

What is the profit from this transaction if the price of the stock does indeed move up to, say, $75 by the expiration date on the call? The answer is that we will earn $25 ($75 -$50) on each of the 100 shares of stock in the call— or a total gross profit of some $2,500; and all from a $500 investment.

This is so since we can buy 100 shares of the stock— from the option writer— at a price of $50 each and immediately turn around and sell them in the market for $75 a share. We could have made the same profit by investing directly in the common stock, but because we would have had to invest $5,000 (100 shares x $50 per share), our rate of return would have been much lower. Obviously, there is a considerable difference between the profit potential of common stocks and calls; and it is this differential which attracts investors and speculators to calls whenever the price (outlook for the underlying financial asset is upward.

(Note that although our illustration is couched in terms of common stock, this same valuation principle is applicable to any of the other securities that may underlie call options, such as bonds, foreign currencies, or futures contracts.)

A similar situation can also be worked out for puts. Assume that for the same $50 stock we could buy a put to sell 100 shares of the stock at $50 for $500. Now we, as the buyer of a put, want the price of the stock to drop, so that we can use the put as a way to make money.

Assume our expectations are correct and the price of the stock does indeed drop, to $25 a share. Here again, we would realize a profit of $25 for each of the 100 shares in the put. We can do this by going to the market and buying 100 shares of the stock at a price of $25 a share, and immediately turning around and selling them to the writer of the put at a price of $50 per share.

Fortunately, put -and call investors do not have to exercise these options and make simultaneous buy and sell transactions in order to receive their profit, since options do have value and can be traded in the secondary market.

The value of both puts and calls is directly linked to the market price of the underlying financial asset. The value of calls increases as the market price of the underlying security rises, whereas the value of puts increases as the price of the security declines.

Advantages and disadvantages

The major advantage of investing in puts and calls is their leverage feature. This feature also carries the advantage of being able to limit risk exposure, since there is only a set amount of money that can be lost (the purchase price of the option). Also appealing is the fact that puts and calls can be used profitably when the price of the underlying security goes up or down. Finally, some unusual tax advantages can be obtained by using puts and calls in fairly specialized investment profiles.

A major disadvantage of puts and calls is that the holder enjoys no interest or dividend income or any other ownership benefit. Moreover, because the instruments have limited lives, the investor has a limited time frame in which to capture desired price behavior. Another disadvantage is the fact that puts and calls cannot be margined. And the issues themselves are a bit unusual and many of their trading strategies are complex; because of this, investors must possess special knowledge and fully understand the subtleties of this trading vehicle.

Options Markets

Although the concept of options can be traced back to the writings of Aristotle, option trading in the United States did not begin until the late 1700s, and until the early 1970s this market remained fairly small, largely unorganized, and the almost private domain of a handful of specialists and traders. All this changed, however, on April 26, 1973, when a new securities market was created with the launching of the Chicago Board Options Exchange (the CBOE).

Conventional options

Prior to the creation of the CBOE, put and call option trading was conducted exclusively in the over-the-counter market through a handful of specialized dealers.

Investors who wished to purchase puts and calls dealt with these options dealers via their own brokers, and the dealers would actually find individuals (or institutions) willing to write the options.

If the buyer wished to exercise the option, he or she did so with the writer, and no one else— a system that largely prohibited any secondary trading. On the other hand, there were virtually no limits on what could be written, so long as the buyer was willing to pay the price.

Put and call options were written on New York and American stocks, as well as on regional and over-the-counter securities; and they were written for as short as thirty days and as long as a year.

Over-the-counter options, known today as conventional options, were hard hit by the CBOE and other options exchanges. The conventional market still exists today, although on a reduced scale, and it is still possible for investors to use this market, along the lines set out above, to create conventional options.

Listed options

The creation of the CBOE marked the first time in American capital market history that stock options were traded on listed exchanges. It marked the birth of so-called listed options, a term used to denote put and call options traded on organized exchanges, as opposed to the conventional options traded in the over the-counter market.

The CBOE created the listed options concept by launching trading in calls on 16 firms. These 16 issues quickly doubled to 32, and soon after, the American Stock Exchange also began trading listed calls. The Pacific and Philadelphia stock exchanges followed; and finally, in June 1977, all four options exchanges began trading in puts.

By 1983, the number of issues listed on the options exchanges had grown from the original 16 to over 350, and most of these are written on stocks traded on the New York Stock Exchange.

The listed options concept provided not only a convenient market for the trading of puts and calls, but also standardized the expiration dates and the prices specified on the options. The exchanges created a clearinghouse organization that eliminated direct ties between buyers and writers of options, and reduced the cost of executing put and call transactions. They also developed an active secondary market, with wide distribution of price information. It is now as easy to trade a listed option as a listed stock.

Stock Options

The advent of the CBOE and other listed options exchanges had a quick and dramatic impact on the trading volume of puts and calls. The level of activity in listed stock options grew by more than a hundredfold in just eight years. Eventually, listed options became available on other financial assets. Today, investors can trade listed options on stocks and stock indexes, debt instruments, foreign currencies, and futures contracts.

The creation and continued expansion of listed options exchanges has truly given the field of investments a whole new dimension. But in order to use these instruments correctly and avoid serious (and possibly expensive) mistakes, the individual investor must fully understand the basic features of these securities. In the material that follows, we will look closely at the investment attributes and trading strategies that can be used with stock options; later we'll explore interest rate, currency, and index options, and then take up futures options.

Stock option provisions

There are three major provisions of put and call options that investors should be aware of: (1) the price at which the stock can be bought or sold, (2) the amount of time remaining until expiration, and (3) the purchase price of the option itself.

Striking price. The striking price represents the price contract between the buyer of the option and the writer. For a call, the striking price specifies the price at which each of the 100 shares of stock can be bought; with a put, it represents the price at which the option buyer may sell the stock to the writer.

The striking price is also known as the exercise price. With conventional (OTC) options, there are no constraints on what the striking price must be (although it is usually specified at or near the market price of the stock prevailing at the time the option is written). With listed options, however, for stocks selling at less than $50 per share the striking price must be in increments of $5. For stocks selling between $50 and $200 per share, the options must be written with striking prices in $10 increments. Finally, for stocks that trade at prices in excess of $ 200, the striking price is in $20 increments. The linking price of both conventional and listed options is adjusted for substantial stock dividends and stock splits.

Expiration date. The expiration date is also an important provision because specifies the life of the option much the same way as the maturity date indicates the life of a bond. Expiration dates for options in the conventional market can fall on any working day of the month.

In contrast, expiration dates are standardized in the listed options market. The exchanges have created three expiration date cycles for all listed options, and each issue is assigned to one of the three cycles. One cycle is January, April, July, and October; another is February, May, August, and November; and the third is March, June, September, and December.

Prices are quoted for only three of the four maturities, with the expiration dates rolling over every three months. For example, the January, April, and July expiration dates would be quoted until the January options expire, then the April, July, and October dates would be used.

Options can be bought, sold, or written for any one of the three dates currently outstanding; since no transaction can take place in the fourth (unlisted) expiration date of a cycle, it follows that nine months is the longest option on the listed exchanges.

Given the month of expiration, the actual day of expiration is always the same: the Saturday following the third Friday of each expiration month. Thus, for all practical purposes, all listed options expire the third Friday of the month of expiration.

Premium. The purchase price of an option is known as the premium. With most securities, the term "premium" is used to denote that portion of the purchase price which exceeds some predetermined theoretical value. With puts and calls, "premium" represents the cost of an option and the price the buyer would have to pay to the writer (or seller) in order to acquire the put or call.

The size of the option premium is obviously important to buyers, writers, and sellers. One factor that affects the size of option premiums is the current market price of the underlying stock: The greater the difference between the price of the stock and the striking price on the option, the greater the value of the put or call.

Another factor is the length of time until the expiration date of the option; the longer the time until expiration, the greater the size of the premium. Still another is the volatility of the underlying security, which is important to the extent that it enhances (or detracts from) the speculative appeal of the option. Other, less important variables include the dividend yield of the underlying stock, the trading volume of the option, and the exchange on which the option is listed.

One factor that affects the size of option premiums is the current market price of the underlying stock: The greater the difference between the price of the stock and the striking price on the option, the greater the value of the put or call.

Another factor is the length of time until the expiration date of the option; the longer the time until expiration, the greater the size of the premium. Still another is the volatility of the underlying security, which is important to the extent that it enhances (or detracts from) the speculative appeal of the option. Other, less important variables include the dividend yield of the underlying stock, the trading volume of the option, and the exchange on which the option is listed.

Put and call transactions

Option traders are subject to commission and transaction costs whenever they buy or sell an option, or when an option is written. The writing of puts and calls is subject to normal options transaction cost, since it effectively represents remuneration to the broker or dealer for selling the option. In relation to the number of shares of common stock controlled (100 shares per option), the transaction costs for executing put and call trades is relatively low.

However, when the transaction costs are compared to the size of the transaction itself, we discover that option transactions can be fairly costly.

Listed options also have their own market place and quotation system. Finding the price (or premium) for a listed stock option is fairly easy.

Note that quotes are provided for calls and puts separately, and for each option, there are three expiration dates listed. Along with the striking price, such information is the basis for differentiating among various options. For example, there are numerous puts and calls outstanding on stocks, each with its own expiration date and striking price.

Measuring value

The value of a put and call depends on its exercise price and the prevailing market price of the underlying stock. The value of a call is determined according to the following simple formula:

$$\text{Value of a Call} = \text{Market Price of the Underlying Stock} - \text{Strike Price of the Call} \times 100$$

$$V = (MP - SPC) \times 100$$

In other words, the value of a call is nothing more than the difference between market price and striking price; while it can be a negative number, such figures really have little or no meaning. A simple illustration will show that an option carrying a striking price of $50 on a stock presently trading at $60 has a value of $1,000 [($60 -$50) X 100 = $10 x 100]. A put, on the other hand, cannot be valued in the same way, since the two options allow the holder to do different things. To find the value of a put, simply reverse the order of the equation a bit, so that we have:

difference between market price and striking price; while it can be a negative number, such figures really have little or no meaning. A simple illustration will show that an option carrying a striking price of $50 on a stock presently trading at $60 has a value of
$1,000 [($60 -$50) X 100 = $10 x 100]. A put, on the other hand, cannot be valued in the same way, since the two options allow the holder to do different things. To find the value of a put, simply reverse the order of the equation a bit, so that we have:

$$\text{Value of a Put} = \text{Strike price of the put} - \text{Market Price of the Stock} \times 100$$

$$V = (SPP - MP) \times 100$$

Put and call values denote what the options should be valued and trading at.

Unfortunately, this rarely occurs. Instead, these securities almost always trade at prices higher than their true value, especially for options that still have a long time to run. This difference is known as the investment premium and indicates the amount of "water" or excess value embedded in the quoted price of the put or call. Investment premium can be found as follows:

$$\text{Investment Premium} = \frac{\text{Option Premium} - \text{Value of the Option}}{\text{Value of the option}}$$

For example, if a put has a value $2,000— found according to the valuation formula above— and carries a price (option premium) of $2,200, it would be trading at an investment premium of 10 percent ($2,200 -$2,000) -$2,000 = $200 - $2,000 = .10).

Many of the same factors that affect option premium also affect investment premium; for example, investment premium tends to increase for longer options and for those on highly volatile stock. Unless it can be recovered when the investor sells the option, investment premium represents a form of sunk cost that is lost for good.

In-the-money/out-of-the-money

When written, options do not necessarily have to carry striking prices at the prevailing market price of the underlying common stock. And as options subsequently trade on the listed exchanges, the price of the option will move in response to moves in the price of the underlying common stock.

When a call has a striking price less than the market price of the underlying common stock, it has a positive value and is known as an in-the-money option. A major portion of the option premium is based on (or derived from) the true value of the call.

When the striking price exceeds the market price of the stock, the call has no "real" value and is known as an out-of-the-money option. Since the option has no value, its price is made up solely of investment premium.

These terms are much more than convenient, exotic names given to options, for as we will see below, they characterize the investment behavior of options and can affect return and risk.

A put option, by the way, is "in-the-money" when its striking price is greater than the market price of the stock; it is "out-of-the-money" when the market price of the stock exceeds the striking price.

Trading Strategies

For the most part, stock options can be used in three types of trading strategies:

(1) buying puts and calls for speculation;
(2) hedging with puts and calls; and
(3) option writing and spreading.

Buying for speculation

This is the simplest and most straightforward use of puts and calls. Basically, it is just like buying stock (buy low and sell high) and, in fact, represents an alternative to investing in stock.

For example, if an investor feels the market price of a particular stock is going to move up, one way of capturing that price appreciation is to buy a call on the stock.

In contrast, if an investor feels the stock is about to drop in price, a put could convert the price decline to a profitable situation. In essence, investors buy options rather than stock whenever the options are likely to yield a greater return.

The principle here, of course, is to get the largest return from one's investment dollar as possible— something that can often be done with puts and calls because of the desirable leverage they offer.

To illustrate the essentials of speculating with options, consider a situation where we have uncovered a stock we feel will move up in price over the next six months.

What we would like to find out at this point is this: What would happen if we were to buy a call on this stock rather than investing directly in the firm's common? To find out, let us see what the numbers show; assume the price of the stock is now $49, and we anticipate that within six months it should rise to about $65.

In order to determine the relative merits of our investment alternatives, we need to determine the expected return associated with each course of action. Because call options have short lives, we will use holding period return to measure yield.
Thus, if our expectations about the stock are correct, it should go up by $16 and in so doing provide stockholders with a 33 percent holding period return [($65 $49) -$49 = $16 -$49 = .33]. But there are also some listed options available on this stock, so let us see how they would do.
We will use as illustration two six-month calls that carry $40 and $50 striking prices, respectively. Clearly, either option alternative represents a superior investment to buying the stock. The dollar amount of profit may be a bit more with the stock, but notice that the size of the required investment ($4,900) is also a lot more.

Observe that one of the calls is an in-the-money option (the one with the $40 striking price); the other is out-of-the-money.

The difference in returns generated by these calls is rather typical. Investors are usually able to generate better rates of return with lower-priced (out-of-the-money) options and also enjoy less exposure to loss.

Of course, the major drawback of out-of-the-money options is that their price is made up wholly of investment premium— a sunk cost which would be lost if the stock does not move in price.

To see how investors can speculate in puts, consider the following situation:

Assume that the price of our stock is now $51, but this time we anticipate a drop in price to about $35 within the next six months. Alternatively, an out-of-the money put (with a striking price of $50) can be purchased for, say, $300. Again, if the price of the underlying stock does indeed drop, investors will make money with the put.
Once more, in terms of holding period return, the stock option is the superior investment vehicle— by a wide margin. Of course, not all option investments end up nearly so well as the ones in our examples; clearly, success in this strategy rests on picking the right underlying common stock.

Thus, security analysis and proper stock selection are critical dimensions of this technique. It is a highly risky investment strategy, but it may be well suited for the more speculatively inclined investor.

Hedging

A hedge is really nothing more than a combination of two or more securities into a single investment position for the purpose of reducing risk. This strategy might involve, for example, buying stock and simultaneously buying a put on that stock; or buying stock and then writing a call.

There are many types of hedges, some very sophisticated, some very simple; but they all are used as a way to earn or protect profit without exposing the investor to excessive loss.

An options hedge may be appropriate if you generated a profit from an earlier common stock investment and wish to protect that profit, or if you are about to enter into a common stock investment and wish to protect your capital (by limiting potential capital loss). If you hold a stock that has gone up in price, the purchase of a put would provide the type of downside protection you need.

The purchase of a call would provide protection to a short seller of common stock. Thus, option hedging always involves two transactions— one is the initial common stock position (long or short), and the other involves the simultaneous or subsequent purchase of the option.

Let us examine a simple options hedge by seeing how a put can be used to limit capital loss or protect profit. Consider an investor who wants to buy 100 shares of stock. Being a bit apprehensive about the stock's outlook, this investor decides to use an option hedge to protect his capital against loss.

He therefore simultaneously buys the stock and a put on the stock (which fully covers the 100 shares owned). Preferably, the put would be a low-priced option with a striking price at or near the current market price of the stock. Suppose the investor purchases the common at $25 and pays $150 for a put with a $25 striking price.

Now, no matter what happens to the price of the stock (over the life of the put), the investor can lose no more than $150; at the same time, the gains are almost unlimited. If the stock does not move, the investor will be out the cost of a put; if it drops in price, then whatever is lost on the stock will be made up with the put.

However, if the price of the stock goes up (as hoped), the put becomes useless, but the investor rakes in the capital gains profit from the stock. The $150 paid for the put is sunk cost, and that is lost no matter what happens to the price of the stock; in effect, it is the price paid for the hedge. Moreover, this hedge is good only as long as the investor holds the put. When this put expires, the investor will have to replace it with another put or forget about hedging his or her capital.

The other basic use of an option hedge involves entering into the options position after a profit has already been made on the stock. This could be done because of investment uncertainty in the foreseeable future, or for tax purposes (to carry over a profit to the next taxable year).

For example, if an investor bought 100 shares of stock at $35 and it moved to $75, there would be a profit of $40 per share to protect. The profit could be protected with an option hedge by again buying a put.

Assume the investor buys a three-month put with a $75 striking price at a cost of $250. Now, regardless of what happens to the stock over the life of the put, the investor would be guaranteed a minimum profit of $3,750 (the $4,000 profit in the stock made so far, less the $250 cost of the put).

Notice that if the price of the stock should fall, the worst that can happen is a guaranteed minimum profit of $3,750. And there is no limit to how much profit can be made— as long as the stock goes up, the investor will reap the benefits. (This discussion pertained to put hedges, but it should be clear that call hedges can also be set up to limit the loss or protect a profit on a short sale. For example, when a stock is sold short, a call can be purchased to protect the short seller against a rise in the price of the stock— with the same basic results outlined above.)

Option writing and spreading

The advent of listed options has led to many intriguing options trading strategies.

In spite of the appeal of these exotic techniques, there is one important point that all the experts agree on: Such specialized trading strategies should be left to experienced investors who fully understand their subtleties.

Our goal at this point is not to master these specialized strategies, but to learn in general terms what they are and how they operate. There are two types of specialized options strategies: (1) writing options, and (2) spreading options.

Writing options.

Generally, investors write options because they feel the price of the underlying stock is going to move in their favor; that is, it is not going to rise as much as the buyer of a call expects, or fall as much as the buyer of a put hopes. And more often than not, the option writer is right— that is, he or she is going to make money far more often than the buyer of the put or call! Such favorable odds explain, in part, the underlying economic motivation for writing put and call options.

Options writing represents an investment transaction to the writers, since they receive the full option premium (less normal transaction costs, of course) in exchange for agreeing to live up to the terms of the option.

Investors can write options in one of two ways. One is to write naked options, which are options on stock not owned by the writer. The investor simply writes the put or call, collects the option premium, and hopes that the price of the underlying stock does not move against him or her.

If successful, naked writing can be highly profitable because of the very modest amount of capital required. One thing that should be kept in mind, however, is that the amount of return to the writer is always limited to the amount of option premium received. Yet there is really no limit to loss exposure. And that is the catch: The price of the underlying stock can rise or fall by just about any amount over the life of the option, and in so doing deal a real blow to the naked put or call writer.

Such risk exposure can be partially offset by writing covered options, which involves writing options against stocks the investor (writer) already owns, or has a position in.

An investor, for example, could write a call against stock he or she owns, or a put against stock he or she has short sold. In this way, the investor can use the long or short position to meet the terms of the option. Such a strategy represents a fairly conservative way to generate attractive rates of return. The object is to write a slightly out-of-the-money option, pocket the option premium, and hope that the price of the underlying stock will move up or down to (but not exceed) the option striking price.

In effect, what an investor is doing is adding option premium to the other usual sources of return that accompany stock ownership or short sales (dividends and/or capital gains). But there is more; for while the option premium adds to the return, it also reduces risk exposure, since it can be used to cushion a loss should the price of the stock move against the investor. There is a hitch to all this, however: The amount of return the covered option investor can realize is limited. For once the price of the underlying common stock begins to exceed the striking price on the option, the option becomes valuable. And once this happens, the option writer starts losing money. From this point on, for every dollar the investor makes on the stock position, he or she loses an equal amount on the option position.

Spreading options.

Options spreading is nothing more than combining two or more options into a single transaction. We could create an options spread by simultaneously buying and writing options on the same underlying stock. These cannot be identical options; they must differ with respect to striking price and/or expiration date.

Spreads are a popular use of listed options, and account for a substantial amount of the trading activity on the listed options exchanges. These spreads go by a variety of exotic names, such as "bull spreads," "bear spreads," "money spreads," "calendar spreads," and "butterfly spreads." Each is different and constructed to meet a certain type of investment goal.
For example, bull spreads are used with call options when prices are moving up as a way to capture the benefits of a rising market. Others are used to profit from a falling market, and still others to try to make money when the price of the underlying stock goes up or down! Whatever the objective, most spreads are written to take advantage of differences in prevailing option premiums as a way to capture the benefits of a rising market. Others are used to profit from a falling market, and still others to try to make money when the price of the underlying stock goes up or down!

The payoff from spreading is usually substantial, but so is the risk. In fact, some spreads that seem to involve almost no risk may end up with devastating results if the market and the "spread" (or difference) between option premiums move against the investor.

One variation of this theme involves option straddles, the simultaneous purchase of a put and a call on the same underlying common stock. Unlike spreads, straddles often involve the same striking price and expiration date.

Here the object is to earn a profit from a modest increase or decrease in the price of the underlying stock. Otherwise, the principles of straddles are much like those for spreads: to build an investment position with combinations of options that will enable an investor to capture the benefits of certain types of stock price behavior. But keep in mind that if the price of the underlying stock and/or the option premiums does not behave in the anticipated manner, the investor loses. Spreads and straddles are extremely tricky and should not be used by novice investors.

SUMMARY

Options, unlike common stocks or bonds, do not provide buyers with the privileges of ownership; rather, the owner of an option is entitled only to the right to subsequently buy or sell other securities. Stock options permit the holder to buy or sell shares of stock at a specified price over a specified period of time.

There are three kinds of options: (1) rights, (2) warrants, and (3) puts and calls.

A right has a very short market life (of no more than several weeks) and enables the holder to purchase a new issue of common stock at a subscription price, set below the prevailing market price of the existing outstanding stock. Only if the shareholder exercises the right or sells it will he or she realize any financial benefit from its issue. If the rights are exercised, the investor obtains stock, commission-free; if they are sold, the investor receives the market value of the right. Trading opportunities in rights are limited due to their short life, the narrow range of their price activity, and their irregular issuance.

A warrant is similar to a right but its maturity is much longer. Attached to bond issues as "sweeteners," warrants allow the holder to purchase the corporation's common stock at a set exercise price on or before the stipulated expiration date.

A warrant becomes valuable when the market price of its underlying common stock equals or exceeds the exercise price. Frequently, warrants trade at a premium price due to their speculative value. Warrants offer advantages to their owners in the form of: (1) attractive capital gains (since warrant prices move with stock prices); (2) low unit cost; and (3) the benefits of leverage (which accompanies the low unit cost). In weighing these advantages, the investor must consider the fact that warrants pay no dividends and carry an expiration date.

Trading in warrants is done primarily as a substitute for common stock investing and is based on the magnified capital gains they offer. The value of a warrant changes directly with and generally by the same amount as the underlying common stock; but since a warrant's unit cost is often much lower than common stock, the same dollar change in price represents a considerably larger percentage yield. In addition to using warrants to magnify the amount of dollar return, they may also be used to limit loss exposure.

Other options that offer attractive speculative value and leverage potential are puts and calls. A put enables the holder to sell a certain amount of a specified security at a specified price over a specified time period. A call, in contrast, gives the holder the right to buy the same securities at a specified price over a specified period of time. The three basic features of puts and calls are striking price (or the contract price between the buyer and writer), the expiration date (which determines the life of the option), and the purchase price of the option itself.

The value of a call is the difference in the market price of the underlying security less the striking price designated on the call. The value of a put is its striking price less the market price of the security. The major drawbacks to put and call options include their limited life, the absence of ownership rights (like the receipt of interest and dividends), and the level of specialized knowledge needed to master the trading strategies involved.

Since April 26, 1973, the Chicago Board Options Exchange has made option trading easy and convenient; contracts have been standardized (with regard to striking prices and expiration dates), trading activity has increased, and option trading has become a widely used investment technique. Today, standardized listed put and call options are available on over 1800 common stocks, a number of debt securities (from T-bills to Treasury bonds), about half a dozen foreign currencies, a large and growing number of stock market industry indexes, and commodities and financial futures.

Puts and calls offer a variety of trading strategies. Buying options for their speculative appeal can be used in place of speculating with the underlying securities themselves. Since these options have a lower unit cost than the underlying financial asset, they yield greater returns per investment dollar.

Conservative investors may be attracted to put and call purchases because they offer limited risk in absolute dollar terms. More likely, however, conservative investors will use options to form hedge positions in combination with other securities. A put can be used to provide downside protection for securities held long; a call can be used to provide upside protection in a short sale. Writing and spreading options are two other popular uses of this investment vehicle.

The Generic Strategies You Can Find Anywhere...

This is the chapter about option strategies (like that wasn't obvious). In order for you to understand the trades that I (the blindfolded monkey), did you have to have a small understanding of the basic option strategies used and their corresponding risk profiles.

Well, that my friends is what this chapter is all about. Most of you reading this know that a simple search on any search engine will find the following information or you could just head over to the Chicago Board of Options Exchange and download your free copy of the characteristics and risks of standardized options, because most of this chapter is in there.

I mean if I were looking for basic option information I would head over there because they (the CBOE) is "The Definitive Source For Options Trading Information" SM Or at least that is what their service mark would have you believe.

I used to think I was in competition with the CBOE but now I realize I'm not. I mean really could you see the guys at the CBOE, with all their regulations, throwing darts and picking stocks... I mean, really.

My only competition is another blindfolded monkey. Any way enough rambling on here is some valuable information that the "Talking Heads" think you need to know before we can get into the good stuff, you know the stuff that the Dart-Throw Trader KNOWS you need to know.

Stock & Option Strategy Risk Profiles

The following charts will try to illustrate the profit and loss profiles for many popular option strategies.

The synthetic equivalent of each is the stock or option position (or combination) that has the same profit and loss profile.

The directional risk indicates the risk from a large move, either up or down, in the underlying stock.

Please note: On many positions, you may see "unlimited downside risk," meaning there is potential for unlimited losses if the stock falls. Strictly speaking, this is not unlimited risk since a stock cannot fall below zero. However, since it is extremely rare to see a stock down to a price of zero, this risk is still considered to be unlimited. In these cases, formulas will be given to calculate the true maximum loss if the stock were to trade for zero.

LONG STOCK

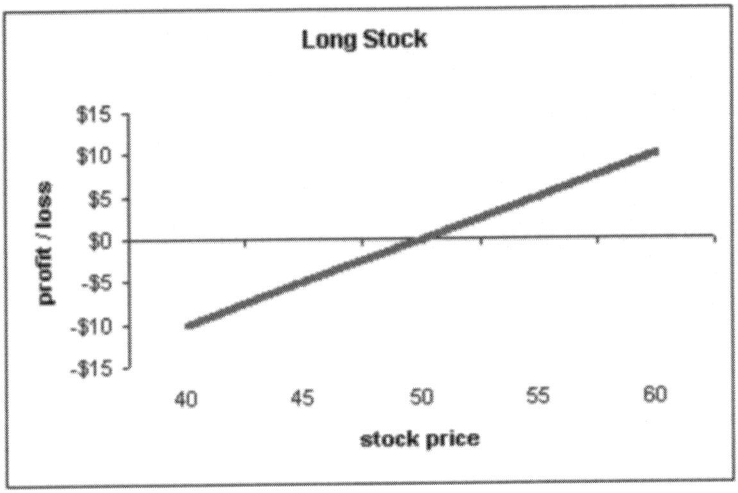

Outlook: Bullish

Directional Risk: Unlimited downside

Max gain: Unlimited

Max loss: Purchase price

Breakeven: Purchase price + commissions

Synthetic option equivalent:

Long call + short put with equal strike prices.
Example: Long $50 call and short $50 put.

SHORT STOCK

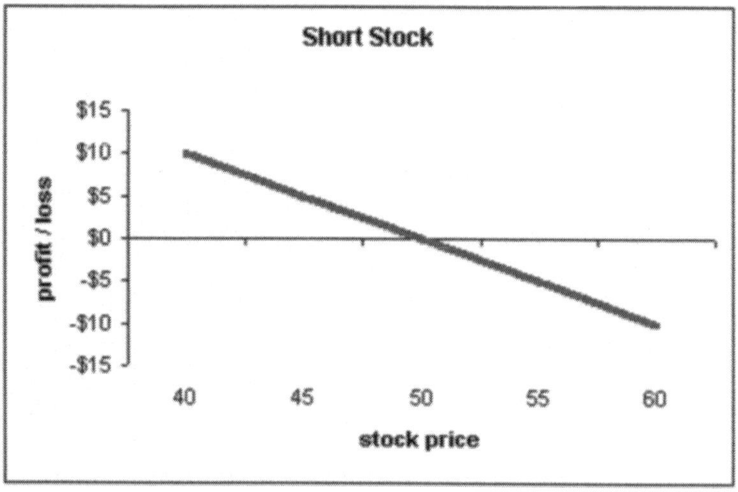

Outlook: Bearish

Directional Risk: Unlimited upside

Max gain: Initial credit

Max loss: Unlimited

Breakeven: Sale price - commissions

Synthetic option equivalent:

Long put + short call with equal strike prices.
Example: Long $50 put and short $50 call.

LONG CALL

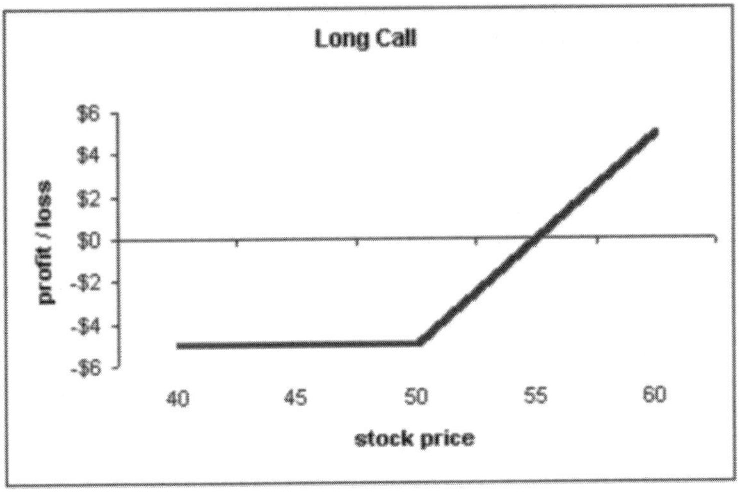

Outlook: Bullish

Directional Risk: Limited downside

Max gain: Unlimited

Max loss: Premium (amount paid). Occurs if stock closes below strike price at expiration.

Breakeven: Strike price + premium

Example: Buy $50 call for $3. Breakeven = $50 + $3 = $53.

Synthetic option equivalent: Long stock + long put

SHORT CALL

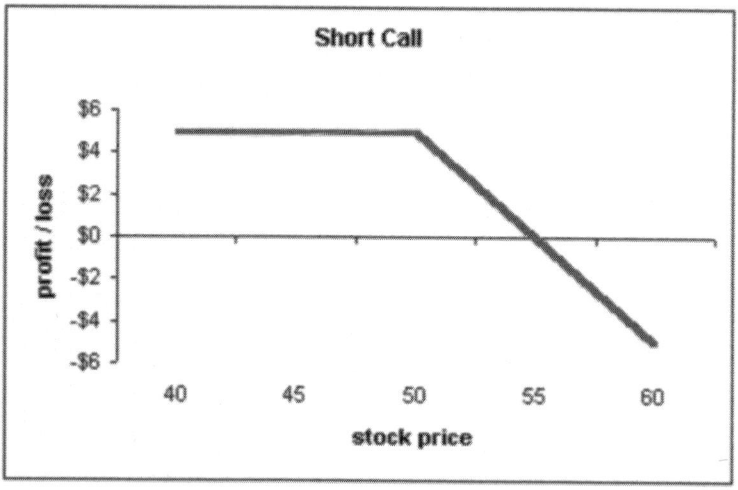

Outlook: Neutral to slightly bearish or slightly bullish

Directional Risk: Unlimited upside

Max gain: Premium (initial credit). Occurs if stock closes below strike price at expiration.

Max loss: Unlimited

Breakeven: Strike price + premium

Example: Sell $50 call for $3. Breakeven is $50 + $3 = $53.

Synthetic option equivalent: Short stock + short put

LONG PUT

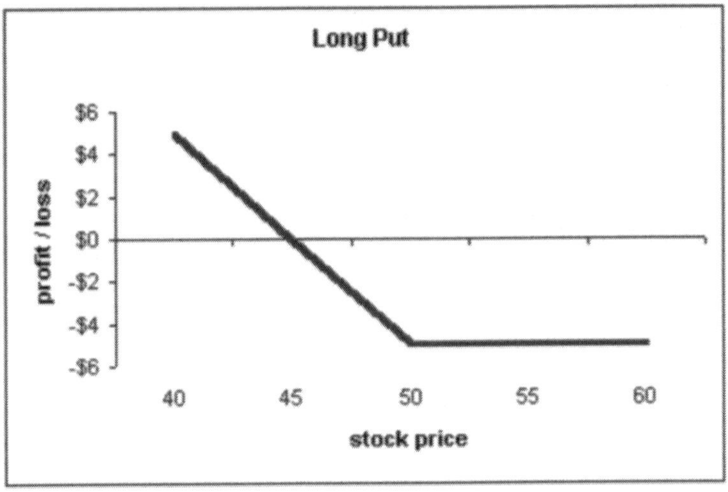

Outlook: Bearish

Directional Risk: Limited upside

Max gain: Strike price - premium

Max loss: Premium (amount paid). Occurs if stock closes above strike price at expiration.

Breakeven: Strike price - premium

Example: Buy $50 put for $3. Breakeven is $50 - $3 = $47.

Synthetic option equivalent: Short stock + long call

SHORT PUT

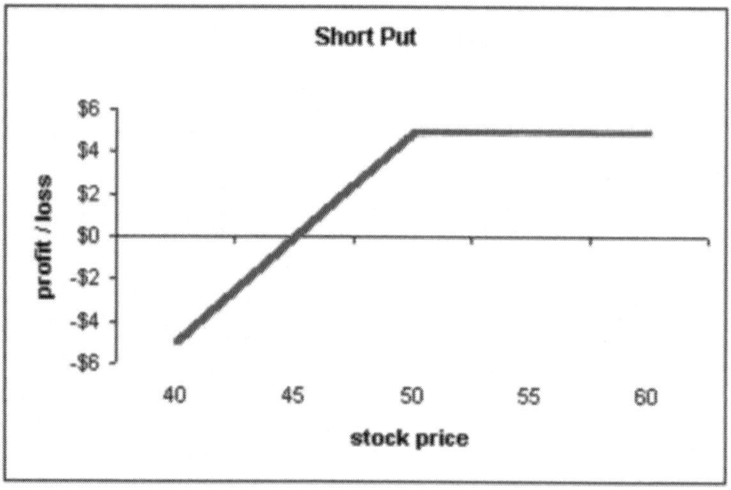

Outlook: Neutral to slightly bullish or slightly bearish

Directional Risk: Unlimited downside

Max gain: Premium (Initial credit). Occurs if stock closes above strike at expiration.

Max loss: Strike - premium

Breakeven: Strike price - premium

Example: Sell $50 put for $3. Breakeven = $50 - $3 = $47.

Synthetic equivalent:

Long stock + short call (covered call position).

COVERED CALL (BUY – WRITE)

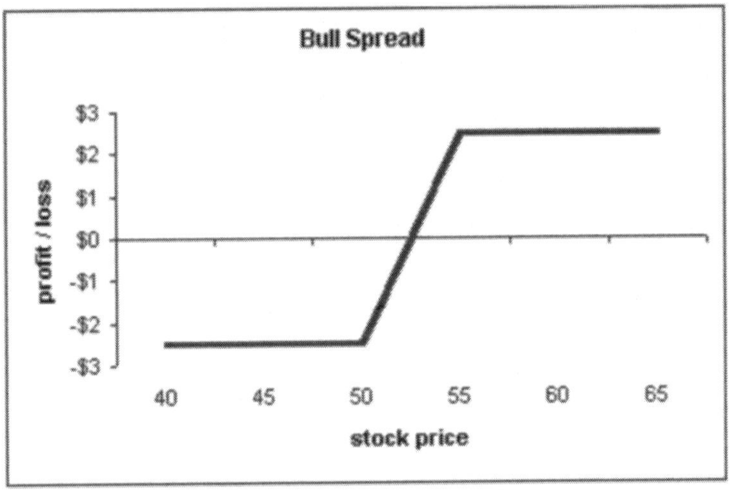

Position: Buy stock and sell calls (equivalent contract amounts) against it.

Example: Buy 300 shares and sell 3 call options

Outlook: Neutral to slightly bullish

Directional Risk: Unlimited downside

Max gain: (2 possible)

(1)Time premium received from calls (occurs if call strike is less than or equal to stock purchase price). Example: Buy stock at $50 and sell the $50 (or lower). The max gain is the *time premium* on the option.

(2)Time premium received plus capital gain (occurs is call strike is higher than stock purchase price). Example: Buy stock at $50 and sell the $55 (or higher) strike. The max gain is the time premium on the option *plus* the capital gain on the stock (difference in strikes).

Max loss: Stock price less the premium received from call (net cost to purchase the stock).

Breakeven: Strike price less premium received. Example: Buy stock at $50 and sell the $50 call for $3 premium.The breakeven point is $50 - $3 = $47.

Synthetic equivalent: Naked put

COVERED PUT (SELL - WRITE)

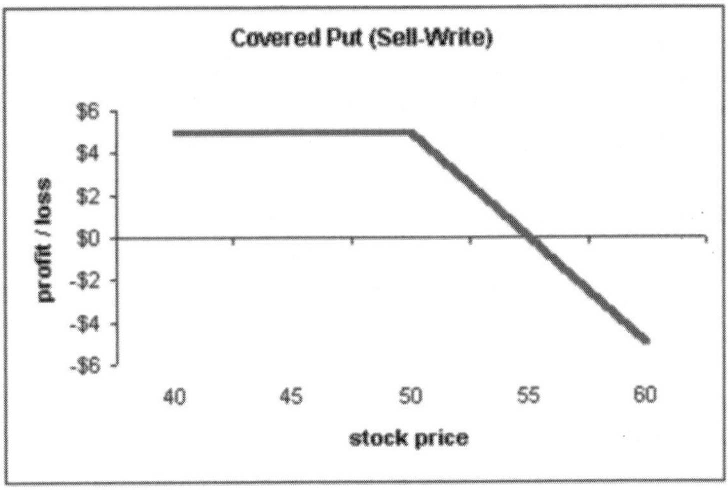

Position: Short stock and sell puts (equivalent contract amounts) against it

Example: Sell short 300 shares and sell 3 put options.

Outlook: Neutral to slightly bearish.

Directional Risk: Unlimited upside.

Max gain:

(1)Time premium received from puts (occurs if put strike is greater than or equal to stock short sale price). Example: Sell short at $50 and sell the $50 (or higher) strike. The max gain is the *time premium* on the option.

(2)Time premium received plus capital gain (occurs is call strike is lower than stock short sale price). Example: Sell short stock at $50 and sell the $45 (or lower) strike. The max gain is the time premium on the option *plus* the capital gain on the stock (difference in strikes).

Max loss: Unlimited

Breakeven: Short sale price plus put option premium received.

Example:
Sell stock short at $50 and sell the $50 put for $3 premium. The breakeven point is $50 + $3 = $53.

Synthetic equivalent: Naked call

LONG STRADDLE

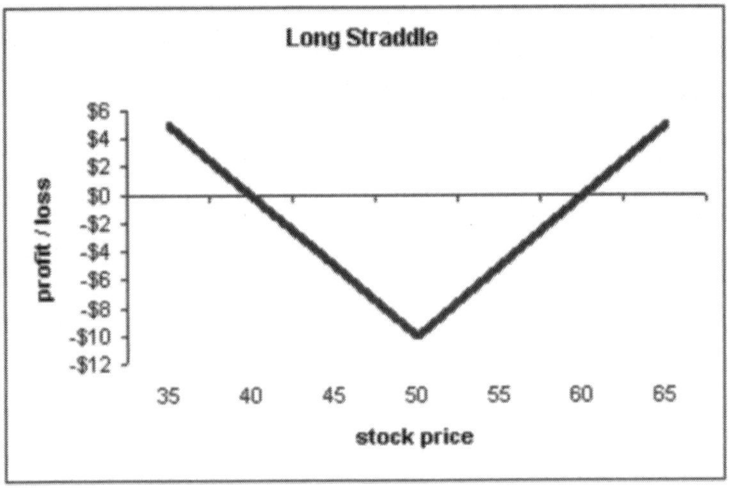

Position: Long call + long put with same strike and time to expiration

Outlook: Extremely bullish or bearish but unsure of direction

Directional Risk: None

Max gain: Unlimited

Max loss: Premiums paid for both options. Occurs if stock closes at strike price at expiration.

Breakeven (2 breakeven points):

Upper: Strike price + call and put premiums

Lower: Strike price - call and put premiums

Example: Buy $50 call for $3 and $50 put for $2
Upper breakeven is $50 + $3 + $2 = $55
Lower breakeven is $50 - $3 - $2 = $45

Synthetic equivalents:

(1)Long stock + double the share equivalent of puts (i.e., buy 100 shares and buy 2 put options)

(2)Short stock + double the share equivalent of calls (i.e.,short 100 shares and buy 2 call options)

(3)Buy 1 call and short half the equivalent shares of stock (i.e., buy 1 call and short 50 shares of stock)

(4)Buy 1 put and buy half the equivalent shares of stock (e.g.,buy 1 put and buy 50 shares of stock)

LONG STRANGLE

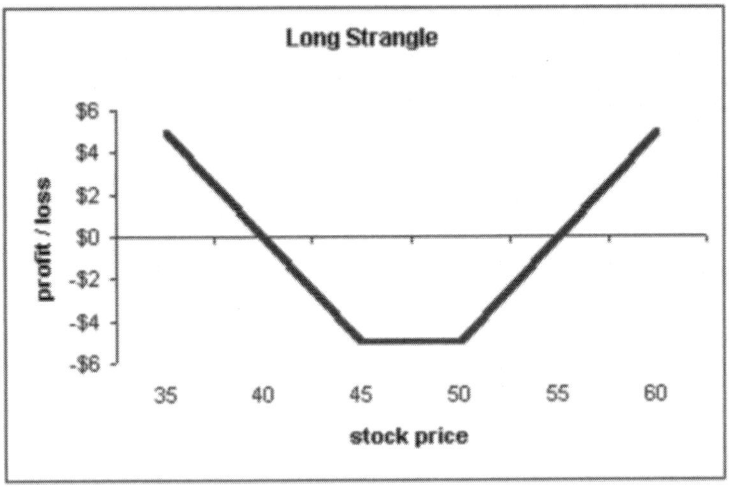

Position: Buy 1 low strike put and buy 1 high strike call

Outlook: Extremely bullish or bearish but uncertain of direction

Directional Risk: None

Max gain: Unlimited.

Max loss: Premiums paid for both options. Occurs if stock stays between strikes at expiration.

Breakeven (2 breakeven points):

Upper: Call strike + call and put premiums

Lower: Put strike - the call and put premiums

Example:
if $5 is paid for both the $45 put and $50 call, the upper breakeven will be $50 + $5 = $55 and the lower breakeven will be $45 - $5 = $40.

Special note: The breakeven points are very different if you are trading an *in-the-money* strangle where the call strike is *lower* than the put strike (also called a "guts" strangle). If $5 is paid for a $45 call and a $50 put, the upper breakeven point is $45 + $5 = $50 and $50 - $5 = $45.

The max loss will also be affected if using in-the-money strangles. The max loss, in this example, is zero since the position must be worth at least the difference in strikes at expiration. This is due to the box position, which guarantees intrinsic value. Remember, if the put strike is greater than the call strike, you must get the difference in strikes back at expiration (although bid-ask spreads may make it slightly less).

Synthetic equivalents:

(1)Long 100 shares + 50 put + 45 put

(2)Short 100 shares + 45 call + 50 call

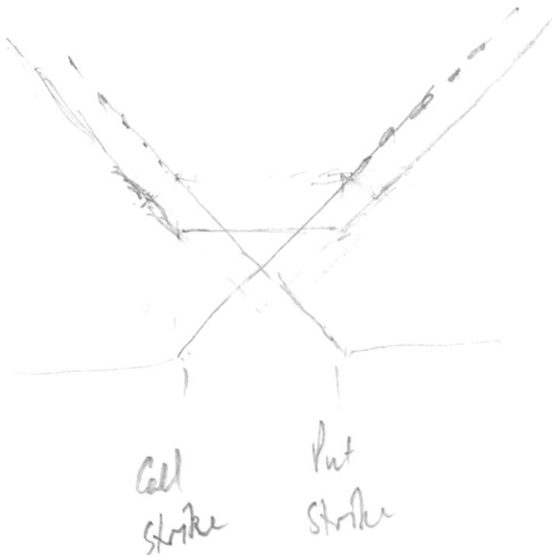

BULL SPREAD

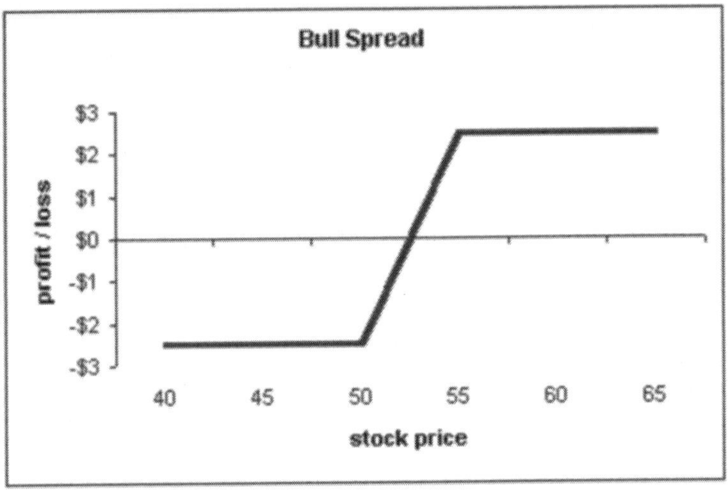

Position (Usually done with either all calls or all puts):

Calls (debit spread): Buy low strike call and sell a higher strike call

Example: Buy $50 call and sell a $55 call.

Puts (credit spread): Sell a high strike put and buy a lower strike put

Example: Sell $55 put and buy $50 put

Outlook:

Calls: Moderately bullish

Puts: Neutral to moderately bullish

Directional Risk: None

Max gain:

Calls: Difference in strike prices less debit.

Example: Buy $50 call and sell $55 call for net debit of $3. Max gain is ($55 - $50) - $3 = $2.

Puts: Credit received

Example: Sell $55 put and buy a $50 put for a net credit of $3. Max gain is $3.

Max loss:

Calls: Premium paid

Puts: Difference in strikes less premium received.

Example: Sell $55 put and buy $50 put for credit of $3. Max loss is ($55 - $50) - $3 = $2.

Breakeven:

Calls: Long call strike plus debit.

Example: Buy $50 call and sell $55 call for net debit of $3. Long call strike = $50 + $3 debit = $53 breakeven.

Puts: High strike put less premium received.

Example: Sell $55 put and buy $50 put for credit of $3. Breakeven = $55 - $3 = $52.

Synthetic equivalent:

Long stock + short high strike call + low strike price put.

Example: Long stock at $50 + Short $55 call + long $45 put

BEAR SPREAD

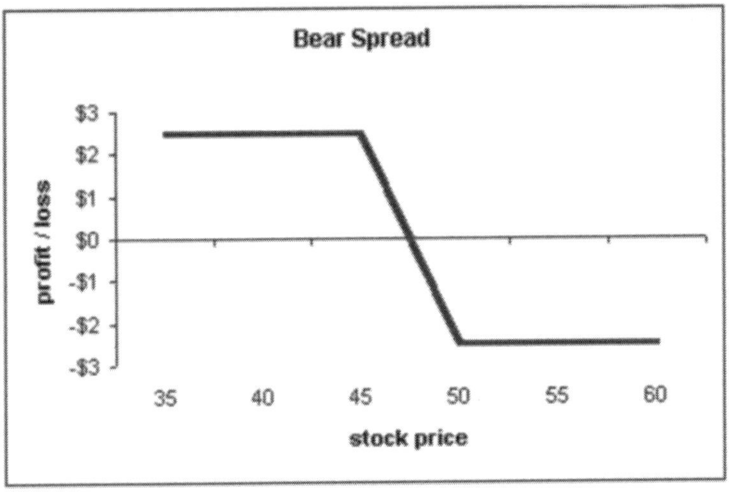

Position (usually done with either all calls or all puts):

Calls (credit spread): Sell a low strike call and buy a higher strike call

Example: Sell the $45 call and buy a $50 call

Puts: (debit spread): Buy high strike put and sell a lower strike put

Example: Buy $50 put and sell $45 put

Outlook:

Calls: Neutral to moderately bearish

Puts: Moderately bearish

Directional Risk: None

Max gain:

Calls: Credit received

Example: Sell the $50 call and buy the $55 call for a net credit of $3. Max gain is $3.

Puts: Difference in strike prices less debit

Example: Buy $55 put and sell $50 put for net debit of $3. Max gain is ($55 - $50) - $3 = $2.

Max loss:

Calls: Difference in strikes less premium received

Example: Sell $45 call and buy $50 call for credit of $3. Max loss is ($50 - $45) - $3 = $2

Puts: Premium paid

Breakeven:

Calls: Short call strike plus premium received. Example: Sell $45 call and buy $50 call for net credit of $3. Breakeven = $45 + $3 = $48 breakeven.

Puts: High strike put less premium received

Example: Buy $50 put and sell $45 put for debit of $3. $50 - $3 = $47.

Synthetic equivalent:

Short stock + long high strike call + short lower strike put

Example: Short stock + long $50 call + short $45 put

CONDOR SPREAD

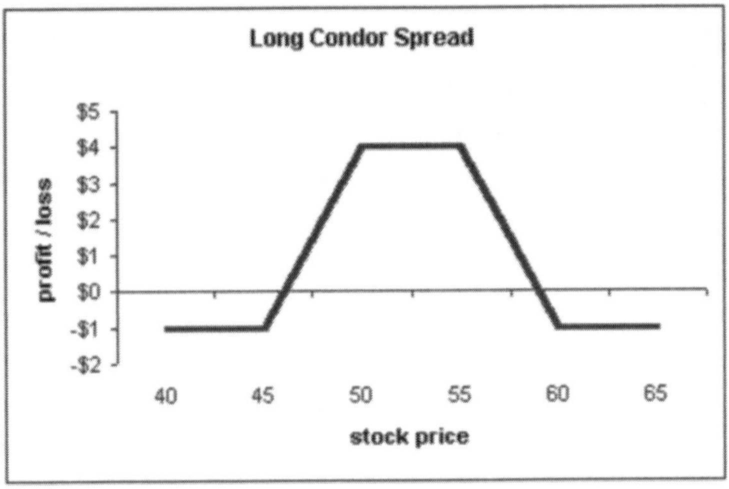

Position (usually done with either all calls or all puts):

Calls or Puts: Buy 1 low strike option, sell 2 successively higher strikes, and buy 1 at an even higher strike. All strikes should be equally spaced with same time to expiration.

Example: Buy 1 $45 call, sell 1 $50 calls, sell 1 $55 call, and buy 1 $60 call. Or, buy 1 $45 put, sell 1 $50 put, sell 1 $55 put, and buy 1 $60 put.

Outlook: Neutral to slightly bullish or bearish

Directional Risk: None

Max gain: Difference in two middle strikes (or any two successive strikes) less premium paid. Occurs if stock closes between middle strike prices at expiration.

Example: Buy 1 $45 call, sell 1 $50 call, sell 1 $55 call, and buy 1 $60 call for net debit of $1. Max gain is ($55 - $50) - $1 = $4.

Max loss: Premium paid

Breakeven (2 breakeven points):

Lower: Low strike + premium

Upper: High strike - premium

Example: Buy 1 $45 call, sell 1 $50 call, sell 1 $55 call, and buy 1 $60 call for net debit of $1. Lower breakeven is $45 + $1 = $46 and upper is $60 - $1 = $59.

Synthetic equivalents (numerous, but most common are):

(1) Long $45 put + short $50 put + short $55 call + long $60 call (also called an "short iron condor"). The iron condor can also be viewed as a long strangle + short strangle or the combination of a bull spread + a bear spread.

(2) Long $45 call + short $50 call + short $55 put + long $60 put (also called an "short iron guts condor"). Can also be viewed as a bull spread + bear spread.

CALL RATIO BACKSPREAD

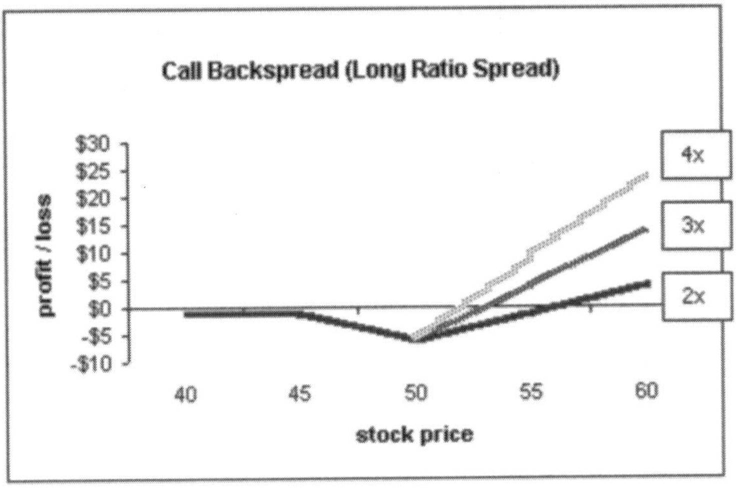

Position: Short low strike call and long more contracts of a higher strike call

Example: Short 1 $45 call and long 2 $50 calls. The more long positions, the higher the slope of the profit and loss diagram as shown in the chart. The diagram shows the effects of buying 2x, 3x and 4x the amount of calls over the short position.

Outlook: Extremely bullish but fearful of a downside move

Directional Risk: Limited downside if debit spread (none if credit spread)

Max gain: Unlimited

Max loss: Per spread, the maximum loss is the difference in strikes + the debit amount (or minus the credit if trade executed for a credit).

Example: Sell $45 call for $7 and buy 2 $50 calls for $5. This is one spread of selling one call and buying two calls, which results in a net debit of $3. This is because $7 was received but $10 was spent (2 long calls at $5). The max loss is ($50 - $45) - $3 = $8.

Breakeven (2 possible breakeven points):

If the trade is executed for a debit, there is one breakeven point:

Long call strike + 1/(R-1) * max loss; where R is the ratio of long calls to short calls (R must be 2 or greater).

Example 1: Sell $45 call for $7 and buy 2 $50 calls for $5 for net debit of $3. This is one -1 x 2 spread (one call sold and two purchased). The ratio (R) is 2 since twice as many calls are purchased. Since the max loss is $8, the breakeven point is $50 + 1/(2-1) * $8 = $58.

Example 2: Sell $45 call for $7 and buy 3 $50 calls for $5. This results in a net debit of +$7 - $15 = $8. The max loss is $13 and the ratio is 3 (three times as many calls purchased). The breakeven is $50 + 1/(3-1) * $13 = $56-1/2.

If the trade is executed for a credit, there will be two breakeven points:

Lower: Short strike plus credit

Upper: Same calculation is used as for debit spread

Example: Sell $45 call for $7 and buy 2 $50 calls for $3 for net credit of $1. Max loss is $4 so lower breakeven will be $45 + $1 = $46.

The formula for the lower breakeven will not change regardless of the number of long calls purchased. This is because the slope of the profit and loss chart is only affected to the right (upper breakeven) of the long strike as shown in the profit and loss diagram above.

Synthetic equivalents (numerous, but most common are):

(1)Long 200 shares + short lower strike call + 2 higher strike puts

Example: Long 200 shares + short $45 call + 2 $50 puts

(2)Short 100 shares + 2 high strike calls + short lower strike put

Example: Short 100 shares + 2 $50 calls + short $45 put

PUT RATIO BACKSPREAD

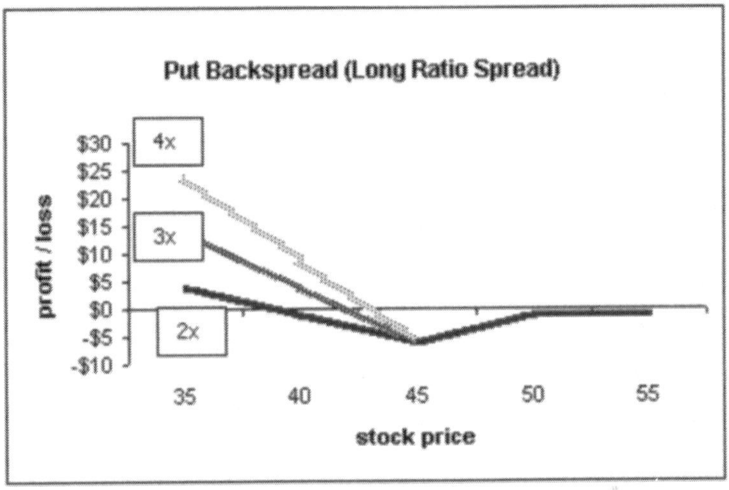

Position: Short a high strike put and long more contracts of a lower strike put

Example: Sell 1 $50 put and buy 2 $45 puts. The more long positions, the steeper the slope of the profit and loss as shown in the diagram. The diagram shows the effects of buying 2x, 3x and 4x the amount of puts over the short position.

Outlook: Extremely bearish but fearful of an upward move

Directional Risk: Limited upside if debit spread (none if credit spread)

Max gain: Strike price of the long less debit (or plus credit). Example: Sell $50 put for $3 and buy 2 $45 puts for $2 each for net debit of $1 (received $3 and paid $4). Max gain is $45 - $1 = $44.

Max loss: Limited. Occurs at strike price of the long position.

Max loss is difference in strikes plus the debit amount (or less the credit amount).

Example: Sell $50 put for $3 and buy 2 $45 puts for $2 each. This is one (-1x2) spread for a net debit of $1 (received $3 and paid $4). The max loss is ($50 - $45) - $1 = $6.

Example 2: Sell $50 put for $3 and buy 2 $45 puts for $1. This results in a net credit of $1. Max loss is now ($50- $45) - $1 = $4.

Breakeven (2 possible breakeven points):

If trade executed for a debit, there is one breakeven point: Long put strike - 1/(R-1) * max loss; where R is the ratio of long puts to short puts (R must be greater than or equal to 2).

Example: Sell 1 $50 put for $3 and buy 2 $45 puts for $2 for net debit of $1. There are twice as many puts purchased, so R = 2. Because the max loss is $6, the breakeven is $45 - 1/(2-1) * $6 = $39.

If the trade is executed for a credit, there will be two breakeven points:

Lower: Same calculation is used as for debit spread

Upper: Short strike - credit

Example: Sell 1 $50 put for $5 and buy 2 $45 puts for $2 for net credit of $1. Upper breakeven is $45 - $1 = $44.

The formula for the upper breakeven will not change regardless of the number of long puts purchased. This is because the slope of the profit and loss chart is only affected to the left (lower breakeven) of the short strike as shown in the profit and loss diagram above.

Synthetic equivalents (numerous, but most common are):

(1)Long 100 shares + short high strike call + long 2 lower strike puts.

Example: Long 100 shares + short $50 call + long 2 $45 puts.

(2)Short 200 shares + long 2 low strike calls + short high strike put.

Example: Short 200 shares + 2 $45 calls + short $50 put.

(3)Short 100 shares + 2 low strike calls + short high strike call

Example: Short 100 shares + 2 $45 calls + short $50 call.

CALENDAR SPREAD

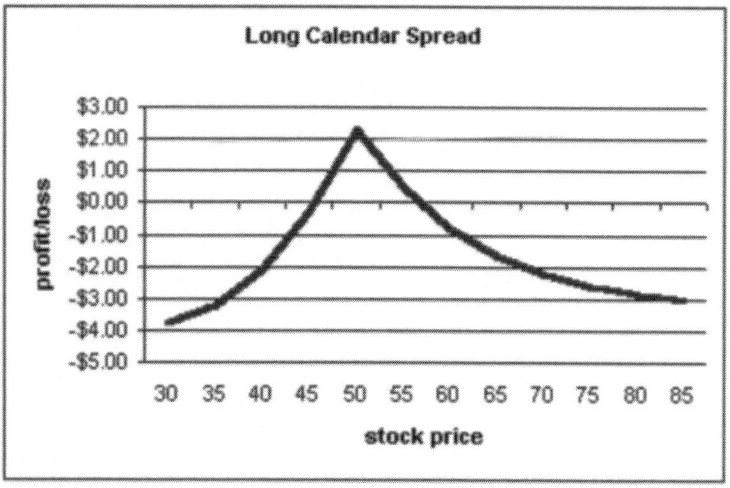

Position: (Can be initiated with either both calls or both puts)

Long a far month contract and short a shorter-term contract with equal strike prices

Example: Buy 1 March $50 call and sell 1 $50 January call

Outlook: Neutral

Directional Risk: Limited upside and downside

Max gain: Limited -- assuming the positions are closed together at expiration of short strike. Occurs if the stock closes at the strike price at expiration of near-term contract. Difficult to say exactly what the max gain will be, as the position is an attempt to exploit time decay, and other factors will move as well.

Max loss: Limited to the net debit. Occurs if: (1) stock closes below strike through both option expirations or (2) if stock makes a large move up or down prior to expiration of near-term strike.

Example: Buy March $50 call for $8, and sell a January $50 call for $5 for net debit of $3. If stock is at or below $50 through January expiration, the short call expires worthless. If the investor continues to hold the long position and the stock closes at or below $50 for March expiration, the trader loses the $3 as both options expired worthless.

Another scenario may happen: if the trader initiates the position and the stock makes a large move upward prior to January expiration, then both options will converge on intrinsic values and lose nearly all of their time premiums. The same is true if the stock collapses. In either case, the trader may lose the entire net debit.

Of course, if the stock collapses during the short-term contract and the position is nearly worthless, one choice for the trader is to close out the short and hold onto the long hoping for a rebound. The trader does not have this choice if the stock makes a large move upward since the short position will exercise and the trader will usually cover with the long position.

Breakeven:

Strike price + net debit.

Example: Long March $50 call and short January $50 call for net debit of $5. At January expiration, breakeven will be $50 + $5 = $55.

These 10 strategies (Covered Call, Covered Put, Long Straddle, Long Strangle, Bull Spread, Bear Spread, Condor, Call Ratio Backspread, Put Ratio Backspread and Calendar Spread) are the most basic option strategies available and the foundation of the Dart-Throw Trader style of trading.

Since the majority of these strategies offer limited risk and limited profit, it is imperative that you pay special attention to the structure of each trade and the risk/reward ratios that each provide.

Each of these strategies can be implemented in any market for a fraction of the cost of buying or selling the underlying asset straight out. Mastering these strategies gives you a strong Dart-Throw Trader foundation, since they are the building blocks of more advanced strategies.

In a following chapter I will give you the specific rules that I follow for structuring each of these specific strategies.

Section 3 – Stuff The Dart-Throw Trader KNOWS You Must Know

"The trend is your friend until it ends, then it becomes your best friend."

- Jimmy Slagle, The Dart-Throw Trader

MACD, Stochastic, Bollinger Bands Fantastic

In this section I am going to cover some terms, techniques and other blindfolded monkey goodies to help you become a more respectable Dart-Throw Trader Apprentice.

I will start with MACD, Stochastic's and Bollinger Band Fantastic... As these are a few of my favorite things. I also believe that if you intend to do any chart reading at all, these should be (at the very least) the starting point of your analysis.

I will also spend a few glorious moments with the most basic and misunderstood technical indicator of them all... the simple, err...I mean, exponential moving average.

Once I am satisfied that I have explained my use of the technical indicators so that a blindfolded monkey can understand them, I will then move on to the meat of the strategy construction models and private underground investors network rules that I use and nobody else can, unless they pay me a gazillion dollars in licensing fees.

So let us step inside the mind of the madness that is the Dart-Throw Trader.

Before I dive too deeply into the technical indicators that I use and why: allow me to give you a simple Dart-Throw Trader understanding of the complex world of technical indicators.
It is my belief that there are roughly 275 Technical indicators although I understand that new ones are being created all the time. In fact, one day I may create my own as well.

Here is the most important thing you should understand about all 275 technical indicators...
Lean in close, it's another secret the "establishment" doesn't want you to know.

Every Technical Indicator Falls Into One of Two Categories

1. **Lagging Indicators** – According to Wikipedia.org - A lagging indicator is an indicator that reacts slowly to changes, and therefore has little predictive value. Generally these types of indicators follow an event; they are historical in nature. To put this in to terms that my family can understand: A lagging indicator "tells us what we already know".
2. **Leading Indicators** – A leading indicator is an indicator that changes before the stock has changed, and therefore provides a predictive value. To put this into terms that my family can understand: A leading indicator "tells us what should happen next".

So, with this newfound market knowledge, allow me to ask you a fair and honest question. Which of these two indicators do you think you should pay more attention to?

Obviously: the leading indicators. Here is the good news for you, of the 275 technical indicators that we know of in existence today. It is estimated that roughly 80% of those indicators are categorized as lagging indicators.

This means that 20% of them are leading indicators. And since the leading indicators are the only ones you want to pay attention to anyway this would imply that there are about 50 technical indicators that one would need to study and learn.

But here is where it gets even better. Of the estimated 50 indicators in existence that fall into the leading category, many of those indicators are simply variations of existing indicators. In other words, many of these leading indicators are simply redundant in the information that they provide.

So, what this all boils down to is that of the leading indicators that exist, there are only about 14 to 16 specific unique leading indicators that need to be learned, understood and applied.

So we take a universe of 275 indicators and narrow it down to a group of 14 to 16 specific unique applicable indicators.

Now that we have identified that there are only a handful of technical indicators that need to be applied to a chart. It is important to understand what each of these technical indicators was created and designed to do.

Every technical indicator created, regardless of whether they're lagging or leading was created to serve one, or more, of three basic purposes.

1. **Alert**
2. **Confirm**
3. **Predict**

So it is simply our responsibility to identify which of the leading indicators alert us of impending behavior, predict future behavior and which of these confirm that behavior.

Allow me to use an analogy to help you understand the power of what I have just shared.

Imagine you are with 300 other guests attending a wedding reception in a hotel ballroom. As the music plays and the guests celebrate, lights begin to flash and a siren begins to wail.

The fire alarm has just gone off. What do you do? Most people would react. They would begin to look for any exit. They would begin to panic.

I, upon hearing the alarm, recognize that it is just an alert. An alert is designed to capture our attention so that we may begin to focus and prepare to respond.

Think of it this way. When the fire alarm goes off, do we for a fact know that there is a fire? No. It could be a drill.

Remember, our responsibility, as Dart-Throw Traders, is to respond when others react.

Here is what we teach blindfolded monkeys. In order to enter a successful trade, we need 1 alert and 3 confirmation's of that alert using leading indicators in order to initiate the correct response.

So let's go back to our fire alarm analogy to put this in perspective. Once the fire alarm goes off we first need to confirm that there is in fact a fire and that this is not just a drill.

Our response to a fire is significantly different than our response to a drill.

The second confirmation we look for is, "where is the fire?" Is it above us, below us, in front, in back or to the side? The last thing we want to do is react and go running into the fire because we did not confirm where it is.

The last confirmation we look for is, "what is the fastest and best escape route?" This confirmation will allow us to quickly exit the building with the highest probability of safety.

Once we have a confirmed alert we can now respond logically while everyone else is reacting emotionally. Do you see the difference? Good.

The Moving Average Convergence / Divergence indicator or as we in the Underground Investors Network call it... "MAC-D".

MACD

From Wikipedia, the free encyclopedia

MACD, which stands for Moving Average Convergence / Divergence, is a technical analysis indicator created by Gerald Appel in the 1960s. It shows the difference between a fast and slow exponential moving average (EMA) of closing prices. During the 1980s MACD proved to be a valuable tool for any trader. The standard periods recommended back in the 1960s by Gerald Appel are 12 and 26 days:

MACD = EMA[12]\,of\,price - EMA[26]\,of\,price

A signal line (or trigger line) is then formed by smoothing this with a further EMA. Sometimes, SMA is used for signal. The standard period for this is 9 days,

signal = EMA[9]\,of\,MACD

The difference between the MACD and the signal line is often calculated and shown not as a line, but a solid block histogram style. This construction was made by Thomas Aspray in 1986. The calculation is simply

histogram = MACD – signal

The set of periods for the averages, often written as say 12,26,9, can be varied. Appel and others have experimented with various combinations.

Interpretation

MACD is a trend following indicator, and is designed to identify trend changes. It's generally not recommended for use in ranging market conditions. Three types of trading signals are generated:

* MACD line crossing the signal line.
* MACD line crossing 0.
* Divergence between price and histogram, or between MACD line and price.

The signal line crossing is the usual trading rule. The standard interpretation is to buy when the MACD crosses up through the signal line, or sell when it crosses down through the signal line. These crossings may occur too frequently, and other tests may have to be applied.

The histogram shows when a crossing occurs. When the MACD line crosses through zero on the histogram it is said that the MACD line has crossed the signal line. The histogram can also help visualizing when the two lines are coming together. Both may still be rising, but coming together, so a falling histogram suggests a crossover may be approaching.

A crossing of the MACD line up through zero is interpreted as bullish, or down through zero as bearish. These crossings are of course simply the original EMA(12) line crossing up or down through the slower EMA(26) line.

Positive divergence between MACD and price arises when price makes a new sell-off low, but the MACD doesn't make a new low (i.e. it remains above where it fell to on that previous price low). This is interpreted as bullish, suggesting the downtrend may be nearly over. Negative divergence is the same thing when rising (i.e. price makes a new rally high, but MACD doesn't rise as high as before), this is interpreted as bearish.

Divergence may be similarly interpreted on the price versus the histogram, where the new price levels are not confirmed by new histogram levels. Longer and sharper divergences (distinct peaks or troughs) are regarded as more significant than small shallow patterns in this case.

It is recommended to look at a MACD on a weekly scale before looking at a daily scale to avoid making short term trades against the direction of the intermediate trend.[1]

Sometimes it is prudent to apply a price filter to the Bullish Moving Average Crossover to ensure that it will hold. An example of a price filter would be to buy if MACD breaks above the 9-day EMA and remains above for three days. The buy signal would then commence at the end of the third day.

Creator

Gerald Appel developed the Moving Average Convergence-Divergence (MACD) Indicator, and has written twelve books relating to investment strategies, including Winning Market Systems, Double Your Money Every Three Years, Stock Market Trading Systems, The Big Move, New Directions in Technical Analysis (co-author, Dr. Martin E. Zweig), and Time-Trend III.

In addition, Gerald has had many articles published in such publications as Money, Barron's, and Stocks and Commodities magazines. He has also produced and appeared in a number of videotapes related to technical investment strategies. Gerald has presented at a number of seminars within the United States and abroad, and has appeared on "Wall Street Week" with Louis Rukeyser and is a frequent guest on other television programs on the financial news networks and elsewhere.

Mr Appel published frequently in the 1970s & 1980s, in a time when computerized tools became available to professional investors but were much less accessible to retail investors. As computerized technical analysis relies on back-testing, it is not surprising that strategies announced year-by-year by Mr. Appel became vulnerable, year-by-year, to failure, as "past results do not guarantee future success". Nevertheless, the author's research has been respectable & innovative.

Signal Processing

The MACD is a filtered measure of the velocity. The velocity has been passed through two first order linear low pass filters. The "signal line" is that resulting velocity, filtered again. The difference between those two, the histogram, is a measure of the acceleration, with all three filters applied. The "MACD crossing the signal line" suggests that the direction of the acceleration is changing. "MACD line crossing zero" suggests that the average velocity is changing direction.

There you have the wikipedia definition of MACD. Honestly I used that definition because… it's accurate, complete and I am too lazy to try to say it in my own words.

Now that we have a working definition, it is time to take some experience and testing to massage the standard definition into something a Dart-Throw Trader can actually use.

This won't take long (because I am teaching it to a blindfolded monkey) and no offense to Gerald Appel (the creator), but as it is wikipedily defined, it doesn't work for me. So, here is my skew of the MACD and why.

I am not going to mess with the core structure of the MACD (that would be insane) I am only going to change the time frame of the exponential Moving Averages it interprets.

Gerald Appel suggested (in the 1960's) to use the 12 day EMA, the 26 day EMA, and a 9 day SMA as the signal line. You know what, it probably worked for him… It does not, however, work for me.

I have decided that the 15 day EMA, the 50 day EMA and a 10 day SMA work better.

Stop wondering why and let me explain. The vast majority of investors that I know would unanimously agree that the 15 day moving average and the 50 day moving average are two of the most recognized and followed moving averages in the investing universe.

Since these are two of the most followed (and reacted to) moving averages we can identify, it is reasonable to assume that there will be a significant amount of emotional reactions that occur as asset prices approach either of these two moving average lines.

To help you better understand these moving averages let me share with you my thoughts and feelings about the 15 Day EMA, the 50 Day EMA and the 200 Day EMA.

First, a definition:

Exponential moving average

From Wikipedia, the free encyclopedia

An exponential moving average (EMA), sometimes also called an exponentially weighted moving average (EWMA), applies weighting factors which decrease exponentially. The weighting for each older data point decreases exponentially, giving much more importance to recent observations while still not discarding older observations entirely.

What?

Blindfolded Monkey Definition. An exponential moving average is the average price of an asset over a specified period of time that pays more attention to what is happening currently in time as opposed to what happened in the past.

"Do Stocks bounce off of support because investors are buying them or do investors buy them because they bounce of support?"

- Jimmy Slagle, The Dart-Throw Trader

The Trading Gridiron...
I Love Football And Trading

When I think about the 15, 50 and 200 day EMA's my mind drifts towards football.

In football, there is a first line of defense, a second line of defense, and a third line of defense. So here is how I interpret these three moving average lines.

In my world, the 15 day exponential moving average (DEMA) is a stocks first line of defense. Much of the time (especially in trending situations) the 15 DEMA line will act as a level of support or resistance depending on where the asset price is in relation to the 15 DEMA.

If the asset price is below the 15 DEMA, it often acts as a level of resistance. If the asset price is above the 15 DEMA, it frequently acts as a level of support.

So I imagine that the 15 DEMA is the first line of defense. It is the nose guard and tackles on the trading gridiron. The job of the first line of defense is to stop the price from moving to far. If the asset can manage to break through the first line of defense, emotions run high because there is usually a small area of playing field before it reaches the second line of defense.

If the asset breaks through the first line of defense, it then becomes the job of the 50 DEMA to keep the asset in check. The 50 DEMA is a much stronger line of defense. It consists of the linebackers on the trading gridiron. (If you know anything about linebackers you know how aggressive they can be in defending their territory.)

If the asset manages to break through the second line of defense, emotions on the field will intensify further as the spectators get more excited, because there is usually a larger area of playing field before it reaches the third line of defense.

The third line of defense is the 200 DEMA, the equivalent of the safeties and cornerbacks on the trading gridiron. This is an aggressive bunch that lives for the open field smack-down.

If the asset manages to break through this final line of defense, emotions on the field will reach critical mass as the game becomes a "foot race" to the goal line.

In terms of the 15, 50 and 200 DEMA's acting as support or resistance: the 15 DEMA is good, the 50 DEMA is better, and the 200 DEMA is bestest (is that even a word?).

Because of the emotions that surround these three moving averages, they are effective tools in being able to RESPOND when others REACT. This is one of the reasons why I chose to use them in the calculation of my MAC-D indicator.

Allow me to illustrate how this applies in the real Dart-Throw Trader world.

I share all of this with you to help you understand the mindset of the Dart-Throw Trader. There are two approaches to entering a Dart-Throw Trade.

1. Throw a dart, pick a stock, and enter an immediate trade based on the stock's current behavior using one of the 10 foundational strategies. This is what the Dart-Throw Trader Challenge was all about.

2. Throw a dart, pick a stock, and wait for a trade to come to you based on the alert and three-confirmation system described above.

The beauty of being a Dart-Throw Trader is that you can do either one. Stay with me and I promise I will show you how to do both.

The next technical indicator I want to share with you is the Stochastic Oscillator.

Stochastic oscillator

From Wikipedia, the free encyclopedia

The stochastic oscillator is a momentum indicator used in technical analysis, introduced by George Lane in the 1950s, to compare the closing price of an asset to its price range over a given time span.

This indicator is usually calculated as:

$$STS = 100 \; \frac{\text{Closing Price} - \text{Price Low}}{\text{Price High} - \text{Price Low}}$$

and can be manipulated by changing the period considered for highs and lows.

Interpretation

The idea behind this indicator is that prices tend to close near their past highs in bull markets, and near their lows in bear markets. Transaction signals can be spotted when the stochastic oscillator crosses its moving average.

Two stochastic oscillator indicators are typically calculated to assess future variations in prices, a fast (%K) and slow (%D). Comparisons of these statistics are a good indicator of speed at which prices are changing or the Impulse of Price. %K is the same as Williams %R, though on a scale 0 to 100 instead of -100 to 0, but the terminology for the two are kept separate.

The %K and %D oscillators range from 0 to 100 and are often visualized using a line plot. Levels near the extremes 100 and 0, for either %K or %D, indicate strength or weakness (respectively) because prices have made or are near new N-day highs or lows.

There are two well-known methods for using the %K and %D indicators to make decisions about when to buy or sell stocks. The first involves crossing of %K and %D signals, the second involves basing buy and sell decisions on the assumption that %K and %D oscillate.

In the first case, %D acts as a trigger or signal line for %K. A buy signal is given when %K crosses up through %D, or a sell signal when it crosses down through %D. Such crossovers can occur too often, and to avoid repeated whipsaws one can wait for crossovers occurring together with an overbought/oversold pullback, or only after a peak or trough in the %D line. If price volatility is high, a simple moving average of the Stoch %D indicator may be taken. This statistic smoothes out rapid fluctuations in price.

In the second case, some analysts argue that %K or %D levels above 80 and below 20 can be interpreted as overbought or oversold. On the theory that the prices oscillate, many analysts (including George Lane) recommend that buying and selling be timed to the return from these thresholds.[2][1] In other words, one should buy or sell after a bit of a reversal. Practically, this means that once the price exceeds one of these thresholds, the investor should wait for prices to return through those thresholds (e.g. if the oscillator were to go above 80, the investor waits until it falls below 80 to sell).

The third way that traders will use this indicator is to watch for divergences where the Stochastic trends in the opposite direction of price. As with the RSI, this is an indication that the momentum in the market is waning and a reversal may be in the making. For further confirmation, many traders will wait for the cross below the 80 or above the 20 line before entering a trade on divergence.

George Lane, a financial analyst from the 1950s is one of the first to publish on the use of stochastic oscillators to forecast prices [1]. According to Lane you use the stochastic's indicator with a good knowledge of "Elliot Wave Theory". A Center piece of his teaching is the divergence and convergence of trend lines drawn on stochastics as diverging/ converging to trend lines drawn on price cycles. Stochastics has the power to predict tops and bottoms.

It should be noted that the existence of price oscillations is hypothetical and statistical at best--stock price movements are a consequence of the actions of human decision-makers and past behavior of market variables does not necessarily predict future behavior.

What?

Blindfolded Monkey Definition: In the Dart-Throw Trader world the Stochastic oscillator serves two distinct purposes.

1. It acts as an alert (remember the fire alarm).

2. It helps us identify support and resistance.

Both purposes allow me to use the indicator based on the type of trade I want to construct: either a "Throw a dart do it now trade" or a "Throw a dart and wait for the alert and confirmations before entry".

Examine the chart below to see the two interpretations.

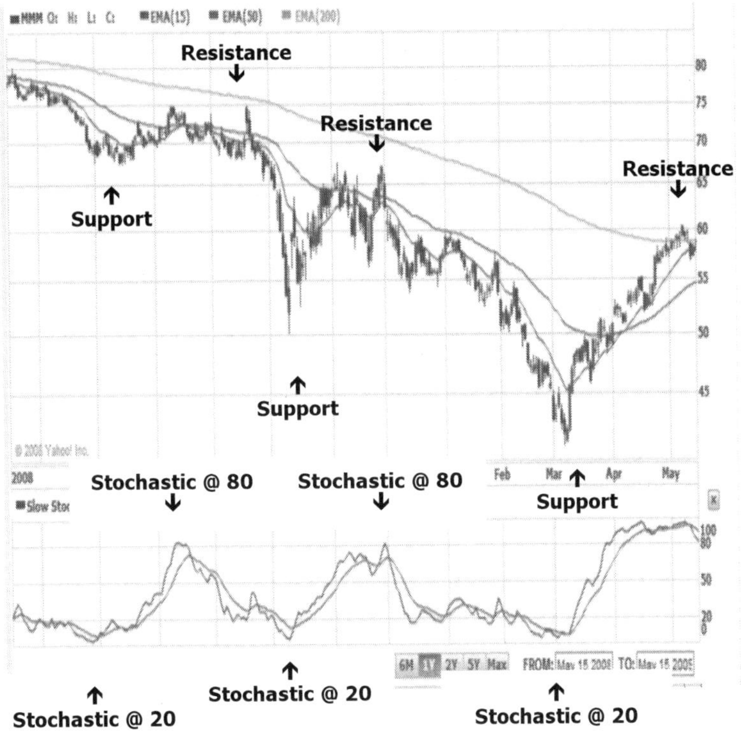

Here is an illustration of the stochastic oscillator being used to identify support and resistance.

When the Stochastic Oscillator is at 20 or below it would suggest that the asset in question is at a level of support. (1)

When the Stochastic Oscillator is at 80 or above it would suggest that the asset in question is a level of resistance. (2)

Here is an illustration of the Stochastic Oscillator being used as a Bull/Bear ALERT.

The Stochastic Oscillator crosses above 20 it is time to start THINKING about becoming bullish.

The Stochastic Oscillator crosses below 80 it is time to start THINKING about becoming bearish.

There is one final indicator I would like to bring to your attention as it relates to the Dart-Throw Trader style of trading and that is the Bollinger Band Indicator.

Bollinger Bands

from Wikipedia, the free encyclopedia

Bollinger Bands are a technical analysis tool invented by John Bollinger in the 1980s. Having evolved from the concept of trading bands, Bollinger Bands can be used to measure the highness or lowness of the price relative to previous trades.

Bollinger Bands consist of:

* a middle band being an N-period simple moving average

* an upper band at K times an N-period standard deviation above the middle band

* a lower band at K times an N-period standard deviation below the middle band

Typical values for N and K are 20 and 2, respectively. The default choice for the average is a simple moving average, but other types of averages can be employed as needed. Exponential moving averages are a common second choice. Usually the same period is used for both the middle band and the calculation of standard deviation.

Purpose

The purpose of Bollinger Bands is to provide a relative definition of high and low. By definition, prices are high at the upper band and low at the lower band. This definition can aid in rigorous pattern recognition and is useful in comparing price action to the action of indicators to arrive at systematic trading decisions.

Interpretation

The use of Bollinger Bands varies wildly among traders. Some traders buy when price touches the lower Bollinger Band and exit when price touches the moving average in the center of the bands. Other traders buy when price breaks above the upper Bollinger Band or sell when price falls below the lower

Bollinger Band. Moreover, the use of Bollinger Bands is not confined to stock traders; options traders, most notably implied volatility traders, often sell options when Bollinger Bands are historically far apart or buy options when the Bollinger Bands are historically close together, in both instances, expecting volatility to revert back towards the average historical volatility level for the stock.-technical analysis.

When the bands lie close together a period of low volatility in stock price is indicated. When they are far apart a period of high volatility in price is indicated. When the bands have only a slight slope and lie approximately parallel for an extended time the price of a stock will be found to oscillate up and down between the bands as though in a channel.

As always, traders are inclined to use Bollinger Bands with other indicators to see if there is confirmation. In particular, the use of an oscillator like Bollinger Bands will often be coupled with a non-oscillator indicator like chart patterns or a trendline; if these indicators confirm the recommendation of the Bollinger Bands, the trader will have greater evidence that what the Bands forecast is correct.

What?

Blindfolded Monkey Definition: In the world of the Dart-Throw Trader the Bollinger Bands help us to...

1. Identify the current trading range of the asset; this is great for structuring calendar spreads and condors.

2. Identify support and resistance.

3. Identify an impending breakout.

Let's examine the following chart to illustrate all three points.

To bring this technical indicator discussion home lets throw the dart… pick a stock at random and do an "immediate" trade evaluation and an "alert – 3 confirmation" trade evaluation, on the same stock.

The dart has been thrown and ANF (Abercrombie & Fitch Co.) was chosen. Let's examine the chart on the next page.

From a throw the dart and place a trade perspective, this one is fairly basic…

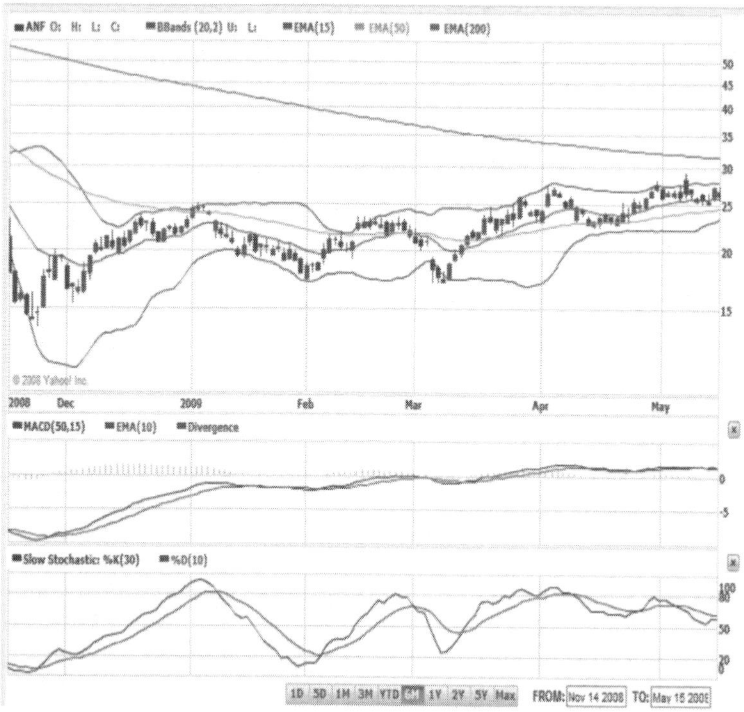

1. MACD is above the zero line indicating it is in a bullish trend.
2. The MACD line is fairly flat indicating the trend is slow.
3. Stochastic is @ 50 therefore ANF is neither oversold or overbought.
4. Bollinger Bands indicate a 3-4 dollar trading range.
5. ANF is at the higher range of the Bollinger Bands (possible resistance)

Overall I would suggest that ANF is in a stagnant to mildly bullish range. Possible strategies to use... Calendar Spread or Condor depends on Risk/Reward ratio.

From a Throw the Dart and wait for an alert and 3 confirmation perspective let's use hind-sight to explain foresight.

1. February – Stochastic moves above the 20 line... ALERT. Time to start thinking bullish because ANF was in a bearish trend.

2. February – MACD Crosses above its signal line... 1st Confirmation. Time to start thinking bullish because ANF was in a bearish trend.

3. March – ANF breaks above the (50DEMA)... 1st Confirmation.

4. March – MACD Crosses Above the zero line... 2nd Confirmation.

5. I would like to see ANF close above its 200 DEMA... This would be a 3rd Confirmation. At that point I would consider a Bull Spread, or long call.

The most important thing to remember when it comes to investing/trading the stock market is this: when all is said and done, a stock is either going to go UP in price, DOWN in price, or STAY the same... it can't do anything else.

The goal is to determine its CURRENT behavior, and trade using any strategy that will afford you the greatest amount of potential profit with the least amount of risk.

Conclusion

There are 275 technical indicators that one can add to a chart to help them make better trading decisions about the current and future expected behavior of any stock. These are the ones I use. Now you know why.

This is what works for me. It may not work for you. You must be diligent and prudent in your analysis at all times.

The Dart-Throw Trader Trading Strategies: Throw Darts – Pick Stocks – Make Money

In previous pages I have shared with you the 10 most fundamental strategies I use as a Dart-Throw Trader. In this section I am going to share with you my exclusive rules for entry.

Remember, you can NOT use these rules in your own trading unless you agree to…

1. **Hold me harmless when you lose all of your money.**
2. **Pay me a gazillion dollars upfront as a licensing fee.**

So with a deep breath and a big smile I now share the Dart-Throw Trader Secret Strategy Rules.

If structured correctly, the collar can be a very low risk, high probability trade. This strategy involves the simultaneous purchase of stock, at-the-money LEAPS puts, and the sale of out-of-the-money LEAPS calls.

To enter this position, we first start with the purchase of at least 100 shares of a selected stock. Once we own the stock, our first goal is to protect our investment. To accomplish this protection, we must purchase an at-the-money or slightly in-the-money protective put. Once we own the stock and have protected the down-side risk of our long stock, we must then sell an out-of-the-money call for the same expiration month of our long protective put.

This trade allows us to profit from three different scenarios. If the stock moves higher in price during the duration of the trade, we profit by selling the stock at the strike price of our short call. If the stock moves lower in price during the duration of the trade, we profit from the increased value of our long put. If the stock doesn't move or trades in a range, our long put and short call expire worthless, allowing us to hold the stock and restructure the trade.

Dart-Throw Traders Guidelines for Entry.

1. For this strategy we are looking for Bullish Trending stocks.

2. Buy 100 shares of stock for each position you want to enter.

3. Because of the structure of this trade, you can purchase this stock on margin, (without the fear of a margin call).

4. Once you own the stock you are then positioned to protect this investment by purchasing an at-the-money or slightly out-of-the-money protective put.

   (To best structure this trade use a LEAPS put.)

5. Now that you have protected your downside, it is now time to sell an out-of-the-money LEAPS call for enough premium to pay for the LEAPS put that you purchased.

6. When you short the LEAPS call make sure it is, at minimum, 2 strikes above the current price of the stock and the premium will cover the cost of the long LEAPS put completely. (Best case is to short a LEAPS call that will not only cover the cost of the LEAPS put but also leave a small credit to your account. This should cover some, if not all, of your margin cost and give you a slight profit if the stock becomes worthless.)

Dart-Throw Traders Guidelines for Exit.

1. This trade is intended to be held until the expiration of the long and short LEAPS options.

2. On expiration, if the stock has moved above the strike of the call you are short, simply deliver the stock at that strike and realize the profit. (the put will expire worthless.)

3. On expiration, if the stock has dropped in value, simply exercise your long put and your short call will expire worthless... or you could simply sell the put for its increased value and continue to hold the stock with a lower cost basis.

4. On expiration, if the stock is between the strikes of the long put and short call, let both options expire worthless. At this point you will still own the stock and can restructure a new collar position... or simply sell the stock for its current price.

5. If the stock makes a strong bullish move prior to expiration, you can always unwind the current collar position by buying back you short LEAPS call and selling back your long LEAPS put. Once you have unwound your original position you can structure a new position at the current stock price.

The Bull Call Spread

The bull call spread consists of the purchase of one call and the sale of a higher call. For example, one might purchase the XYZ November 95 call for 3-1/2 and the sale of the XYZ November 100 call for 1-3/4 with XYZ stock trading at 96. The resulting debit is 1-3/4. If the stock price advances, the spread may become profitable. If XYZ closes above 96-3/4 at expiration, the position is profitable.

This is because the debit was 1-3/4; that is, the entire position cost you that much plus commission. The greatest amount of profit will be realized if XYZ closes at 100 at expiration. In this example, the long call is worth 5, and the short call expires worthless for an additional profit of 1-3/4. This would yield a profit of 1-1/2 + 1-3/4 = 3-1/4.

Break even point = lower strike price + net debit of the spread

Maximum profit potential = higher strike price - lower strike price - net debit of the spread.

The reason an investor would use the bull spread strategy is that he is bullish, but not overly sure. If he were totally sure, he would buy the call outright.

An investor can establish the bull spread using an out-of-the-money call for each leg of the spread. This is extremely aggressive. Or, the investor can establish the spread with a lower call which is in-the-money and the higher call out-of-the-money. This is less aggressive. And the least aggressive strategy is to establish the spread with both legs in the money.

Follow Up Action

The investor needs to keep an eye on this spread. If the underlying security moves up in price too steeply, too quickly, the time value premium of the short call could rise substantially. If this happens, that call may need to be bought back early. Also, if the price of the underlying security rises too high, the short call may go in-the-money. The trader should be aware of this and buy the call back before it is exercised.

If the underlying security declines in price, the trader may want to buy back the short side of the spread. He would then be trying to leg out the long side of the spread looking for price to rise again. I don't recommend doing this unless it can be bought back for 1/16, 1/8, or at most 1/4. Buying it back for 1/8 or 1/4 is buying it back for next to nothing.

Under no circumstances is it recommended for the trader to close out the long side of the spread and try to leg out the short side of the spread after a rise in price. The trader would be looking for the price to decline. The risk is way, way, way, too large. The trader would be leaving himself with an uncovered short position. Theoretically, the risk is unlimited.

Dart-Throw Trader Guidelines for Entry.

1. For this strategy we are looking for Bullish Trending stocks.

2. Buy some time, 3-6 months until expiration. 4 months is optimal.

3. Enter this trade so that the net cost is 40% or less than the trades spread.

There are three ways to get your cost to 40% or below of spread.

Widen the spread, eg; $20, $30, $40... spreads.

Move the spread out of the money.

Shorten the time frame.* (Never shorten the time frame below 3 months unless you understand and are fully prepared to accept the additional risk.)

4. Enter spread with a net position Delta of .25 or greater.

Dart-Throw Trader Guidelines for Exit:

1. You can always exit this trade on expiration, (in fact you will be forced to).

2. You can exit this trade when you have reached a net value that is equal to 80% of the total spread.

3. I like to exit these trades when I have made a 40% return on my risk, or...

4. When I have lost 40% of my risk (cost).

5. If halfway through the life of the trade I have not made at least a 40% return on my risk (cost), I will exit or adjust the trade.

These five guidelines force me to evaluate the trade at very specific intervals.

Ticker ________ Current Price $________ Date ________

Buy ls	________	(-)________
Sell hs	________	(+)________
Max Risk		(=)________
Max Profit		(=)________
Break Even Price		(=)________
Max Gain Price		(=)________

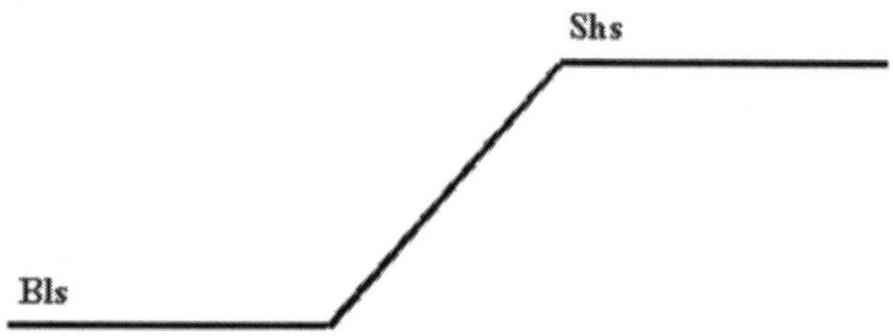

Bull Call Spread

The Bull Put Spread

The options strategy bull spread with puts consists of the purchase of one put, and the sale of another put with a higher strike price. With a stock trading at 37, one might sell the November 40 put and purchase the November 35 put.

For example, assume XYZ is trading at 67. Further assume that the XYZ November 70 put is trading at 5-3/4 and the XYZ November 65 put is trading at 3-1/2. The investor constructing a bull spread with puts would purchase the November 65 put at 3-1/2 and sell the XYZ November 70 put for 5-3/4.

This transaction would yield a credit of 2-1/4. This is also the maximum amount of profit the investor can receive. Because the spread is a credit spread, the investor must collateralize the transaction.

Maximum profit = the net credit received

Maximum risk = the difference between the strike prices - the net credit received.

Break even point = the higher strike price - the net credit.

In our example, if XYZ closes above 70 at expiration, both options expire worthless and the investor profits by the full amount of the initial credit of 2-1/4. The maximum loss is incurred if XYZ closes anywhere below 65 at expiration.

The investor needs to keep in mind that, in this options strategy, the short put can be exercised at any time. Thus, the bull spread with puts is a spread which carries a considerable amount of risk. Should the short put option get exercised, the investor would get stuck paying extra stock commissions. Therefore, should the underlying security decline in price rather than rise in price, the investor should seriously consider closing the transaction.

Dart-Throw Traders Guidelines for Entry.

1. For this strategy we are looking for Bullish Trending stocks.

2. Buy some time, 3-6 months until expiration. 4 months is optimal.

3. Enter this trade so that the net risk is 40% or less than the trades spread.

There are three ways to get your cost to 40% or below of spread.

Widen the spread, ie; $20, $30, $40... spreads.

Move the spread out of the money.

Shorten the time frame.* (Never shorten the time frame below 3 months unless you understand and are fully prepared to accept the additional risk.)

4. Enter spread with a net position Delta of .25 or greater.

Dart-Throw Traders Guidelines for Exit.

1. You can always exit this trade on expiration (in fact you will be forced to).

2. You can exit this trade when you have reached a net value that is equal to 80% of the total spread.

3. I like to exit these trades when I have made a 40% return on my risk. or...

4. When I have lost 40% of my risk (cost).

5. If halfway through the life of the trade I have not made at least a 40% return on my risk (cost), I will exit or adjust the trade.

These Five guidelines force me to evaluate the trade at very specific intervals.

Ticker __________ Current Price $__________ Date ________

Buy ls _________ (-)_________

Sell hs _________ (+)_________

Max Risk (=)_________

Max Profit (=)_________

Break Even Price (=)_________

Max Gain Price (=)_________

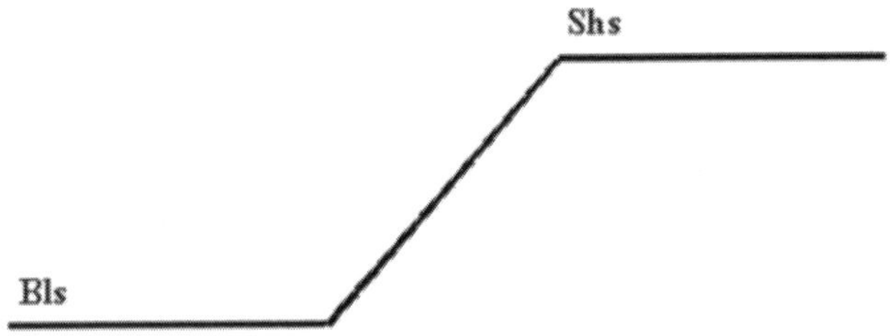

Bull Put Spread

Notes:

____

____

____

____

____

____

The Bear Put Spread

The options strategy "bear spread with puts" involves the sale of one put with a lower strike and the purchase of another put with a higher strike price. For example, one might sell the November 70 put, and simultaneously purchase the November 75 put. In my opinion, the bear spread with puts is superior to the bear spread with calls. An investor risks early exercise with a call bear spread. However, this is not a problem with a put bear spread. In the put bear spread, an out-of-the money put is sold.

An example of the options strategy bear spread with puts is as follows: Assume XYZ is trading at 69. Further assume that the XYZ November 70 puts are trading at 5-3/4, and the XYZ November 65 puts are trading at 3-1/2. An investor would buy the XYZ November 70 put at 5-3/4 and sell the XYZ November 65 put for 3-1/2. This transaction would cost the investor the amount of the debit which is 2-1/4. Don't forget commissions.

At November expiration if XYZ closes above 70 the investor realizes the maximum loss. In this case it's the debit of 2-1/4. However, at November expiration, if XYZ closes below 65, the investor realizes the maximum profit, which in this case is 2-3/4.

Maximum risk = the initial debit.

Maximum profit = the difference between the two strikes - the initial debit.

Break even point = higher strike price - initial debit.

Follow up action would include monitoring the short put if the option is about to go in-the-money. At that point, the bear spread with puts should be closed to avoid the possibility of an exercise. The investor doesn't want to pay extra stock commissions in the event of an exercise. This is a very viable options strategy for many investors who are slightly bearish on the particular index or equity.

Dart-Throw Traders Guidelines for Entry:

1. For this strategy we are looking for Bearish Trending stocks.

2. Buy some time, 2-4 months until expiration. 3 months is optimal.

3. Enter this trade so that the net cost is 40% or less than the trades spread.

There are three ways to get your cost to 40% or below of spread.

Widen the spread, ie; $20, $30, $40... spreads.

Move the spread out of the money.

Shorten the time frame.* (Never shorten the time frame below 3 months unless you understand and are fully prepared to accept the additional risk.)

4. Enter spread with a net position Delta of .25 or greater.

Dart-Throw Traders Guidelines for Exit:

1. You can always exit this trade on expiration, (in fact you will be forced to).

2. You can exit this trade when you have reached a net value that is equal to 80% of the total spread.

3. I like to exit these trades when I have made a 40% return on my risk. or...

4. When I have lost 40% of my risk (cost).

5. If 1/2 way through the life of the trade I have not made at least a 40% return on my risk (cost) I will exit or adjust the trade.

These Five guidelines force me to evaluate the trade at very specific intervals.

Ticker ________ **Current Price $**________ **Date** ________

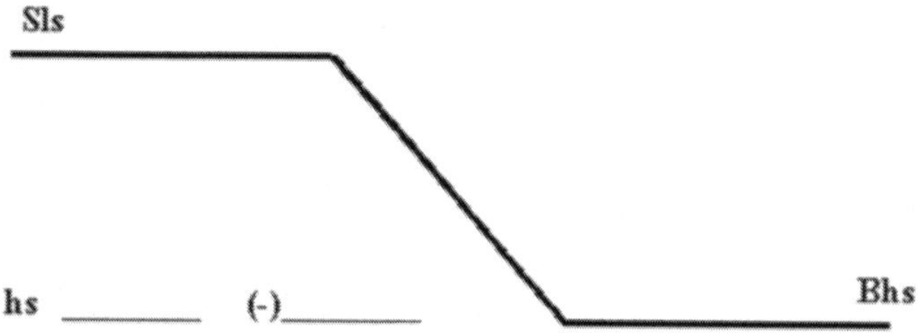

Buy hs ________ (-)________
Sell ls ________ (+)________
Max Risk (=)________
Max Profit (=)________
Break Even Price (=)________
Max Gain Price (=)________

Bear Put Spread

Notes:

____

____

____

____

The Bear Call Spread

The options strategy "bear spread with calls" involves the purchase of one call (higher strike) and the sale of a call with a strike price lower than the long call. This is done as a credit spread. The amount of profit id determined when the spread is initiated. The maximum profit is the amount of the credit. The objective is for both options to expire worthless. The spread becomes profitable if the underlying security which was sold, closes below the strike price. Both options have the same expiration date.

As an example, XYZ is trading at 96. The XYZ November 100 call is trading at 1-3/4. The XYZ November 95 call is trading at 3-1/2. The investor buys the XYZ November 100 call at 1-3/4. And he sells the XYZ November 95 call for 3-1/2. Thus, he is left with a credit of 1-3/4. The amount of maximum profit is 1-3/4. The total amount of risk is 3-1/4 (don't forget commission).

Maximum profit = net amount of the credit received

Maximum risk = difference between the two strike prices - net credit received + commissions

With a bear spread options strategy, the trader is looking for price to decline. If the price rises, the most the trader can lose is predetermined. The greater the maximum profit potential, the greater the risk. The further the short call is in-the-money, the greater the profit potential. However, this carries greater risk as it is more likely the short call will close in-the-money. It is aggressive in the sense that the security needs to decline further in price. The further the security needs to fall, the greater the risk.

Unlike the bear spread done with puts, the bear spread done with calls has an uncovered short call. That is, the long call is not equal to or lower than the sold call. Most brokerage firms will require a larger amount of equity in the account to cover any potential losses. Therefore, this is not a preferred options strategy.

Follow up action would require the investor to be on guard and watch for the time value premium to erode. Should time value premium erode to nothing or very little, the investor risks the short leg being exercised. The spread should be closed regardless of how much time remains in the spread.

Despite the fact that the bear spread done with calls is a credit spread requiring no actual outlay of cash, it is a riskier strategy than the bear spread done with puts. This is because there is a greater risk of early exercise of the short call. Thus, the investor risks higher transaction costs with the extra commissions should the short call be exercised. The debit bear spread done with puts is, in my opinion, a superior options strategy.

Dart-Throw Traders Guidelines for Entry.

1. For this strategy we are looking for **Bearish Trending** stocks.

2. Buy some time, 2-4 months until expiration. **3 months is optimal**.

3. Enter this trade so that the net risk is **40% or less** than the trades spread.

There are three ways to get your cost to 40% or below of spread.

Widen the spread, ie; $20, $30, $40... spreads.

Move the spread out of the money.

Shorten the time frame.* (Never shorten the time frame below 3 months unless you understand and are fully prepared to accept the additional risk.)

4. Enter spread with a **net position Delta of .25** or greater.

Dart-Throw Traders Guidelines for Exit.

1. You can always exit this trade on expiration, (in fact you will be forced to).

2. You can exit this trade when you have reached a net value that is equal to 80% of the total spread.

3. I like to exit these trades when I have made a 40% return on my risk. or...

4. When I have lost 40% of my risk (cost).

5. If halfway through the life of the trade I have not made at least a 40% return on my risk (cost), I will exit or adjust the trade.

These five guidelines force me to evaluate the trade at very specific intervals.

Ticker ________ Current Price $________ Date ________

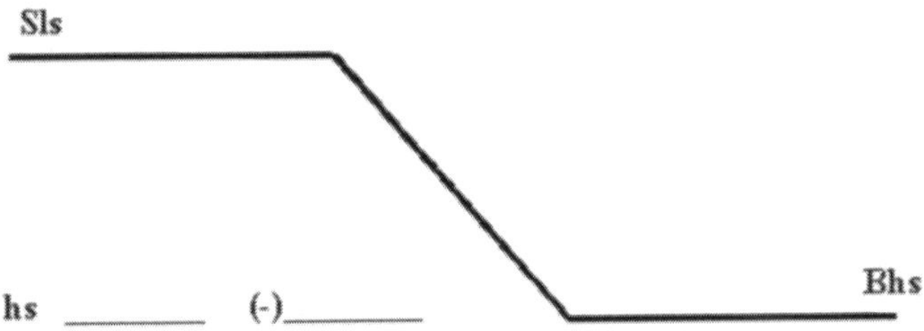

Buy hs ________ (-)________
Sell ls ________ (+)________
Max Risk (=)________
Max Profit (=)________
Break Even Price (=)________
Max Gain Price (=)________

Bear Call Spread

The Call Calendar Spread

A calendar spread (time spread) options strategy consists of the sale of one call and the simultaneous purchase of a call of the same underlying security with the same strike price but with a strike price further out.

An example would be the sale of an XYZ April 95 call for 3-1/2, and the simultaneous purchase of the XYZ October 95 call for 10. Assume XYZ common stock is presently trading at 90. The object is to have XYZ stock close below 95 at the close of April expiration.

Should XYZ close below 95 at April expiration, the April 95 call would expire worthless for a 3-1/2 point profit. The XYZ October 95 call would probably be worth about 7-1/2. The original position cost the investor the difference between the call sold and the call purchased (plus commission).

Thus, the original cost (debit) for the investor was 6-1/2. At April expiration, the investor could close the calendar spread out. The result would be the 7-1/2 points received from the long call. Subtract from this the original debit of 6-1/2, and the result is a profit of 1 point. The underlying security only has to be at about the strike price of the sold call. Profit can be made in a narrow range. However, if the underlying security is far above or below the sold strike price, a loss may occur.

The options strategy just described is a neutral outlook strategy. In other words, the investor doesn't think that the underlying security is going to move much in either direction prior to the April expiration.

However, the investor can also create an aggressive and bullish calendar spread with call. In this case, with XYZ trading at about 96, he might sell the XYZ April 100 call for 1-3/4, and buy the XYZ June 100 call for 3-3/4. First, the investor wants the April 100 call to expire worthless; and second, he wants the price of the underlying security to rise in price after April expiration. If this happens, he will own the June 100 call at a price of 2. This is the amount of the original debit. At this point, the break even point would be 102. It's not unreasonable to expect that a volatile stock like XYZ could move 6 points in two months.

Follow up action for the neutral calendar spread is to close the spread if the sold call is trading near parity. The investor wants to avoid an early exercise with this options strategy since this would involve additional stock commission costs.

Should the underlying security rise quickly after the calendar spread is established, the investor has two choices. First, he can close out the calendar spread early for a small loss. Or second, he can ride out the spread until April expiration hoping for the stock to decline. Should the underlying security decline in price sharply after the spread is initiated, he could sell the long call in an effort to recover a little something and keep the short call on. This is a dangerous options strategy. The trader is left with a naked short call. If the stock remains depressed, the call expires worthless and the trader will profit. However, if the underlying security rises in price drastically prior to April expiration, the losses are potentially unlimited. I don't ever recommend leaving an uncovered (naked) option. The risk is just too great in any options strategy.

Follow up action for the trader who initiated the bullish calendar spread is to close the spread if the underlying security moves up in price too high, and the spread is profitable. A small loss is the preferred options strategy.

It is not recommended to close the short leg and ride out the long leg. If the underlying security declines in price, a larger loss may occur. It is also not recommended to leg out both sides of the bullish calendar spread. The concept behind this type of spread is that the more frequent small losses will be overwhelmed by the less frequent large gains.

There is one other possible options strategy one can use when initiating a calendar spread: buy a longer-term option and sell the near-term option. An example would be to sell the XYZ April 95 call for 3-1/2, and buy the XYZ January 95 call for 8-1/2. At April expiration, assuming the price of XYZ is below 95, the April call would expire worthless, and the January call would be worth about 6.

The investor could then sell an XYZ May 95 call for about 3-1/2. At May expiration, assuming the price of XYZ was still below 95, the investor would have brought in 7 points against the 8-1/2 points the investor originally paid for the January 95 call. Thus, at May expiration, he would be holding a January 95 call worth about 3-1/2 points for an overall cost of 1-1/2. He could then sell the January call and realize his 2 points profit, or hold the call if he expected the price of XYZ to rise by January. This is an options strategy which is not used as much as it could be by traders using calendar spreads.

Dart-Throw Traders Guidelines for (Call Calendar) Entry
(scroll down for Put Calendar rules)

1. For this strategy we are looking for Stagnant to Mildly Bullish stocks.

2. Buy (long) slightly ITM (in the money) Calls.

3. Buy the long call with 6 months or longer in time until expiration.

4. Sell (short) slightly OTM (out of the money) Calls.

5. Sell the short call with with 1 month or less in time until expiration.

6. Buy and Sell equal numbers of options (never sell more than you buy).

7. The short call should be worth 25% or more than the long call (this will cover time decay and commissions if the stock does not move).

(scroll up for Call Calendar rules)

1. For this strategy we are looking for Stagnant to Mildly Bearish stocks.

2. Buy (long) slightly ITM (in the money) Puts.

3. Buy the long put with 6 months or longer in time until expiration.

4. Sell (short) slightly OTM (out of the money) Puts.

5. Sell the short put with with 1 month or less in time until expiration.

6. Buy and Sell equal numbers of options (never sell more than you buy).

7. The short put should be worth 25% or more than the long put (this will cover time decay and commissions if the stock does not move).

Dart-Throw Traders Guidelines for Exit. (Call Calendar, Put Calendar rules to follow)

1. Exit this trade if the short call is 1/4 point or more ITM (in the money); exit even if there is a possibility that it will move a 1/4 ITM.

2. If when approaching expiration of the short call the stock has moved up in price, re-evaluate the position. If you would enter it again, following the above rules, buy back your short and sell the next expiration month available. If you would not enter the trade, based on the above rules, exit the entire trade. If you continue to short calls each month, remember to roll your long call into a further month when you get to the long calls last 3 months of life (at this point time decay works strongly against you).

3. If when approaching expiration of the short call the stock has NOT moved in price, re-evaluate the position. If you would enter it again, following the above rules, buy back your short and sell the next expiration month available. If you would not enter the trade, based on the above rules, exit the entire trade.

4. If when approaching expiration of the short call the stock has moved DOWN in price, re-evaluate the position. I would suggest closing the entire trade and minimizing your loss. If you feel the stock may retrace to its previous price, re-evaluate the position according to the above entry rules.

Put Calendar Exit Rules

1. Exit this trade if the short put is 1/4 point or more ITM (in the money); exit even if there is a possibility that it will move a 1/4 ITM.

2. If when approaching expiration of the short put the stock has moved Down in price, re-evaluate the position. If you would enter it again, following the above rules, buy back your short and sell the next expiration month available. If you would not enter the trade, based on the above rules, exit the entire trade. If you continue to short puts each month, remember to roll your long put into a further month when you get to the long puts' last 3 months of life (at this point time decay works strongly against you).

3. If when approaching expiration of the short put the stock has NOT moved in price, re-evaluate the position. If you would enter it again, following the above rules, buy back your short and sell the next expiration month available. If you would not enter the trade, based on the above rules, exit the entire trade.

4. If when approaching expiration of the short put the stock has moved UP in price, re-evaluate the position. I would suggest closing the entire trade and minimizing your loss. If you feel the stock may retrace to its previous price, re-evaluate the position according to the above entry rules.

The Butterfly & Condor

The butterfly spread is a neutral options strategy position most often involving three different strike price calls. One call is bought at the lowest strike price. Two calls are sold at the middle strike price. And one call is bought at the highest strike price (although it can also be implemented using puts). The investor would use this options strategy if he feels that the underlying security is not too volatile and won't experience too much of a net rise or fall by expiration. Both risk and profit are limited. And commission costs are high. The maximum net amount of profit is realized if the stock price closes at expiration at the strike price of the written options.

Using XYZ as an example, assume the following: An XYZ April 90 call is bought for 6-1/2; two XYZ April 100 calls are sold for 3-1/2 each; and one XYZ April 110 call is purchased for 2 points.

Buy 1 April 90 call = ($650.00)

Sell 2 April 100 calls = $700.00

Buy 1 April 110 call = ($200.00)

Total Net Debit = ($150.00)

Net collateral investment = distance between the strikes + net debit [The butterfly spread is essentially a combination of two options strategies. It is both a bull spread and a bear spread. Therefore, the collateral requirement is the total required for both the bull spread and the bear spread. Despite the fact that the investor only has a net debit here smaller than the total margin required, there will be a reduction in the additional buying ability in the margin account.]

Maximum risk = net amount of the debit plus commission

Maximum profit = distance between the strikes - net debit

Downside break-even = lowest strike + net debit

Upside break-even = highest strike - net debit

In our butterfly spread options strategy example the maximum risk is $150 plus commissions, the maximum profit is $850, the downside break-even point is $97, the upside break-even point is $103.

The optimal butterfly spread to set up is one where the net debit is small. However, we don't recommend using calls at parity because of the risk of assignment. A small debit limits the amount of overall risk. The other thing to look for is that the stock should be near or at the middle strike price (the calls which are sold). Another thing one should look for is to set the butterfly spread up with a volatile and expensive stock. These stocks have strike prices 10 and sometimes 20 points apart. This gives the spreader an advantage. The spreader is at a disadvantage with a less volatile and less expensive stock. It probably won't have as many strikes available.

The follow up action involved for the butterfly spread options strategy is to first watch for early exercise of the middle options. This would happen if the middle strikes were trading near parity. If the middle calls are exercised, I recommend closing the overall spread. If it looks like the calls may be exercised I also recommend closing out the spread.

Keep a close eye on the stock if it is about to go ex-dividend. It could move the middle strikes in-the-money. The second thing to look for is that if the butterfly spread is profitable, consider closing the position out. This is especially true if the middle options look like they might move away from the middle strike price level.

If the stock looks like it's going to move up above the higher strike or down below the lower strike, one might consider closing the trade. Even though the risk is limited to amount of the net debit, if the butterfly spread was set up with a large debit, closing at break-even might be a viable alternative.

The butterfly spread is the only options strategy I can think of where it is possible to leg out of the spread profitably and safely. Because the butterfly spread consists of a bull spread and a bear spread, one spread may reach its maximum profit.

For example, if the price of XYZ were to drop to about 90 the investor would be in a loss situation with his butterfly spread. However, the bear spread portion of his butterfly spread would be at its maximum profit potential. If he bought back the short leg of the bear spread portion for about 1 point and sold the long 100 call for about 1/2, he would have a bull spread which cost 2 points. He increased his risk by 1/2 point from 1-1/2 to 2. Should the price of XYZ increase above 95 he would be able to realize most of the initial profit from the butterfly spread.

Because four different options are involved in setting up the butterfly spread, it becomes a very expensive options strategy to set up. Four different commissions are involved. Generally, the butterfly spread is set up by traders who have very low commission costs. The commission costs with this options strategy are an important consideration to take into account prior to initiating the trade.

Dart-Throw Traders Guidelines for Entry.

1. For this strategy we are looking for Stagnant stocks (3 months or longer).

2. First we want to establish this stocks 3 month trading range.

3. Once the range has been established, we need to identify the current resistance price.

4. Next we need to identify the current support price.

5. Next we need to identify the mid-price between the current support and resistance prices.

6. Once we have identified these three price points, our goal is to sell the strike price closest to the mid-price point (short 2 of these strikes for each butterfly you want to construct).

7. Our Next goal is to buy (long) the strike price closest to the resistance price point we have identified (buy [long] 1 of these strikes for each butterfly you want to construct).

8. Our next goal is to buy (long) the strike price closest to the support price point we have identified (buy [long] 1 of these strikes for each butterfly you want to construct).

9. Enter this trade with options that have 30 days or less until expiration.

10. Enter this trade with a 1:1 reward to risk ratio (never risk more than you can make).

Note: When this trade has been entered correctly you will be in a bull call spread and a bear call spread at the same time, which will enable you to receive your maximum profit if the stock closes at the exact price of the strikes you are short.

Dart-Throw Traders Guidelines for Exit.

1. You must exit this trade, especially if the stock closes at the exact price of the strikes you are short.

2. On expiration if the stock has broken out of its trading range, you only need to close the spread that is profitable. In other words, if the stock breaks-out to the upside, close out the bull call spread. If it breaks out to the downside, close out the bear call spread.

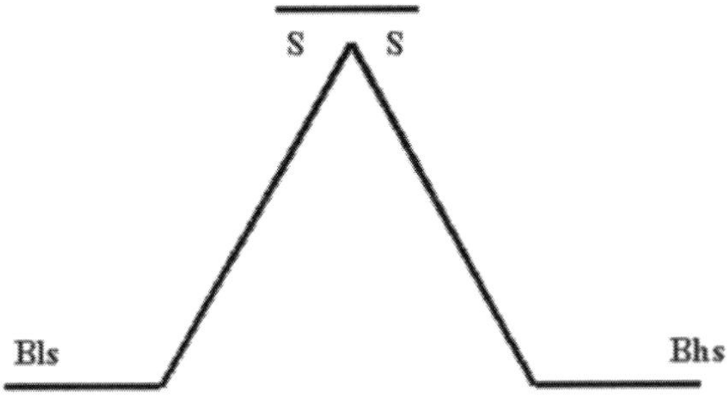

Buy ________	(-)________	Sell ________	(+) ________
Buy ________	(-)________	Sell ________	(+) ________
Max Risk	(=)________	Break Even Upside	________
Max Profit	(=)________	Break Even Downside	________

Ticker ________ Current Price $________ Butterfly

The Call Ratio Back Spread

The Call Ratio Back-Spread consists of the purchase of two or more calls and the sale of 1 lower strike call. For example, one might purchase 2 XYZ November 95 calls for 3-1/2 each and then sell one of the XYZ November 85 calls for 7-3/4 with XYZ stock trading at 86. The resulting credit is 3/4. If the stock price advances, the spread may become profitable. If XYZ closes above 94 1/4 at expiration, the position is profitable. This is because the credit was 3/4; that is, the entire position cost you that much plus commission. The greatest amount of profit is infinite the higher XYZ closes above 95 at expiration.

There are two break even points in this trade.

Lower break even point = lower strike price + net credit of the spread.

Higher break even point = higher strike price - net credit of the spread.

Maximum profit potential is unlimited the higher the stock closes above 95.

The reason an investor would use the call ratio back spread strategy is that he is strongly bullish, but would like a "hedged" position.

An investor can establish the put ratio backspread using out-of-the-money calls for each leg of the spread. This is extremely aggressive. Or, the investor can establish the spread with the short call which is in the money and the long calls out of the money. This is less aggressive. The least aggressive strategy, however, is to establish the spread with both legs in the money.

Dart-Throw Traders Guidelines for Entry.

1. For this strategy we are looking for Strongly Bullish stocks.

2. Buy some time, 3-6 months until expiration. The more time the better.

3. Purchase ATM or slightly OTM calls.

4. Sell ITM calls.

5. Try to limit your spreads to $5 - $10.

6. Buy more calls than you sell in ratios; Short (1) - Long (2), Short (2) - Long (3), Short (1) - Long (3 or 4 or 5...).

7. ALWAYS enter this trade with a net credit.

Dart-Throw Traders Guidelines for Exit.

1. This trade is designed to be held until expiration.

2. You can exit this trade when you have reached a net profit that is acceptable to you.

3. I like to exit these trades when I have made a 80% return on my risk. or...

4. When I have lost 40% of my risk (cost).

5. If halfway through the life of the trade I have not made at least a 40% return on my risk (cost), I will exit or adjust the trade.

These five guidelines force me to evaluate the trade at very specific intervals.

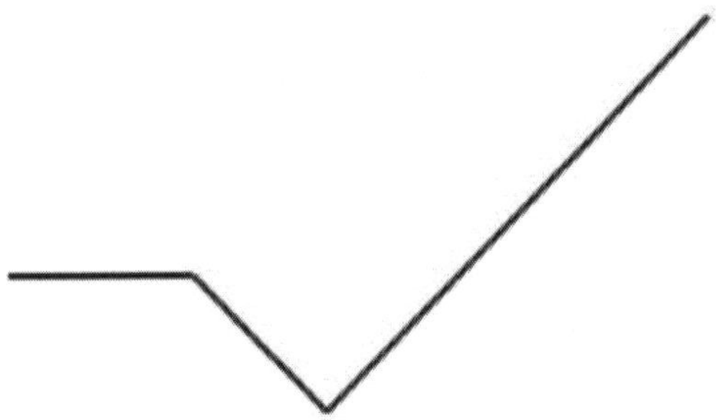

Sell ls (__)	_____	(+)	________	Break Even lwr	______
Buy hs (__)	_____	(-)	________	Break Even hgr	______
Net Debit or Credit		(=)	________		
Max Risk		(=)	________		
Max Gain		(=)	________		

Notes:

____

____

____

____

The Put Ratio Back Spread

The Put Ratio Back Spread consists of the purchase of two or more Puts and the sale of 1 higher strike put. For example, one might purchase 2 XYZ November 85 puts for 3-1/2 each and then sell one of the XYZ November 95 puts for 7-3/4 with XYZ stock trading at 96. The resulting credit is 3/4. If the stock price declines, the spread may become profitable. If XYZ closes below 84 1/4 at expiration, the position is profitable. This is because the credit was 3/4; that is, the entire position cost you that much plus commission. The greatest amount of profit is infinite the lower XYZ closes below 85 at expiration.

There are two break-even points in this trade.

Lower break even point = lower strike price + net credit of the spread.

Higher break even point = higher strike price - net credit of the spread.

Maximum profit potential is unlimited the lower the stock closes below 85.

The reason an investor would use the put ratio backspread strategy is that he is strongly bearish, but would prefer a "hedged" position.

An investor can establish the put ratio backspread using out-of-the-money puts for each leg of the spread. This is extremely aggressive. Or, the investor can establish the spread with the short put which is in the money and the long puts out of the money. This is less aggressive. And the least aggressive strategy is to establish the spread with both legs in the money.

Dart-Throw Traders Guidelines for Entry.

1. For this strategy we are looking for Strongly Bearish stocks.

2. Buy some time, 3-6 months until expiration. The more time the better.

3. Purchase ATM or slightly OTM puts.

4. Sell ITM puts.

5. Try to limit your spreads to $5 - $10.

6. Buy more puts than you sell in ratios; Short (1) - Long (2),

Short (2) - Long (3), Short (1) - Long (3 or 4 or 5...).

7. ALWAYS enter this trade with a net credit.

Dart-Throw Traders Guidelines for Exit.

1. This trade is designed to be held until expiration.

2. You can exit this trade when you have reached a net profit that is acceptable to you.

3. I like to exit these trades when I have made a 80% return on my risk. or...

4. When I have lost 40% of my risk (cost).

5. If halfway through the life of the trade I have not made at least a 40% return on my risk (cost) I will exit or adjust the trade.

These five guidelines force me to evaluate the trade at very specific intervals.

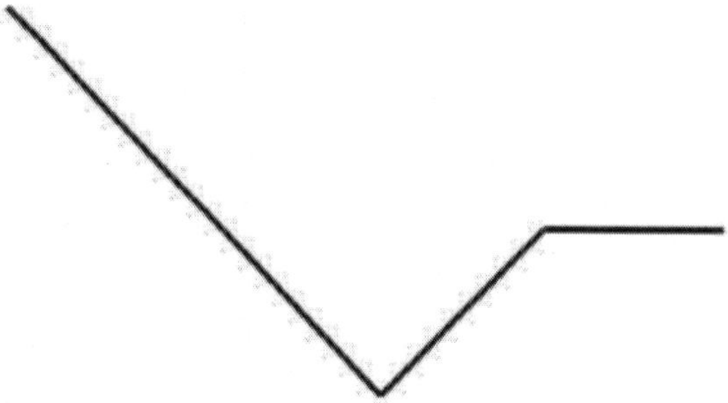

Sell hs (__) _____ (+) ________ Break Even lwr ______
Buy ls (__) _____ (-) ________ Break Even hgr ______
Net Debit or Credit (=) ________
Max Risk (=) ________
Max Gain (=) ________

Put Ratio Backspread

Notes:

As I walk through these 52 trades I want to make it abundantly clear that the next few chapters will read like journal entries, because that is what they are.

I also want to give a small insight into my stock trading evaluation style. As a trader, I have but one objective… too profit as quickly as possible with the least amount of risk.

What that means is simply this… I will not spend a lot of time detailing what I see as I evaluate a stock, I am looking for specific things to help me make a trading decision.

I will be looking at several different technical indicators and obviously surrounding news events and market conditions. My notes reflect my thoughts at the time of the trade and will be posted as they were written in my journal during the evaluation.

As you read through my notes on each stock and subsequent trade you will begin to see patterns emerge in my thoughts and evaluation process.

To help you better understand the trades that were done you will find specific chapters in this book of each strategy I selected and the rules that I follow for the entry and exit of those trades.

I have also included a chapter on technical analysis explaining the indicators that I use and the time frames I select... Keep in mind these are personal preferences based on my particular style of trading.

January 2006

USB – US Bancorp
Ratio Call Calendar Spread - $140.00 (28%) 169

CDWC – CDW Corp.
Horizontal Call Calendar Spread + $80.00 23% 173

SYMC – Symantec Corp.
Ratio Put Calendar Spread - $30.00 (08%) 177

GPS – GAP, Inc.
Ratio Call Calendar Spread +$280.00 79% 181

January Results – 2 Wins vs. 2 Losses.

Net result $190.00 Profit.

If you want true success... STOP trying to make the "right" decision and concentrate on making your decisions "right".

- Jimmy Slagle, The Dart-Throw Trader

January 30, 2006: USB

January 03, 2006 – USB is currently in a weakening bullish trend as evidenced by the MACD indicator. USB is above its 200 DMA and 50 DMA, although stochastics is showing some weakness it is merely a reflection of the previous 4 day sell off. USB sold off to the 50 DMA and bottom BB and made a strong bullish bounce I believe that the 50 dma will act as support going forward.

It appears to me that support is at worst the 200 DMA and resistance is 31, which has been tested 3 times. USB is beginning to show significant range bound behavior. Based on the current behavior I would classify the trend as range bound between 29 and 31. I believe that USB will have a difficult time breaking out of this range for the short term. Based on this evaluation I would suggest a Ratio Call Calendar Spread.

Symbol: usb (30.28) Date: 1/3/2006

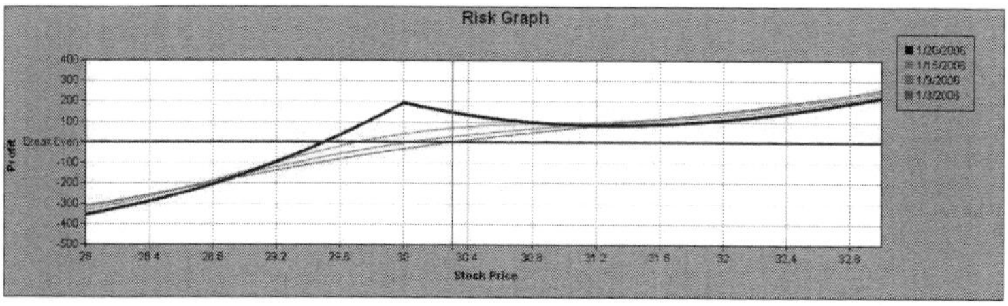

Summary

Cost of Trade	500	Max Reward	219	Delta	103.3
Current Value	500	Probable Reward	0	Theta	$3.95
Profit/Loss	0	Risk/Max Reward	61.7%	Gamma	-41.8
Max Risk	-355	Risk/Prb Reward	0%	Vega	$27.23

Trade Details

Type	Qty	CostBasis	CurrValue	Strike	Expiration	Total Cost	Profit	IV	Delta
call	8	1.1500	1.1500	30	Mar 2006	920	0	17.7700	461.66
call	-6	0.7000	0.7000	30	Jan 2006	-420	0	20.6700	-358.36

Break Evens

	Expiration	Jan 15	Jan 09	Today
Upper B/E	29.50	29.72	30.04	30.28
Lower B/E	29.50	29.72	30.04	30.28

Based on my current outlook I have chosen to enter a Ratio Call Calendar Spread. To enter this trade I will long 8 of the March 2006 30 strike calls @ 1.15 each and short 6 of the January 2006 30 strike calls @ .70 each.

This will give me a total cost of trade of $500 and an immediate risk of $355 based on my outlook (stagnant to mildly bullish) this trade should produce a potential reward of 60%.

Jan 20, 2006 – This trade was beautiful… until today. I should have exited the trade yesterday for a profit but I was holding out for expiration to save a commission. Live and learn. On the sell off today I am going to experience a loss of about $140, but a least I don't have to pay a commission to close the short leg. Looking back I should have done a standard horizontal call calendar spread.

Symbol: usb (29.03) Date: 1/20/2006

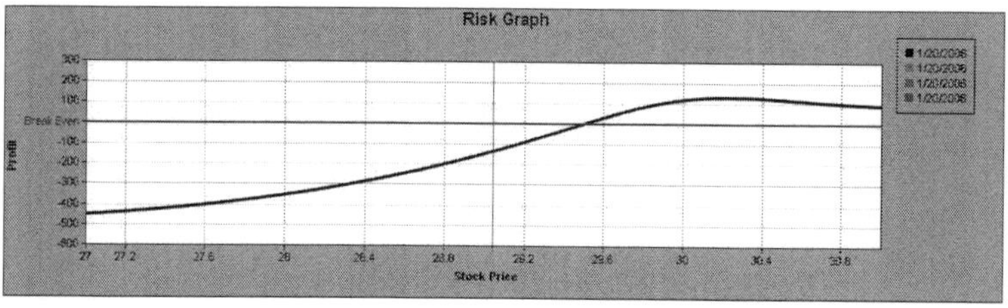

Summary

Cost of Trade	500	Max Reward	132	Delta	275.2
Current Value	360	Probable Reward	0	Theta	NaN
Profit/Loss	-140	Risk/Max Reward	29.4%	Gamma	144.8
Max Risk	-450	Risk/Prb Reward	0%	Vega	$33.48

Trade Details

Type	Qty	CostBasis	CurrValue	Strike	Expiration	Total Cost	Profit	IV	Delta
call	8	1.1500	0.4500	30	Mar 2006	920	-560	17.8800	275.22
call	-6	0.7000	0.0001	30	Jan 2006	-420	420	3437.5000	0.00

Break Evens

	Expiration	Jan 20	Jan 20	Today
Upper B/E	29.50	29.50	29.50	29.50
Lower B/E	29.50	29.50	29.50	29.50

January 20, 2006 – The USB trade has come to a close and unfortunately a loss. I was right about the outlook but wrong about the strategy. Looking back I should have done a standard horizontal call calendar spread.

January 10, 2006 – CDWC.

I love a stock that is trading in a range. CDWC has been range bound for a year bouncing between 55 and 65. This is the type of behavior that is easy to profit from. As of today it appears that CDWC wants to move to the higher end of its trading range which is evident by a MACD cross into a bullish trend, a stochastic cross, a bullish bounce of the Bollinger Bands, a series of higher lows.

I believe that although CDWC is showing bullish behavior it will have a difficult time breaking upward resistance of 65. In fact I believe CDWC will have a short term sell off before moving to the higher end of this range. To take advantage of this bullish skewed range bound behavior, I believe a call calendar spread is the trade of choice.

Symbol: cdwc (60.38) **DT2 CDWC call calendar** Date: 1/10/2006

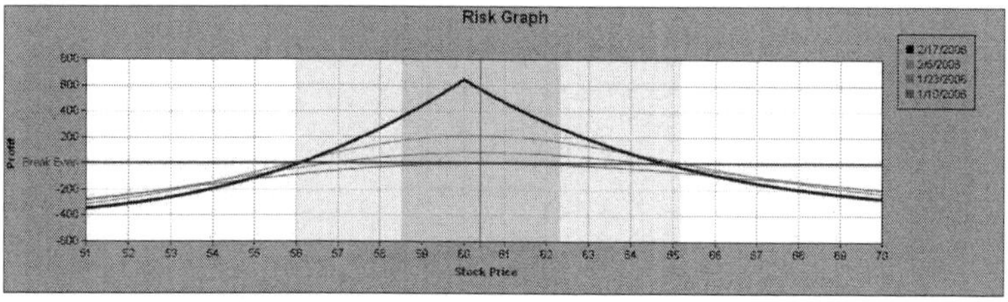

Summary

Cost of Trade	420	Max Reward	643	Delta	2.4
Current Value	420	Probable Reward	293	Theta	$5.64
Profit/Loss	0	Risk/Max Reward	185.5%	Gamma	-8.2
Max Risk	-347	Risk/Prb Reward	84.5%	Vega	$19.33

Trade Details

Type	Qty	CostBasis	CurrValue	Strike	Expiration	Total Cost	Profit	IV	Delta
call	-4	2.5500	2.5500	60	Feb 2006	-1,020	0	29.7900	-220.68
call	4	3.6000	3.6000	60	Apr 2006	1,440	0	26.0100	223.04

Break Evens

	Expiration	Feb 05	Jan 23	Today
Upper B/E	64.85	65.30	64.50	61.00
Lower B/E	56.10	55.90	56.85	60.40

Based on my current outlook of stagnant to mildly bullish I have chosen a horizontal Call Calendar Spread. To enter this trade I will long 4 of the April 2006 calls at 3.60 each and short 4 of the February 2006 calls at 2.55 each. This will give me a cost of trade of $400 and an immediate risk of $347, with a maximum potential return of 185%.

Symbol: cdwc (57.16) **DT2 CDWC call calendar** Date: 2/17/2006

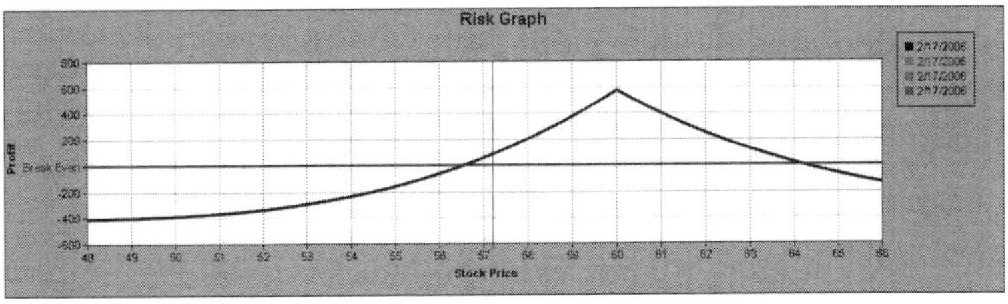

Summary

Cost of Trade	420	Max Reward	575	Delta	137.2
Current Value	500	Probable Reward	0	Theta	-$7.03
Profit/Loss	80	Risk/Max Reward	140.7%	Gamma	25.5
Max Risk	-409	Risk/Prb Reward	0%	Vega	$34.92

Trade Details

Type	Qty	CostBasis	CurrValue	Strike	Expiration	Total Cost	Profit	IV	Delta
call	-4	2.5500	0.0000	60	Feb 2006	-1,020	1,020	0.0000	0.00
call	4	3.6000	1.2500	60	Apr 2006	1,440	-940	24.2800	137.15

Break Evens

	Expiration	Feb 17	Feb 17	Today
Upper B/E	64.25	64.25	64.25	64.25
Lower B/E	56.55	56.55	56.55	56.55

February 17, 2006 – I am beginning to believe in the urban legend of "Max Pain". Max Pain is the belief that on expiration Friday, option traders will manipulate the price of the stock to the price point that will cause the greatest majority of options to expire worthless. To my knowledge, it has never been proven, however, based on the last two trades I have done (USB and CDWC) it appears to be real.

The good news is that although I was correct in my evaluation the sell-off on expiration Friday has once again wrecked havoc with my trade, fortunately this time I ended with a profit. An $80 profit on a $347 risk is equal to a 23% return... I will take it.

"If you know what you are doing you can simply place the stock page on a wall, throw a dart, randomly pick a stock and make money."

- Jimmy Slagle, The Dart-Throw Trader

January 17, 2006 – SYMC.

This stock is going to be fun. In November there was a strong sell off of the stock, which caused a gap down and subsequent downward trend.

This was followed by a bullish reversal at the end of December causing the price to migrate back to the open after the gap. History would suggest that this price point, roughly 20 will now become resistance. If that is true then we would have support at roughly 17 and resistance at 20.

Currently SYMC is showing a bullish outlook MACD has crossed its signal line, Stochastics has moved higher, though now flat and it has moved back above its 50 DMA.

I believe that the rally to 20 is cause for a retracement to at least 18 to test that level of support before moving higher to try and fill the gap. Therefore I believe that a trade that takes advantage of the 17 to 20 range will be the most profitable. With my opinion that the stock will go down before it goes up I think a Ratio Put Calendar Spread offers the best potential for profit.

Symbol: symc (19.36) **DT3 SYMC put ratio calendar** Date: 1/17/2006

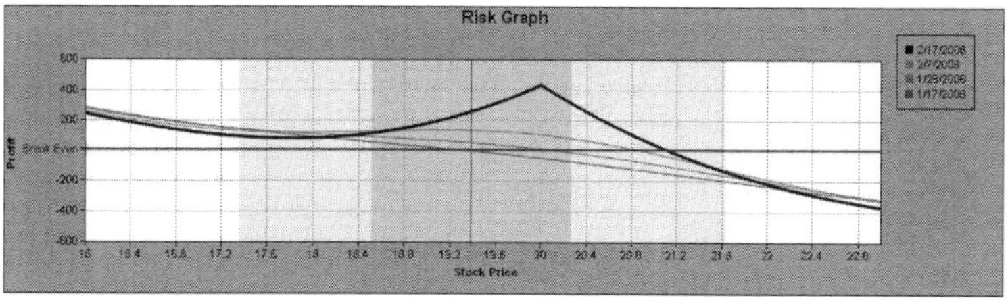

Summary

Cost of Trade	540	Max Reward	431	Delta	-71.1
Current Value	540	Probable Reward	167	Theta	$4.45
Profit/Loss	0	Risk/Max Reward	116.8%	Gamma	-12.9
Max Risk	-369	Risk/Prb Reward	45.3%	Vega	$21.42

Trade Details

Type	Qty	CostBasis	CurrValue	Strike	Expiration	Total Cost	Profit	IV	Delta
put	10	1.5000	1.5000	20	Apr 2006	1,500	0	30.1500	-544.13
put	-8	1.2000	1.2000	20	Feb 2006	-960	0	37.5400	473.06

Break Evens

	Expiration	Feb 07	Jan 28	Today
Upper B/E	21.14	20.90	20.16	19.38
Lower B/E	21.14	20.90	20.16	19.38

With my current outlook of stagnant to mildly bearish I would like to see SYMC Sell off to 17 before trying to refill the gap. This trade gives me the greatest potential for profit if the stock sells off to 17 and retraces or even if it breaks support at 17.

To structure the trade I will long 10 of the April 2006 puts @ 1.50 each and short 8 of the February 2006 puts @ 1.20 each. This gives me a cost of trade of $540 and immediate risk of $369 with a 116% Maximum upside potential.

February 17, 2006 – SYMC. Once again my analysis is spot on. SYMC sold off to 17 testing that level of support before beginning to climb higher. Unfortunately, it was slow to move causing the trade to experience a small loss of ($30), which is a (8%) loss on risk.

Symbol: symc (17.52) **DT3 SYMC put ratio calendar** Date: 2/17/2006

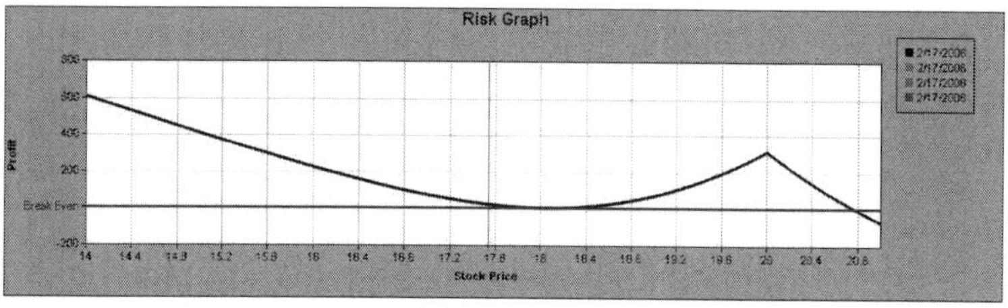

Summary

Cost of Trade	540	Max Reward	609	Delta	-68.7
Current Value	510	Probable Reward	0	Theta	NaN
Profit/Loss	-30	Risk/Max Reward	886.7%	Gamma	110.1
Max Risk	-69	Risk/Prb Reward	0%	Vega	$15.50

Trade Details

Type	Qty	CostBasis	CurrValue	Strike	Expiration	Total Cost	Profit	IV	Delta
put	10	1.5000	2.5500	20	Apr 2006	1,500	1,050	26.5800	-868.70
put	-8	1.2000	2.5500	20	Feb 2006	-960	-1,080	1.0000	800.00

Break Evens

	Expiration	Feb 17	Feb 17	Today
Upper B/E	20.80	20.80	20.80	20.80
Lower B/E	20.80	20.80	20.80	20.80

January 24, 2006 – GPS.

I must enter logical trades expecting emotional reactions. Logically GPS should move down to test 16. The MACD just crossed the center line, the trend is stagnant to bearish. It is below its 200 and 50 DMA's.

But, news and sentiment are more bullish as we move into the spring season. Stochastics says GPS is oversold, it is at the bottom of its Bollinger band, 17 is a tested support… what to do?

My gut says we bounce off of 17 and move back to the 18.50 resistance in the next 30 days, as GPS moves into its earnings. The goal is to make the most amount of money with the least amount of risk.

Symbol: gps (17.06) **DT4 GPS call calendar** Date: 1/24/2006

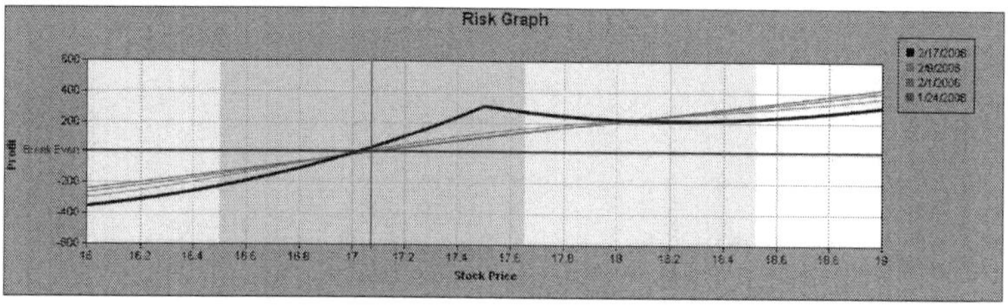

Summary

Cost of Trade	470	Max Reward	308	Delta	231.5
Current Value	470	Probable Reward	33	Theta	-$0.33
Profit/Loss	0	Risk/Max Reward	87.4%	Gamma	-15.1
Max Risk	-352	Risk/Prb Reward	9.5%	Vega	$18.87

Trade Details

Type	Qty	CostBasis	CurrValue	Strike	Expiration	Total Cost	Profit	IV	Delta
call	14	0.5500	0.5500	17.5	Mar 2006	770	0	28.2500	608.00
call	-10	0.3000	0.3000	17.5	Feb 2006	-300	0	27.2900	-376.48

Break Evens

	Expiration	Feb 09	Feb 01	Today
Upper B/E	17.02	17.02	17.06	17.06
Lower B/E	17.02	17.02	17.06	17.06

Based on my outlook of a bullish move (bounce of Bollinger bands and stochasitic's oversold historical rally into earnings) I have chosen to enter a Ratio Call Calendar Spread. This trade allows for a managed risk if the stock breaks support @ 17 but allows for unlimited profit if it moves back into the 18 and beyond price point.

The trade structure is long 14 March 2006 calls and short 10 February 2006 calls for a trade cost of $470 and a risk of $352.

February 17, 2006 – One has to love sentiment and news. GPS rallied into its news and produced an amazing move beyond its resistance.

This trade produced a $280 return on a $352 risk resulting in a 79% return on risk.

Symbol: gps (18.82) **DT4 GPS call calendar** Date: 2/17/2006

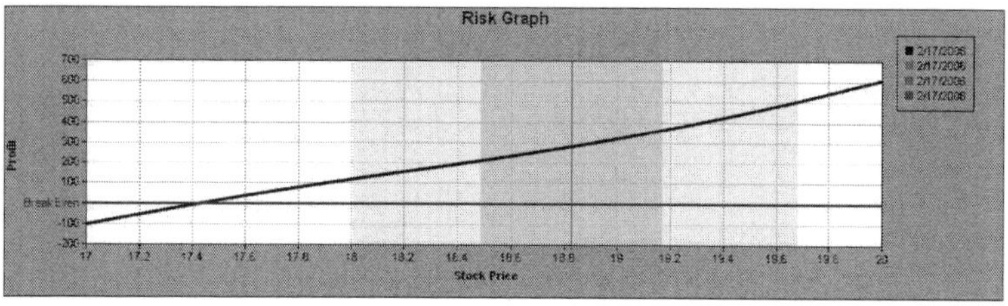

Summary

Cost of Trade	470	Max Reward	608	Delta	149.5
Current Value	750	Probable Reward	285	Theta	NaN
Profit/Loss	280	Risk/Max Reward	592.7%	Gamma	231.0
Max Risk	-103	Risk/Prb Reward	277.4%	Vega	$19.08

Trade Details

Type	Qty	CostBasis	CurrValue	Strike	Expiration	Total Cost	Profit	IV	Delta
call	14	0.5500	1.5000	17.5	Mar 2006	770	1,330	30.4000	1,149.46
call	-10	0.3000	1.3500	17.5	Feb 2006	-300	-1,050	15859.3800	-1,000.00

Break Evens

	Expiration	Feb 17	Feb 17	Today
Upper B/E	17.43	17.43	17.43	17.43
Lower B/E	17.43	17.43	17.43	17.43

February 2006

CSCO – Cisco Systems			
Strangle	+$1320.00	275%	187
DD – DuPont			
Ratio Call Calendar Spread	+ $420.00	250%	191
ROH – Rohm & Haas			
Ratio Call Calendar Spread	+ $725.00	307%	195
LLTC – Linear Tech.			
Put Calendar Spread	+ $180.00	54%	199

February Results – 4 Wins vs. 0 Losses.
Net result $2,645.00 Profit.

"Don't fritter away your time. Create, act, take a place wherever you are and be somebody"

- Theodore Roosevelt

January 31, 2006 – CSCO.

This is a pure earnings play. CSCO likes to move on earnings and this upcoming announcement should not be an exception. August and November announcements both produced downward gaps in price. February's announcement should produce a move as well.

Symbol: csco (18.57) **DT5 CSCO strangle** Date: 1/31/2006

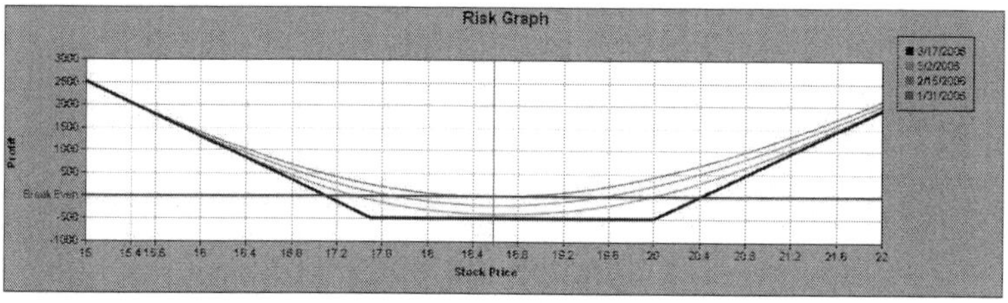

Summary

Cost of Trade	480	Max Reward	2,520	Delta	3.1
Current Value	480	Probable Reward	0	Theta	-$12.55
Profit/Loss	0	Risk/Max Reward	525%	Gamma	445.2
Max Risk	-480	Risk/Prb Reward	0%	Vega	$46.24

Trade Details

Type	Qty	CostBasis	CurrValue	Strike	Expiration	Total Cost	Profit	IV	Delta
call	12	0.2000	0.2000	20	Mar 2006	240	0	25.2800	264.61
put	12	0.2000	0.2000	17.5	Mar 2006	240	0	23.6200	-261.49

Break Evens

	Expiration	Mar 02	Feb 15	Today
Upper B/E	20.40	19.98	19.54	0.00
Lower B/E	17.10	17.38	17.70	0.00

Nothing gives this trader a greater feeling than to be able to enter a delta neutral strangle on a stock that historically moves on earnings... These are the kind of trades I live for... Move - CSCO – Move.

This trade is long 12 March 2006 20 strike calls @ .20 each and Long 12 March 17.50 puts @ .20 each. Total cost $480, total risk $480.

March 17, 2006 – Oh how I do love earnings. CSCO gapped up on its February earnings announcement and continued to run higher. Once the earnings had come out the trade was profitable. I choose to let it run as long a csco continued its trend because the puts were already worthless and the calls continued to multiply in value as the delta continued to increase.

Trade closed on expiration Friday… with a $1,320.00 profit on a $480.00 risk for a 275% return in two months.

Symbol: csco (21.62) **DT5 CSCO strangle** Date: 3/17/2006

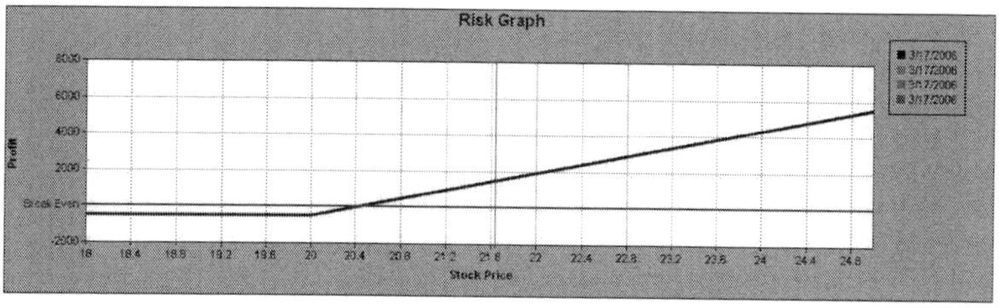

Summary

Cost of Trade	480	Max Reward	5,520	Delta	1,200.0
Current Value	1,800	Probable Reward	0	Theta	NaN
Profit/Loss	1,320	Risk/Max Reward	1150%	Gamma	0.0
Max Risk	-480	Risk/Prb Reward	0%	Vega	$0.00

Trade Details

Type	Qty	CostBasis	CurrValue	Strike	Expiration	Total Cost	Profit	IV	Delta
call	12	0.2000	1.5000	20	Mar 2006	240	1,560	1.0000	1,200.00
put	12	0.2000	0.0000	17.5	Mar 2006	240	-240	0.0000	0.00

Break Evens

	Expiration	Mar 17	Mar 17	Today
Upper B/E	20.40	20.40	20.40	20.40
Lower B/E	20.40	20.40	20.40	20.40

February 7, 2006 – DD.

The lull after the storm. DD just announced earnings at the beginning of Jan. History suggests that we see a move on earnings and then stagnation follows.

MACD is currently bearish, although stochastic's suggests that DD is massively oversold. There is a strong level of support at 38 with resistance at 42. I see no reason why DD should break support or resistance in the short term. Objective is to profit from this current range.

I believe that DD will test the resistance at 42.

Symbol: dd (39.18) **DT6 DD call ratio calendar** Date: 2/7/2006

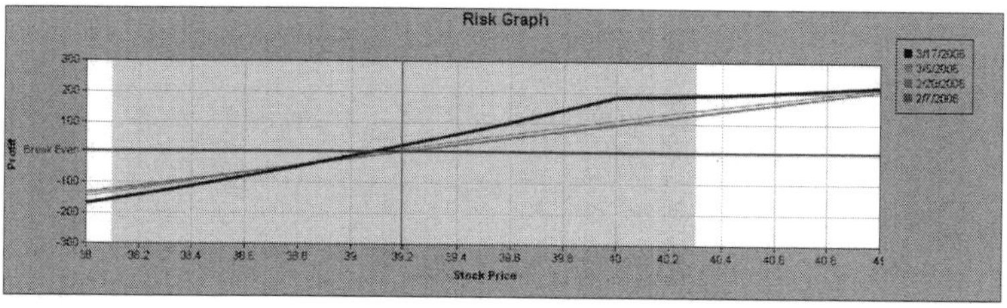

Summary

Cost of Trade	500	Max Reward	220	Delta	113.1
Current Value	500	Probable Reward	33	Theta	-$0.03
Profit/Loss	0	Risk/Max Reward	131%	Gamma	2.2
Max Risk	-168	Risk/Prb Reward	19.5%	Vega	$32.17

Trade Details

Type	Qty	CostBasis	CurrValue	Strike	Expiration	Total Cost	Profit	IV	Delta
call	4	1.5500	1.5500	40	Jul 2006	620	0	17.1900	189.84
call	-2	0.6000	0.6000	40	Mar 2006	-120	0	18.2700	-76.77

Break Evens

	Expiration	Mar 05	Feb 20	Today
Upper B/E	39.07	39.11	39.17	39.19
Lower B/E	39.07	39.11	39.17	39.19

I chose the Ratio Call Calendar spread for many reasons, mostly because there is a minimum risk if DD sells off to 38 before moving higher and this trade gives unlimited upside potential if DD retraces to 42 which is my expectation.

Trade structure is long 4 July 2006 40 strike calls @ 1.55 each and short 2 March 2006 40 strike calls @ .60 each. This gives us a cost of trade @ $500 and an immediate risk of $168 with an unlimited upside profit potential.

March 17, 2006 – DD rallied up to 42 as expected retraced back to 40 where it established a new support level and then moved back to the 43 resistance level as we moved into expiration.

Trade closed on expiration with a $420 profit on a $168 risk producing a 250% ROR.

Symbol: dd (42.56) **DT6 DD call ratio calendar** Date: 3/17/2006

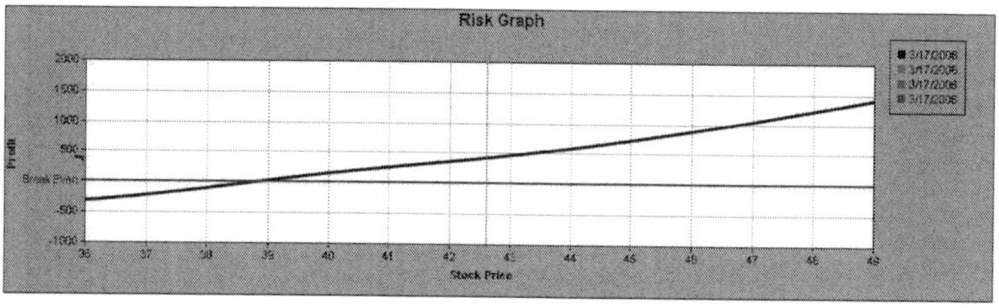

Summary

Cost of Trade	500	Max Reward	1,412	Delta	95.2
Current Value	920	Probable Reward	0	Theta	NaN
Profit/Loss	420	Risk/Max Reward	453.3%	Gamma	26.4
Max Risk	-312	Risk/Prb Reward	0%	Vega	$32.58

Trade Details

Type	Qty	CostBasis	CurrValue	Strike	Expiration	Total Cost	Profit	IV	Delta
call	4	1.5500	3.6000	40	Jul 2006	620	820	19.7700	295.16
call	-2	0.6000	2.6000	40	Mar 2006	-120	-400	12460.9400	-200.00

Break Evens

	Expiration	Mar 17	Mar 17	Today
Upper B/E	38.75	38.75	38.75	38.75
Lower B/E	38.75	38.75	38.75	38.75

February 14, 2006 – ROH.

This one is a bit tricky but that is the beauty of being an intuitive trader. Here is a stock that has had a strong bullish run from 40 to 52. It gapped down from 52 to 48 which is now a level of support based on the previous resistance in February, June – August time frame.

MACD is in a bullish trend, although it is showing weakness, major news is priced in already history suggests range bound behavior. My outlook is that ROH will bounce around between 47 and 52 for the short term therefore allowing a stagnant trading position the opportunity to flourish.

Symbol: roh (50.61) **DT7 ROH call ratio calendar** Date: 2/14/2006

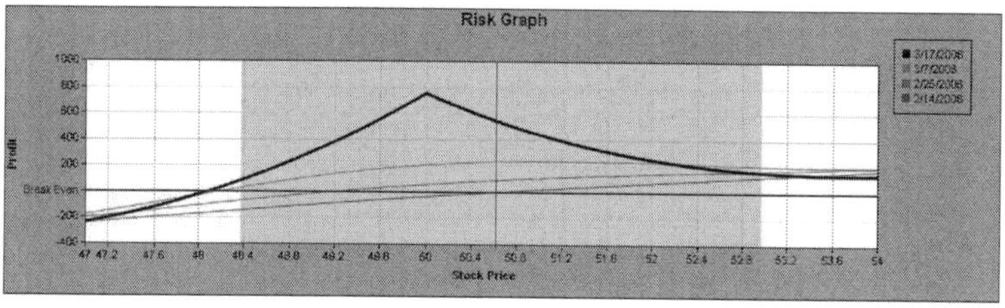

Summary

Cost of Trade	475	Max Reward	755	Delta	56.3
Current Value	475	Probable Reward	199	Theta	$7.36
Profit/Loss	0	Risk/Max Reward	319.6%	Gamma	-6.5
Max Risk	-236	Risk/Prb Reward	84%	Vega	$32.18

Trade Details

Type	Qty	CostBasis	CurrValue	Strike	Expiration	Total Cost	Profit	IV	Delta
call	10	2.0500	2.0500	50	Apr 2006	2,050	0	19.3700	587.58
call	-9	1.7500	1.7500	50	Mar 2006	-1,575	0	23.7400	-531.26

Break Evens

	Expiration	Mar 07	Feb 25	Today
Upper B/E	48.10	48.20	49.20	50.62
Lower B/E	48.10	48.20	49.20	50.62

Based on my 47 – 52 expected trading range outlook I chose the Ratio Call Calendar Spread because it gives me minimal risk if ROH tests its support @ 47 Maximum profit it bounces around and settles in @ 50 (a potential strong level of current support) and is still profitable if it continues to move higher in price.

Trade entry is long 10 April 2006 50 strike calls @ 2.05 each and short 9 March 2006 50 strike calls @ 1.75 each. Total cost $475 with an immediate risk of $236.

Symbol: roh (49.73) **DT7 ROH call ratio calendar** Date: 3/17/2006

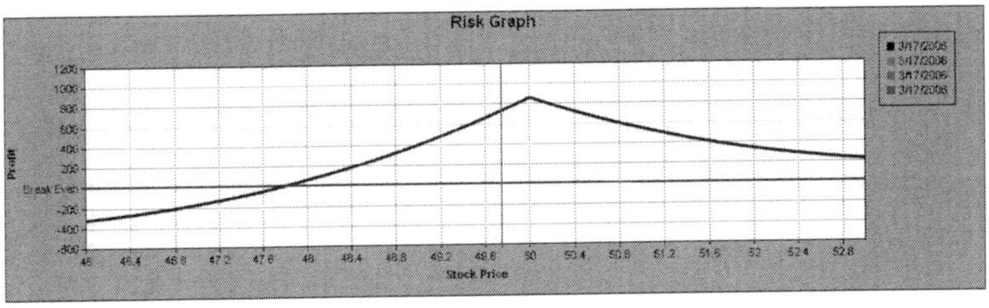

Summary

Cost of Trade	475	Max Reward	861	Delta	488.7
Current Value	1,200	Probable Reward	0	Theta	-$19.43
Profit/Loss	725	Risk/Max Reward	270.1%	Gamma	122.9
Max Risk	-319	Risk/Prb Reward	0%	Vega	$61.41

Trade Details

Type	Qty	CostBasis	CurrValue	Strike	Expiration	Total Cost	Profit	IV	Delta
call	10	2.0500	1.2000	50	Apr 2006	2,050	-850	21.0700	488.70
call	-9	1.7500	0.0000	50	Mar 2006	-1,575	1,575	0.0000	0.00

Break Evens

	Expiration	Mar 17	Mar 17	Today
Upper B/E	47.78	47.78	47.78	47.78
Lower B/E	47.78	47.78	47.78	47.78

March 17, 2006 – ROH chose to hug the $50 price level almost giving us maximum profit in the trade. Trade closed with a $725 profit on a risk of $236 giving me a 307% ROR.

"How many millionaires do you know who have become wealthy by investing in savings accounts? I rest my case."

- Robert G. Allen

February 21, 2006 – LLTC.

This one is another tough one to analyze. The best way to analyze a stock like this in my experience is to simply step back and look at the big picture. Lets examine what we know about its current behavior.

Resistance is 39. Support is 35. MACD is undecided. Stochastics is undecided. Looks like the stock wants to move only the range is too tight for a straddle or strangle. The stock is below the 50 and 200 DMAs and they currently sit on top of one another. News and sentiment is neutral. It is almost a coin toss as to what direction this stock will move.

So the question becomes risk vs reward. The range is 35 – 40, that's easy. Logic would suggest a condor, but there is not enough value in the options. So we go to the traders and get their opinion. Upon careful evaluation of the activity around the calls and puts (volatility and price discrepancy) the action from the floor suggests a more bearish move than bullish in the short term.

If that is the case my only objective can be trade the sentiment but manage the risk.

Symbol: lltc (36.44) **DT8 LLTC put calendar** Date: 2/21/2006

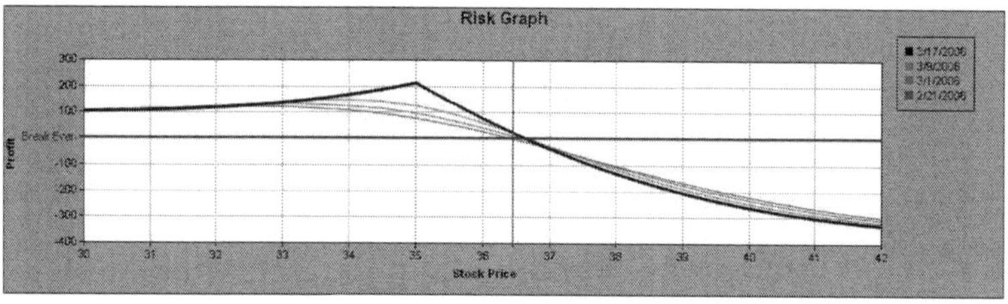

Summary

Cost of Trade	380	Max Reward	213	Delta	-62.7
Current Value	380	Probable Reward	0	Theta	$1.18
Profit/Loss	0	Risk/Max Reward	64.5%	Gamma	-9.1
Max Risk	-330	Risk/Prb Reward	0%	Vega	$8.13

Trade Details

Type	Qty	CostBasis	CurrValue	Strike	Expiration	Total Cost	Profit	IV	Delta
put	2	2.2500	2.2500	37.5	May 2006	450	0	24.3400	-112.07
put	-2	0.3500	0.3500	35	Mar 2006	-70	0	24.7000	49.41

Break Evens

	Expiration	Mar 09	Mar 01	Today
Upper B/E	36.65	36.70	36.60	36.45
Lower B/E	36.65	36.70	36.60	36.45

For the record my gut says "walk away" but I can't because in this challenge it is throw darts – pick stocks – make money. Therefore I have to trade this stock even if I don't want to.

Since the sentiment is bearish, I must enter a range bound to bearish outlook trade that will allow me to profit if the sentiment is correct but to minimize risk if wrong.

The only trade that makes sense is a put calendar spread. This trade gives minimum risk if the stock tests its resistance and profits if it continues to drift lower.

To structure the trade I went long 2 May 2006 37.5 strike Puts @ 2.25 each and short 2 March 2006 35 strike puts @ .35 each, for a cost of trade of $380 and an immediate risk of $330.

March 17, 2006 – The sentiment turned out to be accurate and this trade ended with a profit of $180.00 on a risk of $330 for a 54% ROR.

Symbol: lltc (35.21) **DT8 LLTC put calendar** Date: 3/17/2006

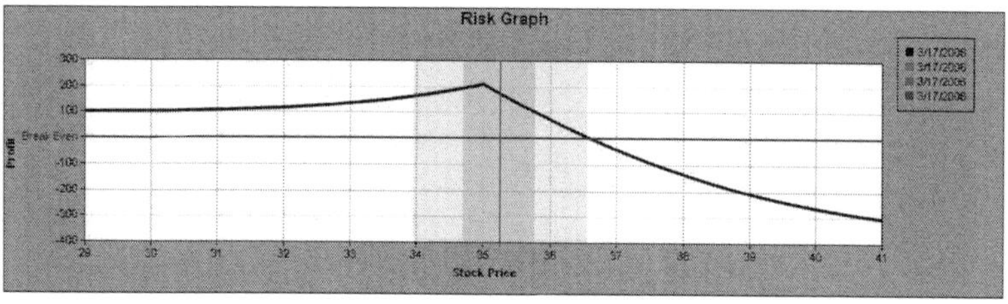

Summary

Cost of Trade	380	Max Reward	210	Delta	-142.1
Current Value	560	Probable Reward	140	Theta	-$1.68
Profit/Loss	180	Risk/Max Reward	69.1%	Gamma	19.4
Max Risk	-304	Risk/Prb Reward	46%	Vega	$10.01

Trade Details

Type	Qty	CostBasis	CurrValue	Strike	Expiration	Total Cost	Profit	IV	Delta
put	2	2.2500	2.8000	37.5	May 2006	450	110	24.0600	-142.08
put	-2	0.3500	0.0000	35	Mar 2006	-70	70	0.0000	0.00

Break Evens

	Expiration	Mar 17	Mar 17	Today
Upper B/E	36.65	36.65	36.65	36.65
Lower B/E	36.65	36.65	36.65	36.65

March 2006

DUK – Duke Energy			
Long Put	+ $180.00	37%	205
CCI – Crown Castle			
Ratio Call Calendar Spread	- $ 80.00	(72%)	209
KBH – KB Homes			
Call Calendar Spread	+ $460.00	172%	213
CNP – Centerpoint Energy			
Long Put	+ $250.00	55%	217

March Results – 3 Wins vs. 1 Losses.

Net result $810.00 Profit.

"If there is anything I would do differently in my life, it is that I would study business more. I'm trying to teach my daughter Chloe at an early age about investing and money so she's not afraid of it."

- Donna Mills

February 28, 2006 – DUK.

Finally... an easy evaluation. DUK has been in a slow almost painful bullish trend back up to firm resistance at 29 and now the stock is destined to rollover and test support. This is simple short term directional bearish trade... the long put.

Symbol: duk (28.4) **DT9 DUK long put** Date: 2/28/2006

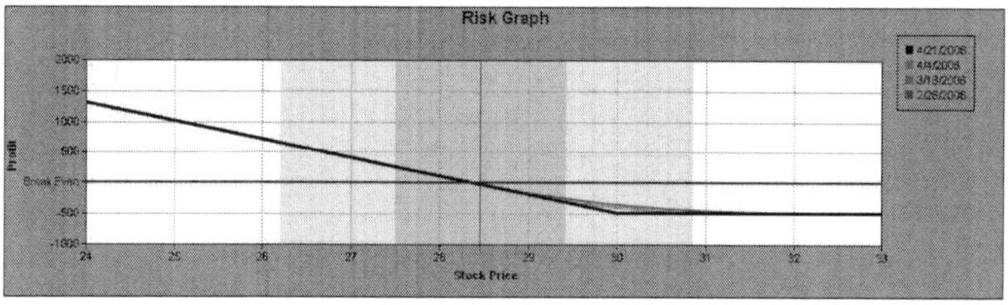

Summary

Cost of Trade	480	Max Reward	1,320	Delta	-266.6
Current Value	480	Probable Reward	14	Theta	-$0.33
Profit/Loss	0	Risk/Max Reward	275%	Gamma	47.2
Max Risk	-480	Risk/Prb Reward	3%	Vega	$6.10

Trade Details

Type	Qty	CostBasis	CurrValue	Strike	Expiration	Total Cost	Profit	IV	Delta
put	3	1.6000	1.6000	30	Apr 2006	480	0	11.2500	-266.56

Break Evens

	Expiration	Apr 04	Mar 18	Today
Upper B/E	28.40	28.40	28.40	28.40
Lower B/E	28.40	28.40	28.40	28.40

This is a straight long put purchase to take advantage of a very short term drop in price. Trade structure is long 3 of the April 2006 30 strike puts at a cost of 1.60 each. Total cost $480, total risk $480, potential reward unlimited.

March 7, 2006. DUK sold off to support, trade closed. Sold the puts for 2.20 each. This gives the trade a $180 profit on a $480 risk for a 37% ROR.

Symbol: duk (27.74) **DT9 DUK long put** Date: 3/7/2006

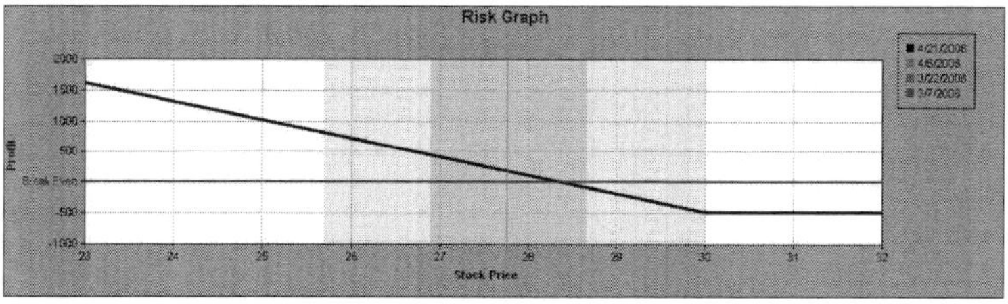

Summary

Cost of Trade	480	Max Reward	1,620	Delta	-300.0
Current Value	660	Probable Reward	190	Theta	$0.37
Profit/Loss	180	Risk/Max Reward	337.5%	Gamma	0.0
Max Risk	-480	Risk/Prb Reward	39.7%	Vega	$0.00

Trade Details

Type	Qty	CostBasis	CurrValue	Strike	Expiration	Total Cost	Profit	IV	Delta
put	3	1.6000	2.2000	30	Apr 2006	480	180	1.0000	-300.00

Break Evens

	Expiration	Apr 06	Mar 22	Today
Upper B/E	28.40	28.40	28.40	28.35
Lower B/E	28.40	28.40	28.40	28.35

March 7, 2006 – CCI.

This one looks too easy. Here we have a bullish trending stock that loves to use its 50 DMA as support as it skips merrily along. MACD is bullish although showing signs of weakness and stochastics is undecided at the moment.

The stock has just hit its 50 DMA again and looks poised to bounce higher and test resistance at 32 as it continues its well established trend.

Easy trade decision take advantage of slow bullish trend while minimizing risk. I choose the Ratio Call Calendar Spread.

Symbol: cci (30.19) **DT10 CCI call ratio calendar** Date: 3/7/2006

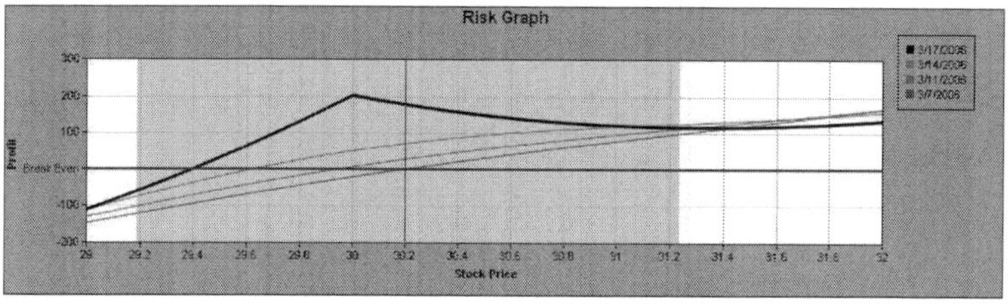

Summary

Cost of Trade	535	Max Reward	202	Delta	106.6
Current Value	535	Probable Reward	71	Theta	$6.77
Profit/Loss	0	Risk/Max Reward	183.2%	Gamma	-28.0
Max Risk	-110	Risk/Prb Reward	64.1%	Vega	$19.49

Trade Details

Type	Qty	CostBasis	CurrValue	Strike	Expiration	Total Cost	Profit	IV	Delta
call	7	1.3000	1.3000	30	Apr 2006	910	0	27.8700	386.85
call	-5	0.7500	0.7500	30	Mar 2006	-375	0	32.4100	-280.24

Break Evens

	Expiration	Mar 14	Mar 11	Today
Upper B/E	29.40	29.63	29.95	30.20
Lower B/E	29.40	29.63	29.95	30.20

This is a simple decision. Trade entry is long 7 April 2006 30 strike calls @ 1.30 each and short 5 March 2006 30 strike calls @ .75 each. Cost of trade is $535 immediate risk is $110 potential return $100+.

March 17, 2006 – Why is it that the simple "No Brainer" trades always mess with you? Here is a stock that is in a firmly established slow moving bullish trend. This stock loves to bounce off its 50 DMA as it sets new highs.

Only this time I place a trade that will take full advantage of its behavior and this stock decides to do the complete opposite of what it has done for six months. It breaks its 50 DMA two days before this trade comes to fruition which extinguishes any hope of profit.

Trade closed with an $80 loss on a risk of $110 a 72% loss… ouch.

Symbol: cci (29.1) **DT10 CCI call ratio calendar** Date: 3/17/2006

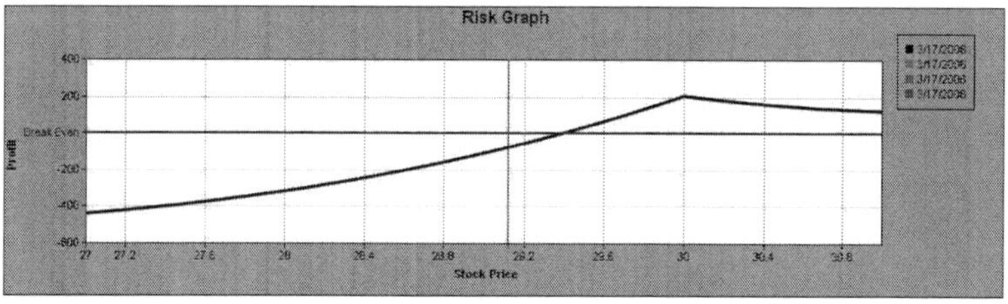

Summary

Cost of Trade	535	Max Reward	206	Delta	269.8
Current Value	455	Probable Reward	0	Theta	-$9.96
Profit/Loss	-80	Risk/Max Reward	47.1%	Gamma	106.0
Max Risk	-438	Risk/Prb Reward	0%	Vega	$24.12

Trade Details

Type	Qty	CostBasis	CurrValue	Strike	Expiration	Total Cost	Profit	IV	Delta
call	7	1.3000	0.6500	30	Apr 2006	910	-455	28.0200	269.84
call	-5	0.7500	0.0000	30	Mar 2006	-375	375	0.0000	0.00

Break Evens

	Expiration	Mar 17	Mar 17	Today
Upper B/E	29.40	29.40	29.40	29.40
Lower B/E	29.40	29.40	29.40	29.40

March 14, 2006 - KBH.

Throw the Dart Pick a stock that has just reacted to news... great. KBH is in a decisive down trend. MACD is bearish, it is below its 50 and 200 DMA's, in fact, it appears that the 50 DMA wants to cross below the 200 DMA.

Now here is the problem. KBH has established support at 61 and has now bounced off of that number on news and stochastics (outrageously oversold) has now bounced and crossed its signal line. What is a trader to do?

The news isn't that good. Remember... I must RESPOND when others REACT. The reaction is a bullish pop, KBH may test resistance at 70 but the overwhelming momentum is bearish. I believe it will try to test 70 before falling back to support.

Symbol: kbh (66.45) **DT11 KBH call calendar** Date: 3/14/2006

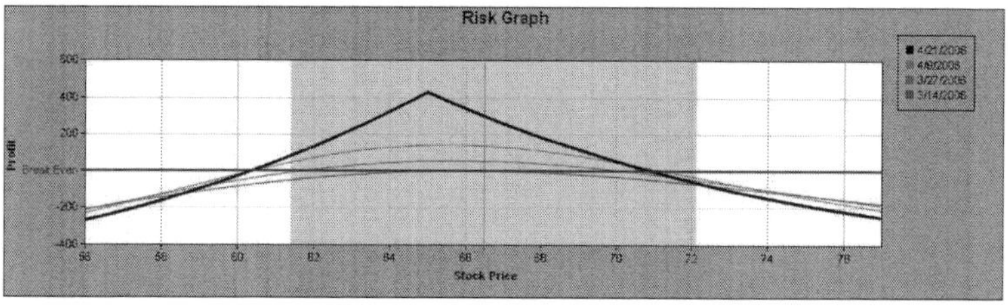

Summary

Cost of Trade	520	Max Reward	428	Delta	-2.0
Current Value	520	Probable Reward	62	Theta	$3.66
Profit/Loss	0	Risk/Max Reward	160.2%	Gamma	-4.4
Max Risk	-267	Risk/Prb Reward	23.2%	Vega	$14.12

Trade Details

Type	Qty	CostBasis	CurrValue	Strike	Expiration	Total Cost	Profit	IV	Delta
call	2	6.5000	6.5000	65	Jul 2006	1,300	0	35.8100	118.58
call	-2	3.9000	3.9000	65	Apr 2006	-780	0	36.2400	-120.55

Break Evens

	Expiration	Apr 09	Mar 27	Today
Upper B/E	71.00	71.30	70.30	66.50
Lower B/E	60.40	60.40	61.70	65.60

Based upon my outlook that KBH would test resistance @ 70 before falling to support I believed a Put Calendar Spread would provide a profit with minimal risk exposure, however after crunching the numbers the Call Calendar Spread proved to be the better choice.

Trade entry long 2 July 2006 65 strike calls @ 6.50 each and short 2 April 2006 65 strike calls @ 3.90 each. Total trade cost $520, immediate risk $267, maximum potential gain $428.

April 21, 2006 – How I love being right. KBH tested 70 three times but just didn't have the courage to break through and each time it tested it drifted back down to 65 which was my max gain price point.

Trade closed with a $460 profit on a $267 risk for a 172% ROR.

Symbol: kbh (65.55) **DT11 KBH call calendar** Date: 4/21/2006

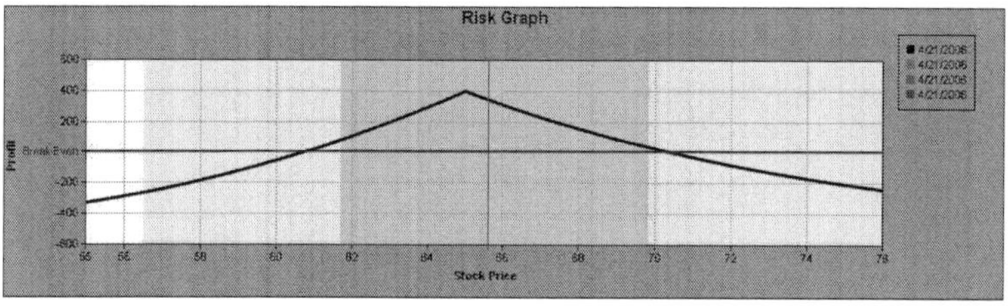

Summary

Cost of Trade	520	Max Reward	399	Delta	112.5
Current Value	980	Probable Reward	71	Theta	-$5.18
Profit/Loss	460	Risk/Max Reward	121.3%	Gamma	6.9
Max Risk	-329	Risk/Prb Reward	21.7%	Vega	$25.80

Trade Details

Type	Qty	CostBasis	CurrValue	Strike	Expiration	Total Cost	Profit	IV	Delta
call	2	6.5000	4.9000	65	Jul 2006	1,300	-320	34.6600	112.46
call	-2	3.9000	0.0000	65	Apr 2006	-780	780	0.0000	0.00

Break Evens

	Expiration	Apr 21	Apr 21	Today
Upper B/E	70.50	70.50	70.50	70.50
Lower B/E	60.80	60.80	60.80	60.80

March 28, 2006 – CNP.

I love these types of setups… although the last one like this turned out to be a bust. Outlook is simple… bearish. CNP broke a 4 month support line, MACD is bearish, 50 DMA has crossed below 200 DMA and the 50 & 200 DMA's are diverging, there is no foreseeable support. The move down is on above average volume. All together now… Long Put.

Symbol: cnp (11.98) **DT12 CNP long put** Date: 3/28/2006

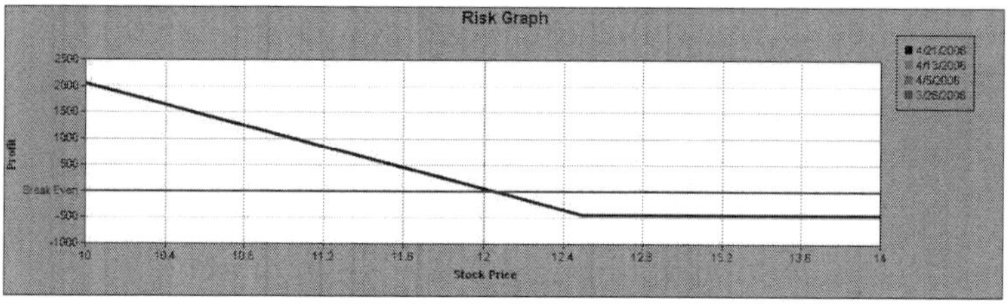

Summary

Cost of Trade	450	Max Reward	2,050	Delta	-1,000.0
Current Value	450	Probable Reward	0	Theta	$0.51
Profit/Loss	0	Risk/Max Reward	455.6%	Gamma	0.0
Max Risk	-450	Risk/Prb Reward	0%	Vega	$0.00

Trade Details

Type	Qty	CostBasis	CurrValue	Strike	Expiration	Total Cost	Profit	IV	Delta
put	10	0.4500	0.4500	12.5	Apr 2006	450	0	1.0000	-1,000.00

Break Evens

	Expiration	Apr 13	Apr 05	Today
Upper B/E	12.06	12.06	12.06	12.04
Lower B/E	12.06	12.06	12.06	12.04

This was a simple decision. Trade setup Long 10 April 2006 12.5 strike puts @ .45 each. Cost of trade $450, risk $450, reward unlimited.

April 12, 2006 – Stock shows some signs of bullish life… so take the money and run.

Trade closed with a $250 profit on a $450 risk for a 55% ROR.

Symbol: cnp (11.73) **DT12 CNP long put** Date: 4/12/2006

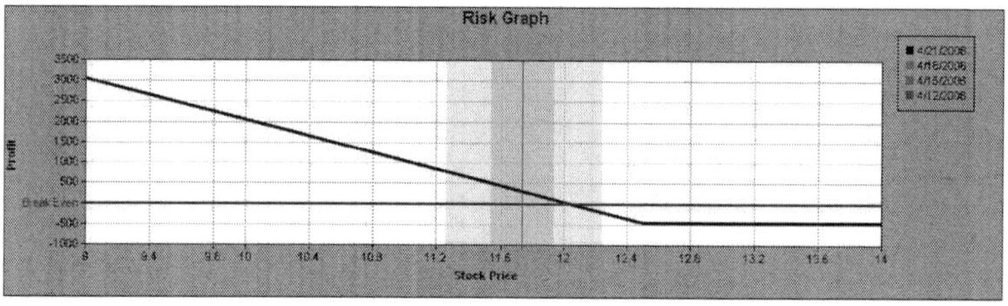

Summary

Cost of Trade	450	Max Reward	3,050	Delta	-1,000.0
Current Value	700	Probable Reward	307	Theta	$0.51
Profit/Loss	250	Risk/Max Reward	677.8%	Gamma	0.0
Max Risk	-450	Risk/Prb Reward	68.2%	Vega	$0.00

Trade Details

Type	Qty	CostBasis	CurrValue	Strike	Expiration	Total Cost	Profit	IV	Delta
put	10	0.4500	0.7000	12.5	Apr 2006	450	250	1.0000	-1,000.00

Break Evens

	Expiration	Apr 18	Apr 15	Today
Upper B/E	12.06	12.06	12.06	12.06
Lower B/E	12.06	12.06	12.06	12.06

April 2006

JNPR – Juniper Networks			
Iron Condor	+ $0.00	0%	223
SWK – Stanley Works			
Call Calendar Spread	+ $460.00	96%	227
KMB – Kimberly Clark			
Long Put	- $ 20.00	(4%)	231
GPS – Gap, Inc.			
Long Put	- $ 70.00	(15%)	235
FRX – Forrest Labs			
Long Put	+ $320.00	72%	239

April Results – 2 Wins vs. 2 Losses & 1 Break

Even Net result $690.00 Profit.

"This is your life, and it's ending one minute at a time."

-Chuck Palahniuk, Fight Club, Chapter 3

March 28, 2006 – JNPR.

Finally a stock that looks like it wants to fit into my favorite strategy. JNPR got destroyed on their last earnings gapping from 21 to 17. It has now filled the gap and is looking to trend back down.

It has a strong resistance at 21 and tested support at 17. It is below its 200 DMA (bearish) MACD is bearish, the 50 DMA appears to also provide resistance. News has come and gone what is an exhausted stock to do but trade in a range.

I propose the short term range will be between 17 and 21. This looks like a great Iron Condor setup.

Symbol: jnpr (19.06) **DT13 JNPR idib** Date: 3/28/2006

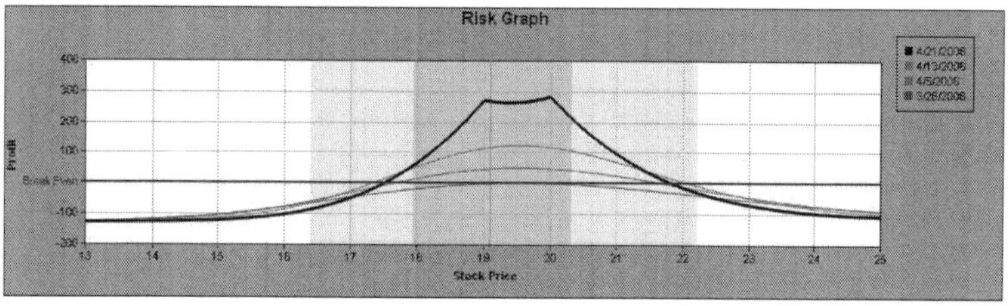

Summary

Cost of Trade	420	Max Reward	284	Delta	7.9
Current Value	420	Probable Reward	116	Theta	$5.08
Profit/Loss	0	Risk/Max Reward	224.3%	Gamma	-16.4
Max Risk	-127	Risk/Prb Reward	91.9%	Vega	$5.48

Trade Details

Type	Qty	CostBasis	CurrValue	Strike	Expiration	Total Cost	Profit	IV	Delta
call	-3	0.6000	0.6000	20	Apr 2006	-180	0	49.7700	-113.98
call	3	1.3000	1.3000	19	May 2006	390	0	43.6900	163.68
put	-3	0.9000	0.9000	19	Apr 2006	-270	0	48.2800	138.61
put	3	1.6000	1.6000	20	May 2006	480	0	37.2500	-180.41

Break Evens

	Expiration	Apr 13	Apr 05	Today
Upper B/E	21.85	22.15	21.75	20.10
Lower B/E	17.55	17.35	17.65	19.10

This is a 4 legged trade and is simply a combination between a call and put calendar spread. It gives the stock room to move but really depends on range bound behavior to reach its full potential.

The structure is simple...
Long 3 May 2006 19 strike calls and short 3 April 2006 20 strike calls (call calendar spread).

Long 3 May 2006 20 strike puts and short 3 April 19 strike puts (put calendar spread)

The combination of the two trades has a net cost of $420 and immediate risk of $127 with a max gain of $284.

April 21, 2006 – Here is another perfect example of a tremendous trade being blown out on expiration day. On April 19 (2 days before expiration JNPR was sitting nicely @ $20 after market close they decide to pre-announce earnings and on April 20th It Gaps down from 20 to 18 basically blowing the trade out. On April 19th this trade was destined to close at about Max Gain… two days later it closes out at break even.

Symbol: jnpr (17.87) **DT13 JNPR idib** Date: 4/21/2006

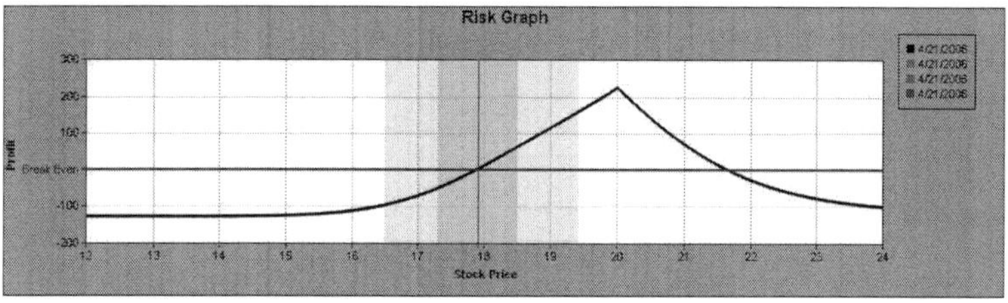

Summary

Cost of Trade	420	Max Reward	225	Delta	137.6
Current Value	420	Probable Reward	12	Theta	NaN
Profit/Loss	0	Risk/Max Reward	177.5%	Gamma	93.5
Max Risk	-127	Risk/Prb Reward	9.7%	Vega	$8.72

Trade Details

Type	Qty	CostBasis	CurrValue	Strike	Expiration	Total Cost	Profit	IV	Delta
call	-3	0.6000	0.0000	20	Apr 2006	-180	180	0.0000	0.00
call	3	1.3000	0.3500	19	May 2006	390	-285	38.4600	91.35
put	-3	0.9000	1.2000	19	Apr 2006	-270	-90	17597.6600	300.00
put	3	1.6000	2.2500	20	May 2006	480	195	37.6000	-253.72

Break Evens

	Expiration	Apr 21	Apr 21	Today
Upper B/E	21.70	21.70	21.70	21.70
Lower B/E	17.90	17.90	17.90	17.90

April 4, 2006 – SWK.

One more nicely trending stock. The evaluation process on this one is easy... bullish trend, 50 DMA acts as support, increasing volume... the only downside is the trend is slow.

Strategy choice Ratio Call Calendar... minimizes risk gives unlimited upside if SWK chooses to make a strong run.

Symbol: swk (51.29) **DT14 SWK call calendar** Date: 4/4/2006

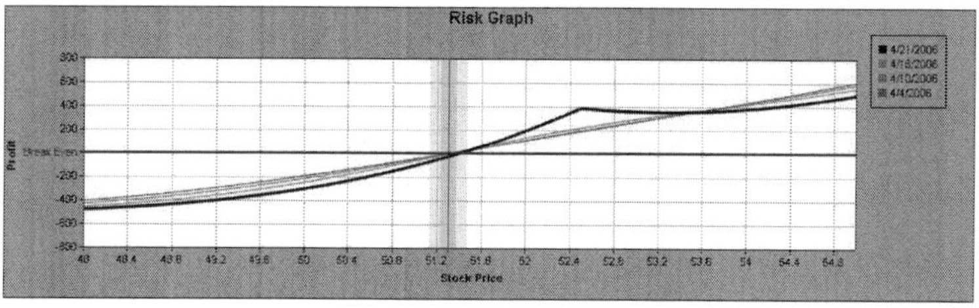

Summary

Cost of Trade	520	Max Reward	498	Delta	157.9
Current Value	520	Probable Reward	-24	Theta	-$1.01
Profit/Loss	0	Risk/Max Reward	104.3%	Gamma	7.3
Max Risk	-477	Risk/Prb Reward	-5%	Vega	$35.82

Trade Details

Type	Qty	CostBasis	CurrValue	Strike	Expiration	Total Cost	Profit	IV	Delta
call	8	0.9000	0.9000	52.5	May 2006	720	0	19.2600	307.87
call	-5	0.4000	0.4000	52.5	Apr 2006	-200	0	19.4100	-149.96

Break Evens

	Expiration	Apr 16	Apr 10	Today
Upper B/E	51.40	51.32	51.32	51.30
Lower B/E	51.40	51.32	51.32	51.30

Trade structure is long 8 May 52.50 strike calls @ .90 each and short 5 April 52.50 strike calls @ .40 each. Trade cost is $520, immediate risk is $477, Max reward is $498.

April 21, 2006 – Finally a stock that does exactly what it is supposed to do. Trade closed with a $460 profit on a $477 risk for a 96% ROR.

Symbol: swk (54.17) **DT14 SWK call calendar** Date: 4/21/2006

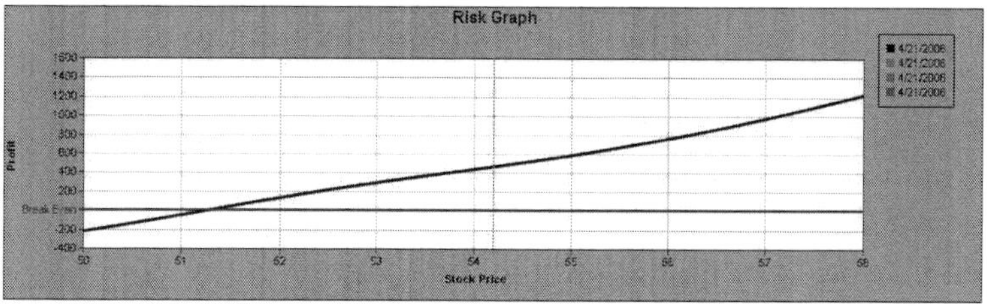

Summary

Cost of Trade	520	Max Reward	1,224	Delta	66.2
Current Value	980	Probable Reward	0	Theta	NaN
Profit/Loss	460	Risk/Max Reward	564.5%	Gamma	81.6
Max Risk	-217	Risk/Prb Reward	0%	Vega	$41.23

Trade Details

Type	Qty	CostBasis	CurrValue	Strike	Expiration	Total Cost	Profit	IV	Delta
call	8	0.9000	2.3500	52.5	May 2006	720	1,160	22.4600	566.20
call	-5	0.4000	1.8000	52.5	Apr 2006	-200	-700	9677.7300	-500.00

Break Evens

	Expiration	Apr 21	Apr 21	Today
Upper B/E	51.30	51.30	51.30	51.30
Lower B/E	51.30	51.30	51.30	51.30

April 11, 2006 – KMB.

The joy of trending stocks. Nothing and I mean nothing makes me a happy trader like a nice trending stock. KMB is bearish. Everything about KMB is bearish and the best news is I have a target... $56. If KMB can drift to 56 I can make some money in a put calendar spread. If it breaks below $56 I can make more.

Strategy Selection Put Calendar Spread.

Symbol: KMB (57.15) **DT15 KMB Long Put** Date: 4/11/2006

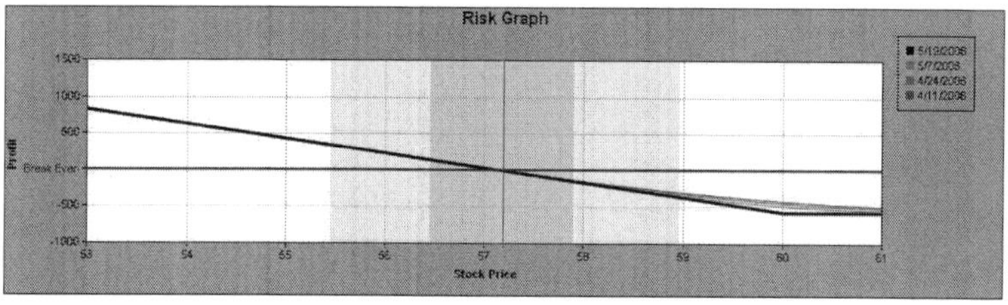

Summary

Cost of Trade	570	Max Reward	830	Delta	-184.9
Current Value	570	Probable Reward	-7	Theta	-$0.40
Profit/Loss	0	Risk/Max Reward	145.6%	Gamma	15.2
Max Risk	-570	Risk/Prb Reward	-1.1%	Vega	$5.24

Trade Details

Type	Qty	CostBasis	CurrValue	Strike	Expiration	Total Cost	Profit	IV	Delta
put	2	2.8500	2.8500	60	May 2006	570	0	10.1600	-184.92

Break Evens

	Expiration	May 07	Apr 24	Today
Upper B/E	57.15	57.15	57.15	57.20
Lower B/E	57.15	57.15	57.15	57.20

This is a simple trade setup… long 2 May 60 strike puts @ 2.85 each. Cost of Trade is $570, risk is $570, reward is unlimited.

April 21, 2006 – I have decided to close this trade out as there is an impending earnings announcement due in a couple of days.

Symbol: KMB (57.19) **DT15 KMB long put** Date: 4/21/2006

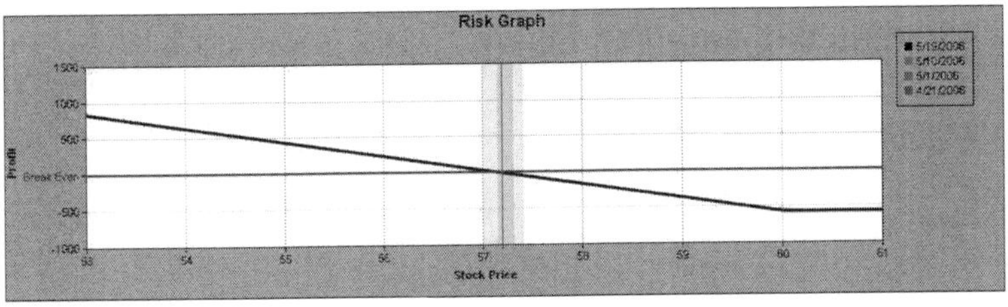

Summary

Cost of Trade	570	Max Reward	830	Delta	-200.0
Current Value	550	Probable Reward	-13	Theta	$0.33
Profit/Loss	-20	Risk/Max Reward	145.6%	Gamma	0.0
Max Risk	-570	Risk/Prb Reward	-2.3%	Vega	$0.00

Trade Details

Type	Qty	CostBasis	CurrValue	Strike	Expiration	Total Cost	Profit	IV	Delta
put	2	2.8500	2.7500	60	May 2006	570	-20	1.0000	-200.00

Break Evens

	Expiration	May 10	May 01	Today
Upper B/E	57.15	57.15	57.15	57.15
Lower B/E	57.15	57.15	57.15	57.15

Trade Closed for a $20 loss and a 4% loss on risk.

"A loss never bothers me after I take it. I forget it overnight. But being wrong-not taking the loss-that is what does damage to the pocketbook and to the soul."

- Jesse Livermore

April 18, 2006 – GPS.

Ha, Ha, Ha. I threw the dart and hit GPS again. The first GPS trade was a Ratio Call Calendar Spread for a $280 profit. I can't wait to see what this analysis reveals.

GPS is range bound between 17 and 19. This is a very narrow trading range. If I wasn't under a challenge I would walk away, however, I must be true to the challenge.

The indicators suggest a mildly bearish move and GPS should test 17 the only real trade I have is a long put.

Symbol: gps (17.69) **DT16 GPS long put** Date: 4/18/2006

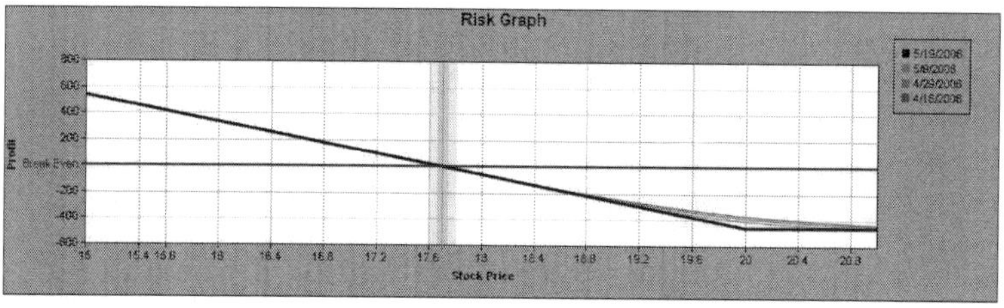

Summary

Cost of Trade	460	Max Reward	540	Delta	-196.2
Current Value	460	Probable Reward	0	Theta	-$0.04
Profit/Loss	0	Risk/Max Reward	117.4%	Gamma	9.0
Max Risk	-460	Risk/Prb Reward	0%	Vega	$0.47

Trade Details

Type	Qty	CostBasis	CurrValue	Strike	Expiration	Total Cost	Profit	IV	Delta
put	2	2.3000	2.3000	20	May 2006	460	0	19.8400	-196.24

Break Evens

	Expiration	May 09	Apr 29	Today
Upper B/E	17.70	17.70	17.70	17.70
Lower B/E	17.70	17.70	17.70	17.70

Trade Structure is long 2 May 20 strike puts @ 2.30 each, looking for a move to 17 or below. Cost of trade is $460, Risk of trade $460, Max Reward Unlimited.

April 26, 2006 – One of the most important aspects of being a good trader is to try to take as much of your emotions out of your trading as possible and cut your losses as quickly as you can.

GPS turned against me and I gave it a week. Since I can't predict the future I would rather take a small loss today than a large one next week.

Trade closed with a $70 loss for a 15% loss on risk.

Symbol: gps (18.02)	**DT16 GPS long put**	Date: 4/26/2006

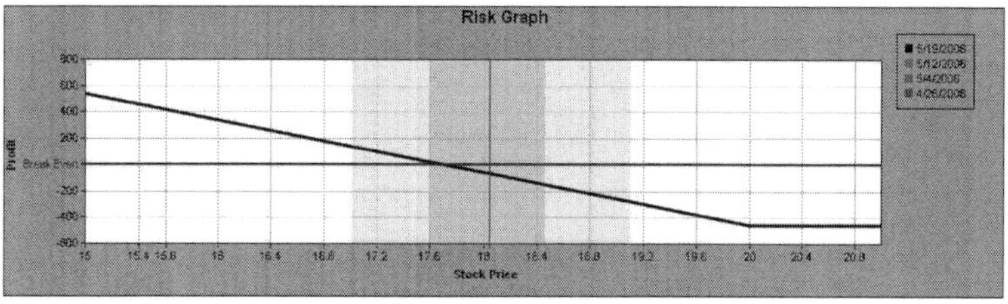

Summary

Cost of Trade	460	Max Reward	540	Delta	-200.0
Current Value	390	Probable Reward	-68	Theta	$0.11
Profit/Loss	-70	Risk/Max Reward	117.4%	Gamma	0.0
Max Risk	-460	Risk/Prb Reward	-14.8%	Vega	$0.00

Trade Details

Type	Qty	CostBasis	CurrValue	Strike	Expiration	Total Cost	Profit	IV	Delta
put	2	2.3000	1.9500	20	May 2006	460	-70	1.0000	-200.00

Break Evens

	Expiration	May 12	May 04	Today
Upper B/E	17.70	17.70	17.70	17.70
Lower B/E	17.70	17.70	17.70	17.70

April 25, 2006 – FRX.

What a day to pick FRX. Bad news is out and FRX has sold off and closed below its 200 DMA. MACD turned bearish a couple of weeks prior to today, the 90 day trend is bearish, it would appear that FRX wants to test the $38 dollar level and may do it fairly quickly. Strategy Selection… Long Put.

Symbol: frx (40.93) **DT17 FRX long put** Date: 4/25/2006

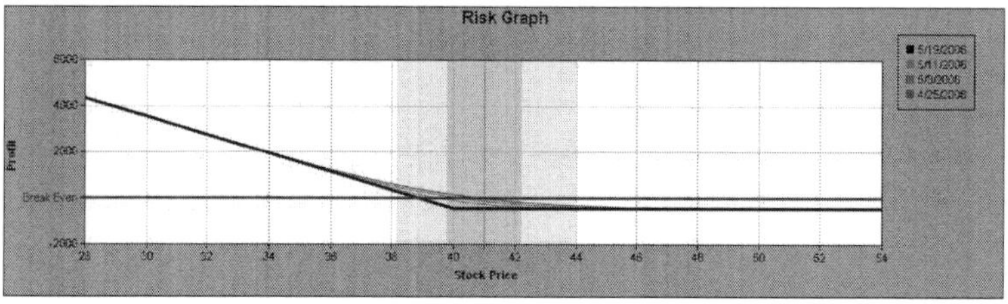

Summary

Cost of Trade	440	Max Reward	4,360	Delta	-153.4
Current Value	440	Probable Reward	-318	Theta	-$12.17
Profit/Loss	0	Risk/Max Reward	990.9%	Gamma	39.3
Max Risk	-440	Risk/Prb Reward	-72.2%	Vega	$16.03

Trade Details

Type	Qty	CostBasis	CurrValue	Strike	Expiration	Total Cost	Profit	IV	Delta
put	4	1.1000	1.1000	40	May 2006	440	0	37.0100	-153.36

Break Evens

	Expiration	May 11	May 03	Today
Upper B/E	38.90	39.60	40.30	41.00
Lower B/E	38.90	39.60	40.30	41.00

Trade structures is simply long 4 May 40 strike puts @ 1.10 each. Trade cost $440, trade risk $440, Max gain unlimited, although my price target is $38.

May 19, 2006 – FRX hit my $38 price target today… it could go lower or it could bounce. My choice, take the profit and be happy.

Trade closed with a $320 profit on a $440 risk for a 72% ROR.

Symbol: frx (38.09)	**DT17 FRX long put**	Date: 5/19/2006

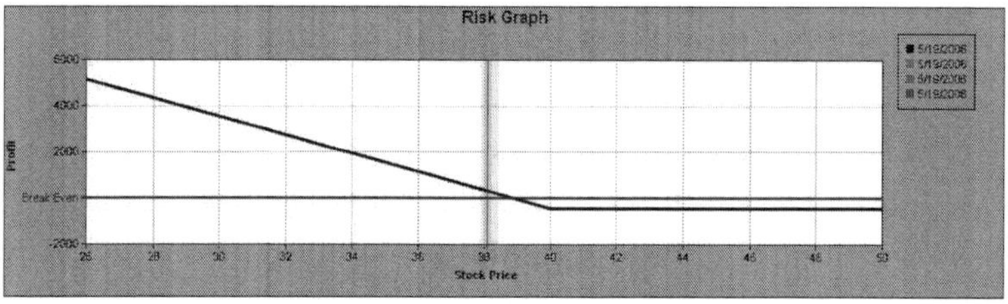

Summary

Cost of Trade	440	Max Reward	5,160	Delta	-400.0
Current Value	760	Probable Reward	304	Theta	NaN
Profit/Loss	320	Risk/Max Reward	1172.7%	Gamma	0.0
Max Risk	-440	Risk/Prb Reward	69.1%	Vega	$0.00

Trade Details

Type	Qty	CostBasis	CurrValue	Strike	Expiration	Total Cost	Profit	IV	Delta
put	4	1.1000	1.9000	40	May 2006	440	320	1.0000	-400.00

Break Evens

	Expiration	May 19	May 19	Today
Upper B/E	38.90	38.90	38.90	38.90
Lower B/E	38.90	38.90	38.90	38.90

May 2006

RYL – Ryland Group			
Bear Put Spread	+ $460.00	96%	245
OCR – Omnicare, Inc.			
Call Calendar Spread	- $125.00	(24%)	249
XTO –			
Long Put	- $130.00	(28%)	253
UST – UST, Inc.			
Long Call	+ $315.00	69%	257

May Results – 2 Wins vs. 2 Losses

Net result $520.00 Profit.

"If we did all the things we are capable of doing, we would literally astound ourselves."

- Thomas Alva Edison

May 2, 2006 – RYL.

Here is another one of those – should be no brainer – trades. RYL was trading in a range between 65 – 75. It has now broken support at 65. MACD is Bearish, It is below its 50 and 200 DMA and the 50 DMA has just crossed below the 200 DMA – Next real support is 55 and it looks as if RYL will test.

Strategy Selection: Bear Put Spread

Symbol: ryl (62.09) **DT18 RYL bear put** Date: 5/2/2006

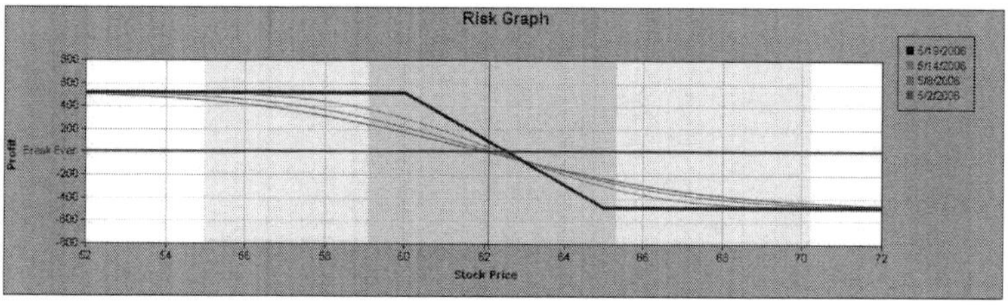

Summary

Cost of Trade	480	Max Reward	520	Delta	-84.4
Current Value	480	Probable Reward	55	Theta	$2.96
Profit/Loss	0	Risk/Max Reward	108.3%	Gamma	1.5
Max Risk	-480	Risk/Prb Reward	11.5%	Vega	-$0.93

Trade Details

Type	Qty	CostBasis	CurrValue	Strike	Expiration	Total Cost	Profit	IV	Delta
put	2	3.5000	3.5000	65	May 2006	700	0	30.7700	-148.40
put	-2	1.1000	1.1000	60	May 2006	-220	0	37.7200	64.05

Break Evens

	Expiration	May 14	May 08	Today
Upper B/E	62.60	62.50	62.30	62.10
Lower B/E	62.60	62.50	62.30	62.10

Trade structure is long 2 May 65 strike puts @ 3.50 and short 2 May 60 strike puts @ 1.10. Trade cost is $480, Trade risk is $480, Max gain is $520.

May 19, 2006 – RYL has hit my price target of $55, everything indicates it could move lower, however I am a firm believer that you will never go broke it you take profits, but you might if you leave them on the table.

Trade closed with a $460 profit on a risk of $480 for a 96% ROR.

Symbol: ryl (53.84) **DT18 RYL bear put** Date: 5/19/2006

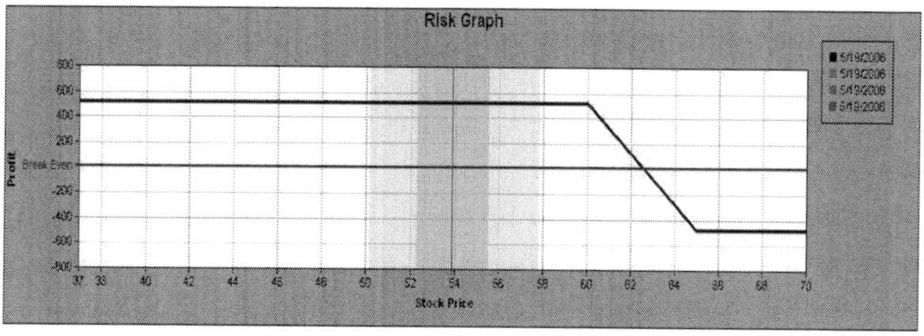

Summary

Cost of Trade	480	Max Reward	520	Delta	0.0
Current Value	940	Probable Reward	519	Theta	NaN
Profit/Loss	460	Risk/Max Reward	108.3%	Gamma	0.0
Max Risk	-480	Risk/Prb Reward	108.1%	Vega	$0.00

Trade Details

Type	Qty	CostBasis	CurrValue	Strike	Expiration	Total Cost	Profit	IV	Delta
put	2	3.5000	11.0000	65	May 2006	700	1,500	1.0000	-200.00
put	-2	1.1000	6.3000	60	May 2006	-220	-1,040	1.0000	200.00

Break Evens

	Expiration	May 19	May 19	Today
Upper B/E	62.60	62.60	62.60	62.60
Lower B/E	62.60	62.60	62.60	62.60

May 9, 2006 – OCR.

This stock like every other stock on the planet (right now) is range bound. OCR's current trading range is 51 to 62. It is currently on the upswing of its roll between the top an bottom of its range.

History suggests that it will roll up to 62 and then roll back down to 51. The goal is to structure a trade that will profit as long as OCR stays in this range. The best trade for that behavior is the Iron Condor.

Strategy Selection: Iron Condor.

Symbol: Ocr (56.33) **DT19 OCR idib** Date: 5/9/2006

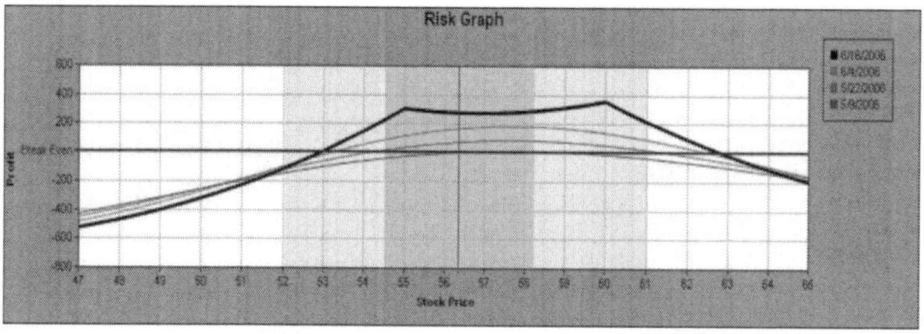

Summary

Cost of Trade	1,690	Max Reward	358	Delta	14.2
Current Value	1,690	Probable Reward	213	Theta	$4.88
Profit/Loss	0	Risk/Max Reward	68.3%	Gamma	-10.1
Max Risk	-524	Risk/Prb Reward	40.6%	Vega	$25.26

Trade Details

Type	Qty	CostBasis	CurrValue	Strike	Expiration	Total Cost	Profit	IV	Delta
call	2	5.3000	5.3000	55	Sep 2006	1,060	0	34.1800	118.70
call	-2	1.0500	1.0500	60	Jun 2006	-210	0	32.6500	-59.16
put	2	5.8000	5.8000	60	Sep 2006	1,160	0	27.8200	-121.87
put	-2	1.6000	1.6000	55	Jun 2006	-320	0	31.0900	76.51

Break Evens

	Expiration	Jun 04	May 22	Today
Upper B/E	62.90	62.60	61.55	59.25
Lower B/E	53.00	53.25	54.20	56.35

Trade structure is long 2 September 55 strike calls @ 5.30 each and short 2 June 60 strike calls @ 1.05 each. (call calendar spread)

Trade structure is long 2 September 60 strike puts @ 5.80 each and short 2 June 55 strike puts @ 1.60 each. (put calendar spread)

Trade cost is $1,690, trade risk is $524 and max gain is $358.

With a trading range between 53 and 63.

May 19, 2006 – Once again the trade was perfect right up until expiration Friday… May 18th the trade was at max gain on the low end… Max Gain. Friday (May 19th) the stock sells off from 55 to 50 effectively blowing the trade out of the water.

Trade closed with a $125 loss or a 24% loss on risk.

Symbol: Ocr (50.62) **DT19 OCR idib** Date: 5/19/2006

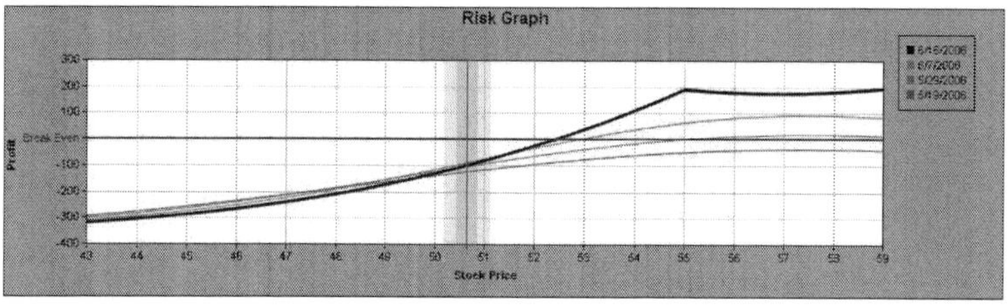

Summary

Cost of Trade	845	Max Reward	195	Delta	23.1
Current Value	720	Probable Reward	-99	Theta	$2.29
Profit/Loss	-125	Risk/Max Reward	61.4%	Gamma	-1.6
Max Risk	-318	Risk/Prb Reward	-31.3%	Vega	$11.82

Trade Details

Type	Qty	CostBasis	CurrValue	Strike	Expiration	Total Cost	Profit	IV	Delta
call	1	5.3000	2.6500	55	Sep 2006	530	-265	37.0400	39.31
call	-1	1.0500	0.2500	60	Jun 2006	-105	80	43.9100	-9.16
put	1	5.8000	9.9000	60	Sep 2006	580	410	28.5700	-82.65
put	-1	1.6000	5.1000	55	Jun 2006	-160	-350	39.6800	75.59

Break Evens

	Expiration	Jun 07	May 29	Today
Upper B/E	52.45	52.90	54.95	0.00
Lower B/E	52.45	52.90	54.95	0.00

May 16, 2006 – XTO.

I would appear that I have hit into a flock of range bound stocks. Actually all stocks are range bound, sometimes the range is just wider than others. XTO is a stock that is currently oversold and has tested support at 32 for the third time in as many months.

The problem with this test however is it is the first time it has broken the 200 DMA with a gap in price. Logic says walk away the Dart-Throw Trader Challenge says place a trade.

Historically when XTO has exhibited this behavior there has been a dead-cat bounce (I know it's not politically correct, but I am not running for office). Does history want to repeat itself now?

Strategy chosen: Long Call

Symbol: xto (41.04) **DT20 XTO long call** Date: 5/16/2006

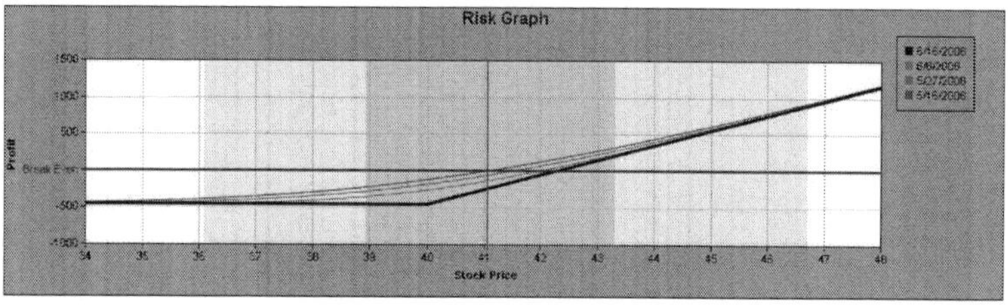

Summary

Cost of Trade	450	Max Reward	1,150	Delta	124.3
Current Value	450	Probable Reward	-90	Theta	-$5.30
Profit/Loss	0	Risk/Max Reward	255.6%	Gamma	18.1
Max Risk	-450	Risk/Prb Reward	-19.9%	Vega	$9.10

Trade Details

Type	Qty	CostBasis	CurrValue	Strike	Expiration	Total Cost	Profit	IV	Delta
call	2	2.2500	2.2500	40	Jun 2006	450	0	35.2300	124.32

Break Evens

	Expiration	Jun 06	May 27	Today
Upper B/E	42.25	42.00	41.50	41.05
Lower B/E	42.25	42.00	41.50	41.05

Trade structure is long 2 June 40 strike calls @ 2.25 each. Trade cost $450, trade risk $450, Max profit unlimited. Price target for XTO is $35.

May 17, 2006 – I have decided to pull the plug on this trade, it does not appear that this cat wants to bounce.

Trade closed $130 loss for a 28% loss on risk.

Symbol: xto (39.86) **DT20 XTO long call** Date: 5/17/2006

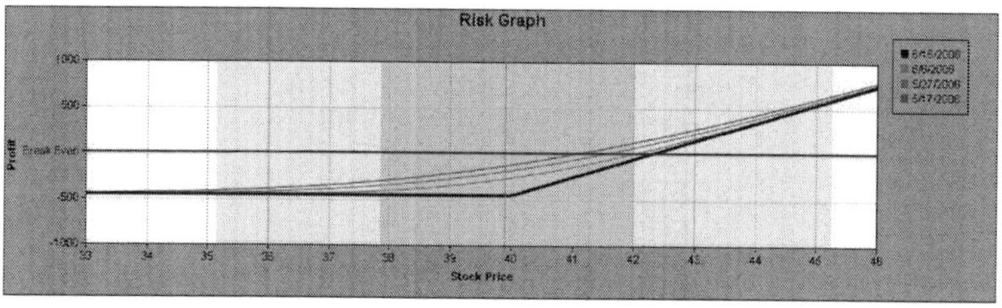

Summary

Cost of Trade	450	Max Reward	750	Delta	102.1
Current Value	320	Probable Reward	-234	Theta	-$5.61
Profit/Loss	-130	Risk/Max Reward	166.7%	Gamma	19.3
Max Risk	-450	Risk/Prb Reward	-52%	Vega	$9.11

Trade Details

Type	Qty	CostBasis	CurrValue	Strike	Expiration	Total Cost	Profit	IV	Delta
call	2	2.2500	1.6000	40	Jun 2006	450	-130	36.2300	102.08

Break Evens

	Expiration	Jun 06	May 27	Today
Upper B/E	42.25	41.95	41.50	41.05
Lower B/E	42.25	41.95	41.50	41.05

May 23, 2006 – UST.

Another slow moving bullish trend. MACD is bullish, although weak. UST's 50 DMA crossed above the 200 DMA (bullish). Earnings have come and gone. Looks as though UST wants to bounce off the bottom BollingerBand, 50 and 200 DMA before continuing this slow moving bullish trend.

Strategy Selection: Long Call

Symbol: ust (43.09) **DT21 UST long call** Date: 5/23/2006

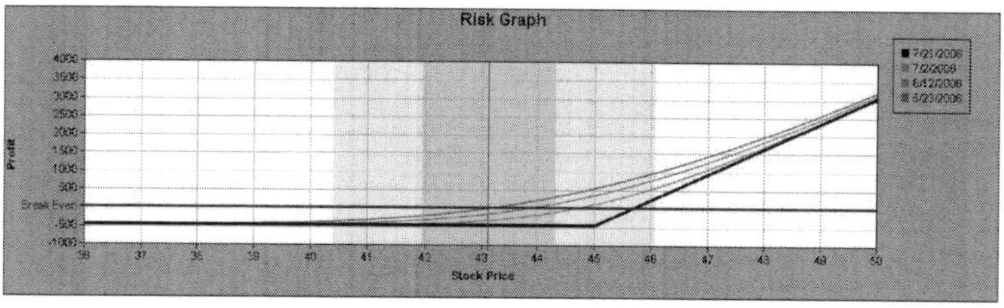

Summary

Cost of Trade	455	Max Reward	3,045	Delta	217.8
Current Value	455	Probable Reward	-364	Theta	-$7.34
Profit/Loss	0	Risk/Max Reward	669.2%	Gamma	73.1
Max Risk	-455	Risk/Prb Reward	-79.9%	Vega	$42.85

Trade Details

Type	Qty	CostBasis	CurrValue	Strike	Expiration	Total Cost	Profit	IV	Delta
call	7	0.6500	0.6500	45	Jul 2006	455	0	19.5300	217.83

Break Evens

	Expiration	Jul 02	Jun 12	Today
Upper B/E	45.65	44.65	43.80	43.10
Lower B/E	45.65	44.65	43.80	43.10

Trade Structure: Long 7 July 45 strike calls @ .65 each. Trade cost $455, trade risk $455 max profit unlimited. Price target 45 (resistance).

June 9, 2006 – UST hit my $45 price target today, it is time to close the trade.

Trade closed $315 profit on $455 risk for a 69% ROR.

Symbol: ust (44.98) **DT21 UST long call** Date: 6/9/2006

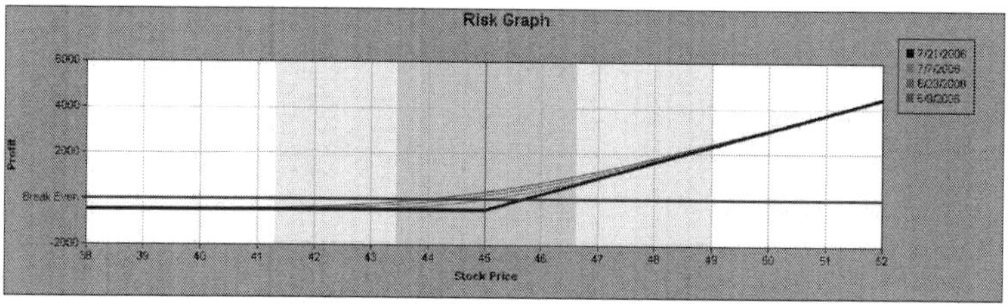

Summary

Cost of Trade	455	Max Reward	4,445	Delta	361.7
Current Value	770	Probable Reward	208	Theta	-$9.46
Profit/Loss	315	Risk/Max Reward	976.9%	Gamma	102.6
Max Risk	-455	Risk/Prb Reward	45.7%	Vega	$42.57

Trade Details

Type	Qty	CostBasis	CurrValue	Strike	Expiration	Total Cost	Profit	IV	Delta
call	7	0.6500	1.1000	45	Jul 2006	455	315	17.8200	361.70

Break Evens

	Expiration	Jul 07	Jun 23	Today
Upper B/E	45.65	45.05	44.50	44.00
Lower B/E	45.65	45.05	44.50	44.00

June 2006

EBAY – EBAY, inc.			
Condor	- $ 50.00	(22%)	263
IBM – IBM			
Long Call	- $220.00	(47%)	267
KIM – Kimco Realty			
Long Call	+ $450.00	107%	271
DOV – Dover Corp			
Long Call	+ $720.00	141%	275
DUK – Duke Energy			
Bear Put Spread	+ $ 30.00	6%	279

May Results – 3 Wins vs. 2 Losses

Net result $930.00 Profit.

"Don't worry about people stealing your ideas. If the ideas are any good, you'll have to ram them down peoples' throats."

- Howard Aiken

May 30, 2006 – EBAY.

Earnings. 3 days ago earnings are announced. Ebay just gapped up 4 dollars on an earnings announcement after being in a decisive bearish trend.

Is the earnings enough to push the stock higher and reverse the trend or is Ebay going to slam back down to 30? At this point technicals are useless this is purely an emotional play.

1st rule of Fight Club… I mean Dart-Throw Trader: Respond when others React.

Ebay has set support at 30 and there is now strong resistance at 37. There is an emotional pull to take ebay to 37 but I don't believe there is enough commitment from the market to reverse the trend. I believe Ebay is going to trade in a range now between 30 and 37. How to profit? Sell Volatility.

Strategy Selection: Condor.

Symbol: ebay (33.21) **DT22 EBAY condor** Date: 5/30/2006

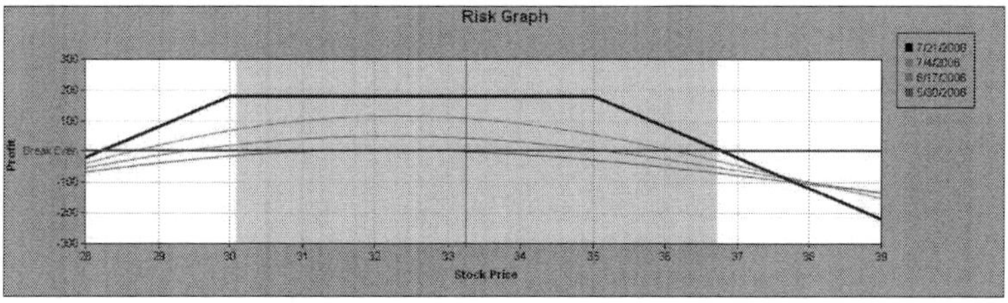

Summary

Cost of Trade	-180	Max Reward	180	Delta	-9.2
Current Value	-180	Probable Reward	82	Theta	$2.13
Profit/Loss	0	Risk/Max Reward	81.8%	Gamma	-7.7
Max Risk	-220	Risk/Prb Reward	37.2%	Vega	-$5.19

Trade Details

Type	Qty	CostBasis	CurrValue	Strike	Expiration	Total Cost	Profit	IV	Delta
call	-1	1.3500	1.3500	35	Jul 2006	-135	0	41.1000	-40.07
put	-1	0.8000	0.8000	30	Jul 2006	-80	0	42.6400	23.55
call	1	0.2500	0.2500	40	Jul 2006	25	0	38.2500	11.38
put	1	0.1000	0.1000	25	Jul 2006	10	0	45.6000	-4.06

Break Evens

	Expiration	Jul 04	Jun 17	Today
Upper B/E	36.80	36.20	35.25	33.25
Lower B/E	28.20	28.65	29.35	31.05

With a now established range of 30 to 37 and volatility rising in the options this trade makes risk/reward sense.

Trade structure: Long 1 July 40 strike call @ .25 and short 1 July 35 strike call @ 1.35.
Long 1 July 25 put @ .10 and short 1 July 30 strike put @ .80.

Trade cost is $180, trade risk is $220, max profit is $220.

June 27, 2006 – After the gap up on earnings Ebay drifts back down to $30 which is great. The stock is sitting at the bottom end of the max gain profile a little bounce up and everybody is happy… but no ebay sits on $30 for 12 days and then on expiration Friday sells off to $28 effectively killing my beautiful, perfect trade.
Trade closed with a $50 loss… should have been a $200 profit.

Symbol: ebay (28.25) **DT22 EBAY condor** Date: 6/27/2006

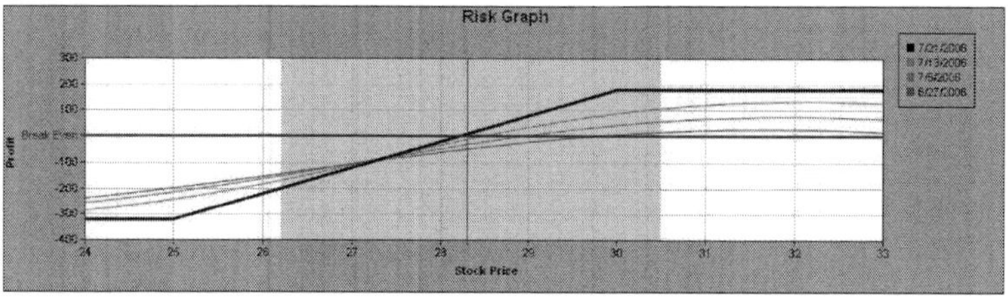

Summary

Cost of Trade	-180	Max Reward	180	Delta	41.0
Current Value	-230	Probable Reward	-16	Theta	$2.09
Profit/Loss	-50	Risk/Max Reward	56.3%	Gamma	-7.4
Max Risk	-320	Risk/Prb Reward	-5.1%	Vega	-$1.99

Trade Details

Type	Qty	CostBasis	CurrValue	Strike	Expiration	Total Cost	Profit	IV	Delta
call	-1	1.3500	0.1500	35	Jul 2006	-135	120	57.3000	-8.37
put	-1	0.8000	2.5000	30	Jul 2006	-80	-170	49.6200	65.68
call	1	0.2500	0.0001	40	Jul 2006	25	-25	36.6200	0.01
put	1	0.1000	0.3500	25	Jul 2006	10	25	52.4700	-16.34

Break Evens

	Expiration	Jul 13	Jul 05	Today
Upper B/E	28.20	28.50	28.95	29.75
Lower B/E	28.20	28.50	28.95	29.75

June 6, 2006 – IBM.

I am beginning to believe I am throwing darts into the range bound river. IBM support @ 78 resistance @ 85… rolling, rolling, rolling, keep those doggies rolling… raw hide.

IBM is sitting on firm support at 78, stochastics shows oversold and logic suggests a bounce and test of at least 81 and probably a move back to 84. Although MACD is bearish and the 50 DMA is diverging from the 200 DMA a bounce to 81 should produce a few dollars from a long call position.

Strategy Selection: Long Call

Symbol: ibm (79.76) **DT23 IBM long call** Date: 6/6/2006

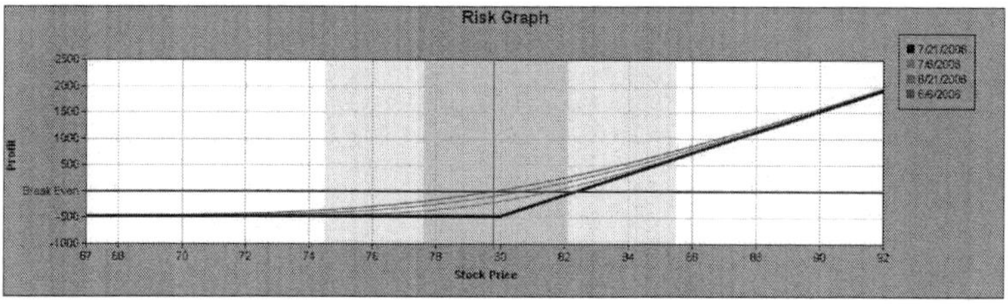

Summary

Cost of Trade	470	Max Reward	1,930	Delta	101.2
Current Value	470	Probable Reward	-214	Theta	-$5.58
Profit/Loss	0	Risk/Max Reward	410.6%	Gamma	13.2:
Max Risk	-470	Risk/Prb Reward	-45.4%	Vega	$22.34

Trade Details

Type	Qty	CostBasis	CurrValue	Strike	Expiration	Total Cost	Profit	IV	Delta
call	2	2.3500	2.3500	80	Jul 2006	470	0	21.6500	101.17

Break Evens

	Expiration	Jul 06	Jun 21	Today
Upper B/E	82.40	81.60	80.70	79.80
Lower B/E	82.40	81.60	80.70	79.80

Trade structure long 2 July 80 strike calls @ 2.35 each. Trade cost $470, trade risk $470, max profit unlimited.

June 8, 2006 – IBM decides to play dirty and blow through support on strong volume. I will pull the plug on this trade and fight another day.

Trade Exit with a $220 loss which is a 47% loss on risk.

Symbol: ibm (77.03) **DT23 IBM long call** Date: 6/8/2006

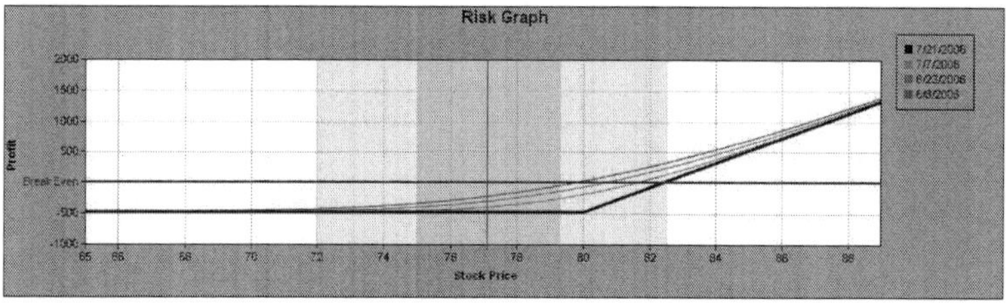

Summary

Cost of Trade	470	Max Reward	1,330	Delta	66.4
Current Value	250	Probable Reward	-403	Theta	-$5.16
Profit/Loss	-220	Risk/Max Reward	283%	Gamma	12.2
Max Risk	-470	Risk/Prb Reward	- 85.7%	Vega	$19.19

Trade Details

Type	Qty	CostBasis	CurrValue	Strike	Expiration	Total Cost	Profit	IV	Delta
call	2	2.3500	1.2500	80	Jul 2006	470	-220	22.5400	66.35

Break Evens

	Expiration	Jul 07	Jun 23	Today
Upper B/E	82.40	81.60	80.60	79.70
Lower B/E	82.40	81.60	80.60	79.70

June 13, 2006 – KIM.

Have you ever done a trade that logically was stupid but intuitively was right on the money? This is where I find myself as I evaluate KIM.

Logically KIM should drop to $34. Lets look at the facts… It has just rolled over from resistance at $38 which it has failed to break through even after numerous tests. Macd is below the zero line (bearish), stochastics is about to cross below its signal line, every thing about this chart says its going to roll down. The logical choice here is a bearish trade specifically a long put because it should drop to 34 and if it breaks 34… wow.

But here is where intuition and behavior steps in. Past performance does NOT guarantee future results, everybody knows that. But here is the thorn in this trades side. Historically, this stock likes to run up in anticipation of earnings during the 3 weeks prior to its announcement and there is no reason to believe it won't happen again. So do I take a short term "sure thing" – stock dropping to 34 or the longer-term historical behavior which will produce a better ROR if correct?

Strategy Chosen: Long Call (two reasons: 1. If Kim rallies into earnings I have unlimited upside with minimal risk. 2. If Kim breaks 34 I turn it into a BearCall Spread and probably make a few dollars. Either way I should win.

Symbol: kim (35.79)	**DT24 KIM long call**	Date: 6/13/2006

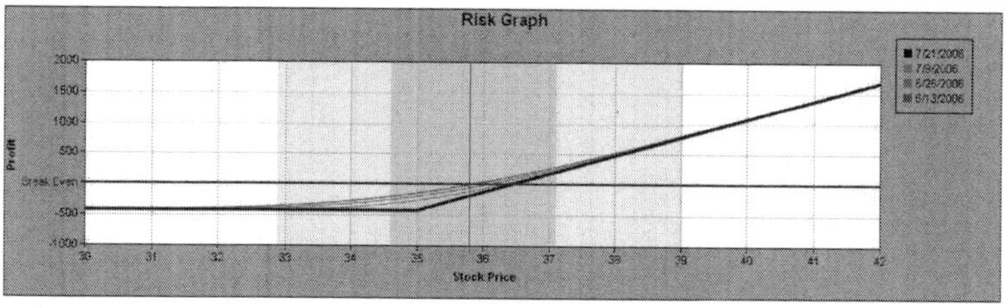

Summary

Cost of Trade	420	Max Reward	1,680	Delta	195.3
Current Value	420	Probable Reward	-49	Theta	-$3.62
Profit/Loss	0	Risk/Max Reward	400%	Gamma	47.1
Max Risk	-420	Risk/Prb Reward	-11.7%	Vega	$12.82

Trade Details

Type	Qty	CostBasis	CurrValue	Strike	Expiration	Total Cost	Profit	IV	Delta
call	3	1.4000	1.4000	35	Jul 2006	420	0	20.4000	195.28

Break Evens

	Expiration	Jul 09	Jun 26	Today
Upper B/E	36.40	36.30	36.05	35.80

Trade structure long 3 July 35 strike calls @ 1.40 each. Trade cost $420, Trade risk $420, Max gain unlimited.

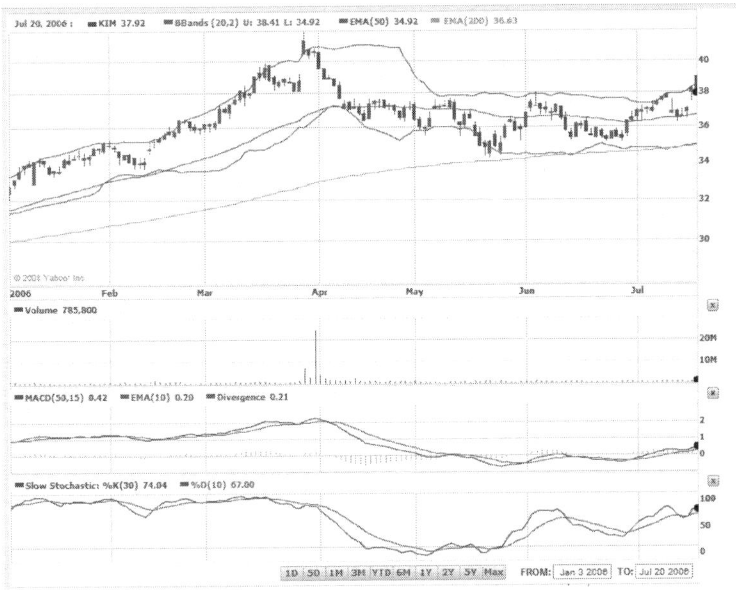

July 20, 2006 – Expiration Friday. I was wrong and I was right about this stock and I am glad I was. My original expectation was that KIM would fall to $34 (support). It didn't, which is good because I was in a long call. Since it didn't fall to 34 I was Wrong.

However I was right because as history suggested KIM rallied into its earnings, rising from $35 to $38 allowing me to close this trade out with a $450 profit on a $420 risk which is a 107% ROR… Sweet.

Symbol: kim (37.92) **DT24 KIM long call** Date: 7/20/2006

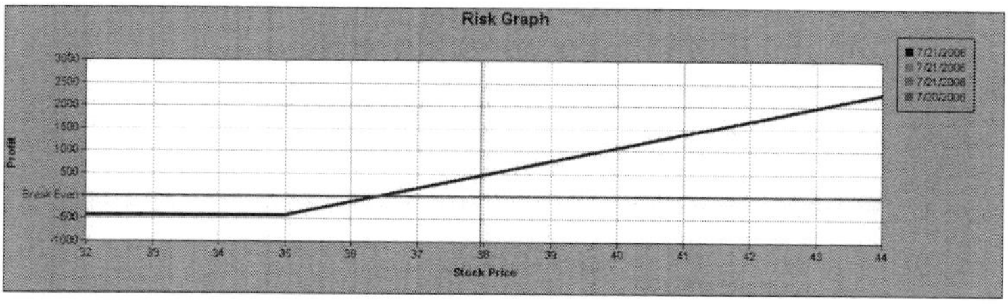

Summary

Cost of Trade	420	Max Reward	2,280	Delta	300.0
Current Value	870	Probable Reward	0	Theta	-$0.29
Profit/Loss	450	Risk/Max Reward	542.9%	Gamma	0.0
Max Risk	-420	Risk/Prb Reward	0%	Vega	$0.00

Trade Details

Type	Qty	CostBasis	CurrValue	Strike	Expiration	Total Cost	Profit	IV	Delta
call	3	1.4000	2.9000	35	Jul 2006	420	450	1.0000	300.00

Break Evens

	Expiration	Jul 21	Jul 21	Today
Upper B/E	36.40	36.40	36.40	36.40
Lower B/E	36.40	36.40	36.40	36.40

June 20, 2006 – DOV.

Here is a stock that is short term oversold and has tested its 200 DMA as support, has given a short term inside bar reversal signal, stochastics trying to cross its signal line, MACD (although bearish) looks to be turning.

Most technicians would look at this chart and suggest that DOV will test its 50 DMA for resistance before heading lower... I would probably agree. Since that is the case why not profit from the test of the 50 DMA make some cash and then ride it south?

Strategy Selected: Long Call Price target 50 DMA (roughly 48).

Symbol: dov (45.81)	**DT25 DOV long call**	Date: 6/20/2006

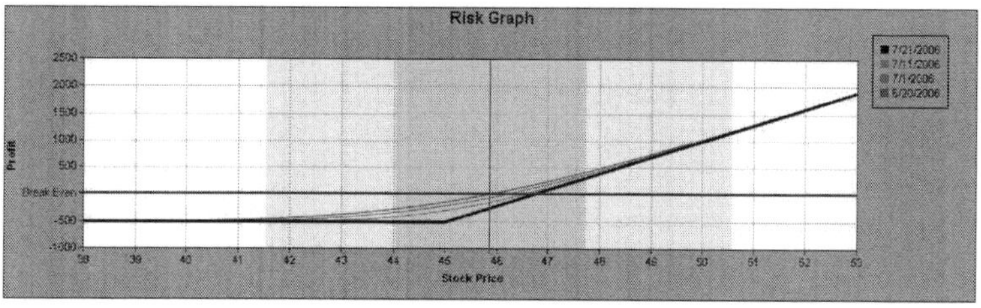

Summary

Cost of Trade	510	Max Reward	1,890	Delta	186.4
Current Value	510	Probable Reward	-46	Theta	-$5.95
Profit/Loss	0	Risk/Max Reward	370.6%	Gamma	36.7
Max Risk	-510	Risk/Prb Reward	-9.1%	Vega	$15.23

Trade Details

Type	Qty	CostBasis	CurrValue	Strike	Expiration	Total Cost	Profit	IV	Delta
call	3	1.7000	1.7000	45	Jul 2006	510	0	23.3100	186.41

Break Evens

	Expiration	Jul 11	Jul 01	Today
Upper B/E	46.70	46.50	46.15	45.85
Lower B/E	46.70	46.50	46.15	45.85

Trade structure is long 3 July 45 strike calls @ 1.70 each. Trade cost is $510, trade risk is $510, trade max profit is unlimited.

June 29, 2006 – My price target was hit today on a strong market open move. My feeling has always been when your target is hit… take the money.

Trade closed with a $720 profit on a $510 risk for a 141% ROR.

Symbol: dov (49.13) **DT25 DOV long call** Date: 6/29/2006

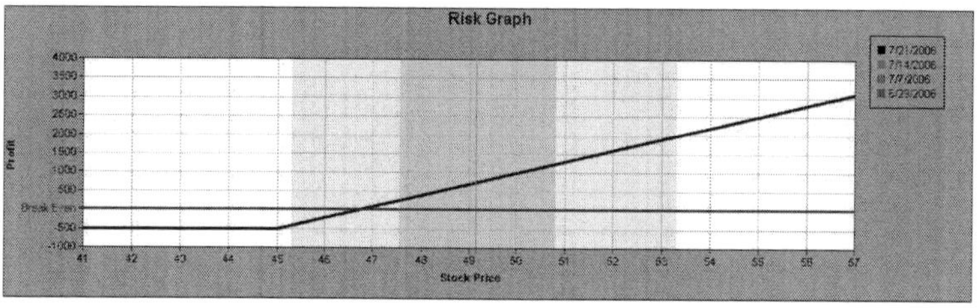

Summary

Cost of Trade	510	Max Reward	3,090	Delta	300.0
Current Value	1,230	Probable Reward	760	Theta	-$0.37
Profit/Loss	720	Risk/Max Reward	605.9%	Gamma	0.0
Max Risk	-510	Risk/Prb Reward	149%	Vega	$0.00

Trade Details

Type	Qty	CostBasis	CurrValue	Strike	Expiration	Total Cost	Profit	IV	Delta
call	3	1.7000	4.1000	45	Jul 2006	510	720	1.0000	300.00

Break Evens

	Expiration	Jul 14	Jul 07	Today
Upper B/E	46.70	46.70	46.70	46.70
Lower B/E	46.70	46.70	46.70	46.70

June 27, 2006 – DUK.

Obviously I need to move the location of my dartboard or change the location I throw from. This is the second time I have hit DUK with a dart. Believe me when I say, I would NOT choose this stock on my own free will.

At best this stock is in a $2 dollar trading range... a $2 range. You can't really trade a stock in a $2 trading range... or can you? I guess we will soon find out.

The main problem I see so far is that we are already in the Middle of the range so it really only has about $1 to move... geez. So I guess the only real trade is to try an profit from the stock either staying above 27 or below 29.50. Basically we just have to figure a way to profit from time decay. The easiest thing to do is to either sell a put and hope it doesn't go down or sell a call and hope it doesn't go up... either way, too much risk. So it is going to have to be one of the four vertical spreads... the decision now is simply risk vs reward.

Strategy Selected: Bear Put spread (it offered the best risk/reward profile).

Symbol: duk (28.52)	**DT26 DUK bear put**	Date: 6/27/2006

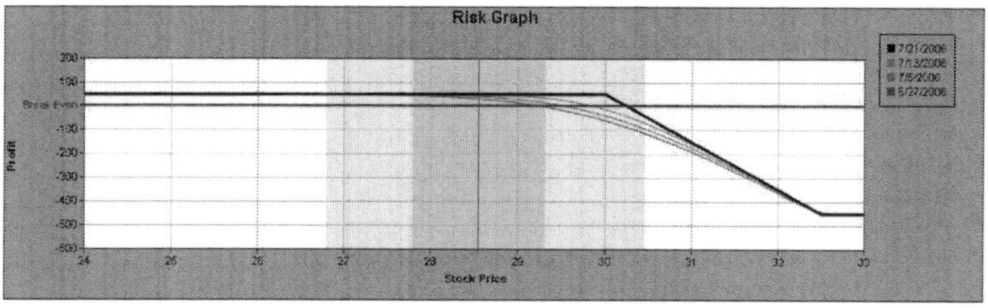

Summary

Cost of Trade	450	Max Reward	50	Delta	-27.9
Current Value	450	Probable Reward	39	Theta	$1.23
Profit/Loss	0	Risk/Max Reward	11.1%	Gamma	-34.5
Max Risk	-450	Risk/Prb Reward	8.6%	Vega	-$3.25

Trade Details

Type	Qty	CostBasis	CurrValue	Strike	Expiration	Total Cost	Profit	IV	Delta
put	2	3.8000	3.8000	32.5	Jul 2006	760	0	1.0000	-200.00
put	-2	1.5500	1.5500	30	Jul 2006	-310	0	17.6200	172.09

Break Evens

	Expiration	Jul 13	Jul 05	Today
Upper B/E	30.25	29.90	29.55	29.30
Lower B/E	30.25	29.90	29.55	29.30

Trade structure is long 2 July 32.50 puts @ 3.80 each and short 2 July 30 puts @ 1.55 each. Trade Cost is $450, trade risk is $450, max profit is $50.

For the record I would rather have walked away.

July 21, 2006 – If I seem frustrated with this trade, it is because I am. Two days after I enter a bearish trade with the sole intent of this stock staying below $30 it gap's up to $29.70. Ok fine that is the top end of DUK's range, no problem. As long as DUK stays below 30 leading to the July expiration this trade makes money.

Three days later its back down to $29... great, I can breathe again. Five days later its back to $29.80... its still below 30, its still below 30... all is well. The next day drifting back down to 29.25... sweet only 4 days to go to expiration.

July 21 – Expiration Day – DUK moves above 30 on open... &*&&%%$$$&**#@!#%. However it chooses to close at $29.93... Can Anyone Say: Max Pain?

Trade closed with a $30 profit on a risk of $450 for a 6% ROR.

Symbol: duk (29.93) **DT26 DUK bear put** Date: 7/21/2006

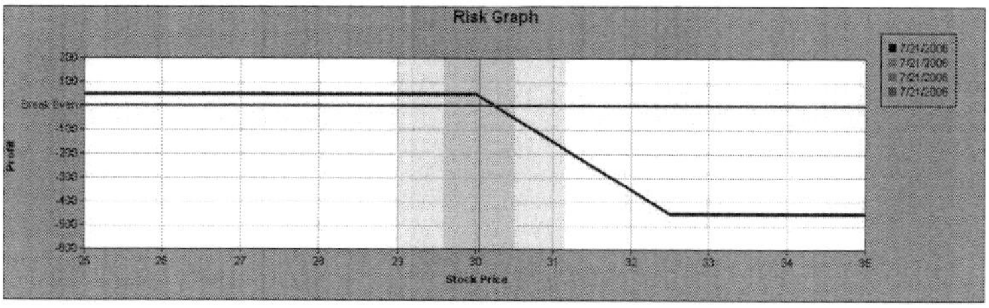

Summary

Cost of Trade	450	Max Reward	50	Delta	-200.0
Current Value	480	Probable Reward	-10	Theta	NaN
Profit/Loss	30	Risk/Max Reward	11.1%	Gamma	0.0
Max Risk	-450	Risk/Prb Reward	-2.1%	Vega	$0.00

Trade Details

Type	Qty	CostBasis	CurrValue	Strike	Expiration	Total Cost	Profit	IV	Delta
put	2	3.8000	2.4000	32.5	Jul 2006	760	-280	1.0000	-200.00
put	-2	1.5500	0.0000	30	Jul 2006	-310	310	0.0000	0.00

July 2006

PG – Proctor & Gamble			
Long Call	+ $690.00	186%	285
PMI – PMI Group, Inc.			
Long Put	+ $210.00	63%	289
TGT – Target Corp			
Long Call	+ $570.00	154%	293
LEG – Leggett & Platt, Inc			
Call Calendar Spread	+ $ 40.00	10%	297

May Results – 4 Wins vs. 0 Losses

Net result $1,510.00 Profit.

"Next..."

- Jimmy Slagle, The Dart-Throw Trader

July 5, 2006 – PG.

Ok. I like the way PG looks right now. First let me say I am bullish… now let me explain why.

The first thing I notice is that PG was in a distinct down trend and now looks to be reversing that trend. MACD has crossed above its signal line and the 2 lines are diverging (even though MACD has not crossed above zero). PG rallied up to its 50 DMA, hit and hovered then broke above it on a gap move. The next day it sold off back down to the 50 DMA and it held. At the Same Time it broke above and closed above its 200 DMA as well.

Now many would suggest that this same "event" occurred at the end of April, and I of course would agree except for the fact that on this move it broke out of the bearish channel. My outlook is bullish.

Strategy Selection: Long call. Price target 58.50.

Symbol: pg (55.93) **DT27 PG long call** Date: 7/5/2006

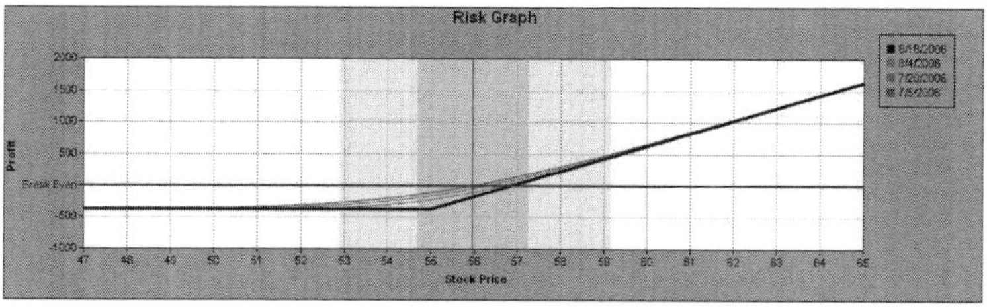

Summary

Cost of Trade	370	Max Reward	1,630	Delta	126.4
Current Value	370	Probable Reward	-101	Theta	-$2.98
Profit/Loss	0	Risk/Max Reward	440.5%	Gamma	23.1
Max Risk	-370	Risk/Prb Reward	-27.2%	Vega	$14.64

Trade Details

Type	Qty	CostBasis	CurrValue	Strike	Expiration	Total Cost	Profit	IV	Delta
call	2	1.8500	1.8500	55	Aug 2006	370	0	16.8200	126.39

Break Evens

	Expiration	Aug 04	Jul 20	Today
Upper B/E	56.85	56.65	56.30	55.95
Lower B/E	56.85	56.65	56.30	55.95

Trade structure is long 2 August 55 strike calls @ 1.85 each. Trade cost is $370, trade risk is $370, max gain is unlimited.

August 18, 2006 – PG hit my price target on August 2 on a gap move. Normally I would close the trade when my target was hit. This time I chose to keep it open simply because the price was hit on a gap move and not a trend move.

Because it was and emotional move, I moved stop order up to 50 and let the trade run until expiration moving the stop to each swing low.

Trade closed with a $690 profit on a $370 risk for a 186% ROR.

Symbol: pg (60.39) **DT27 PG long call** Date: 8/18/2006

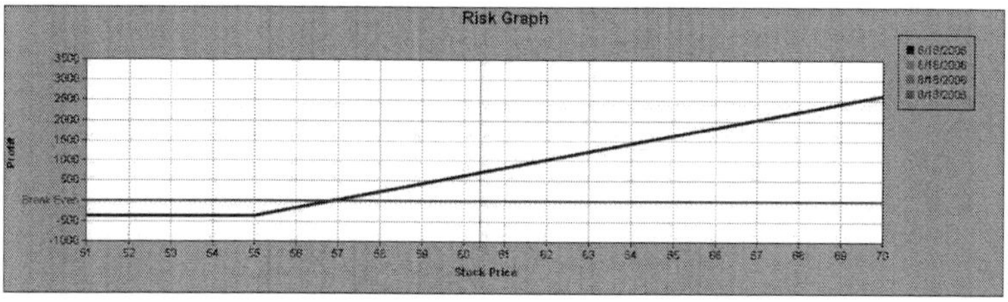

Summary

Cost of Trade	370	Max Reward	2,630	Delta	200.0
Current Value	1,060	Probable Reward	0	Theta	NaN
Profit/Loss	690	Risk/Max Reward	710.8%	Gamma	0.0
Max Risk	-370	Risk/Prb Reward	0%	Vega	$0.00

Trade Details

Type	Qty	CostBasis	CurrValue	Strike	Expiration	Total Cost	Profit	IV	Delta
call	2	1.8500	5.3000	55	Aug 2006	370	690	1.0000	200.00

Break Evens

	Expiration	Aug 18	Aug 18	Today
Upper B/E	56.85	56.85	56.85	56.85
Lower B/E	56.85	56.85	56.85	56.85

July 11, 2006 – PMI.

PMI is in a slow bearish trend that began in May and was confirmed by the MACD in June. All of the indicators are bearish so I won't spend anytime on those. What has my interest is the third lower peak that was established on July 1st. This begins a third wave down and I believe that PMI will test 42.50 which was its support back in april.

Strategy Selection: Long Put. Price target 42.50

Symbol: pmi (43.7) **DT28 PMI long put** Date: 7/11/2006

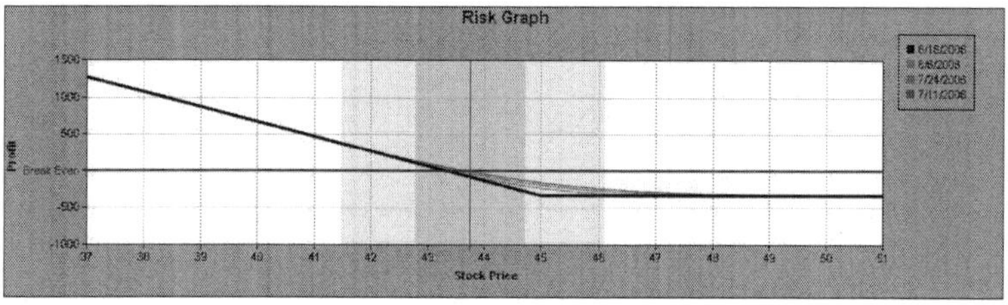

Summary

Cost of Trade	330	Max Reward	1,270	Delta	-141.0
Current Value	330	Probable Reward	-50	Theta	-$1.81
Profit/Loss	0	Risk/Max Reward	384.8%	Gamma	31.5
Max Risk	-330	Risk/Prb Reward	-15.1%	Vega	$9.73

Trade Details

Type	Qty	CostBasis	CurrValue	Strike	Expiration	Total Cost	Profit	IV	Delta
put	2	1.6500	1.6500	45	Aug 2006	330	0	15.5300	-141.02

Break Evens

	Expiration	Aug 06	Jul 24	Today
Upper B/E	43.35	43.45	43.55	43.75
Lower B/E	43.35	43.45	43.55	43.75

Trade structure is long 2 August 45 strike puts @ 1.65 each. Trade cost is $330, trade risk is $330, max profit is unlimited.

August 18, 2006 – PMI hit my price target today on a trend move.

Trade closed with a $210 profit on a $330 risk which is a 63% ROR.

Symbol: pmi (42.37) **DT28 PMI long put** Date: 7/18/2006

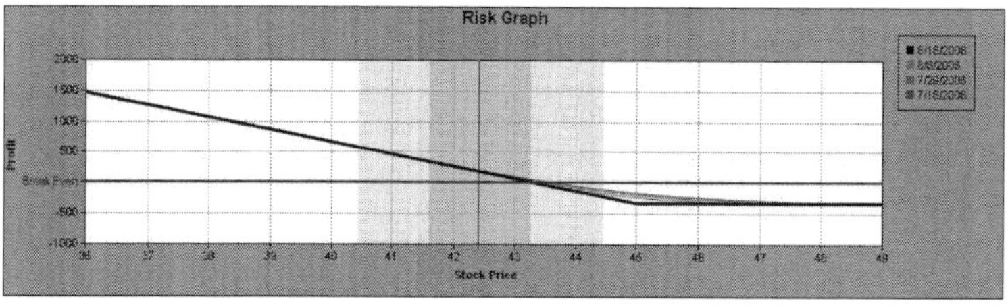

Summary

Cost of Trade	330	Max Reward	1,470	Delta	-177.6
Current Value	540	Probable Reward	189	Theta	-$1.03
Profit/Loss	210	Risk/Max Reward	445.5%	Gamma	18.8
Max Risk	-330	Risk/Prb Reward	57.4%	Vega	$4.71

Trade Details

Type	Qty	CostBasis	CurrValue	Strike	Expiration	Total Cost	Profit	IV	Delta
put	2	1.6500	2.7000	45	Aug 2006	330	210	16.4400	-177.57

Break Evens

	Expiration	Aug 08	Jul 29	Today
Upper B/E	43.35	43.40	43.55	43.70
Lower B/E	43.35	43.40	43.55	43.70

July 18, 2006 – TGT.

TGT just got the rug pulled out from under it on bad earnings news and an analyst downgrade. All indicators are bearish and major support has been massively violated on a gap move. Most traders would suggest a dead cat bounce and I agree it should bounce back to 48 before heading lower.

I am inclined to purchase a call to profit from the expected bounce and if TGT goes lower I will simply roll the trade into a BearCall Spread.

Strategy Selection: Long Call. Price target $48.

Symbol: tgt (45.53) **DT29 TGT long call** Date: 7/18/2006

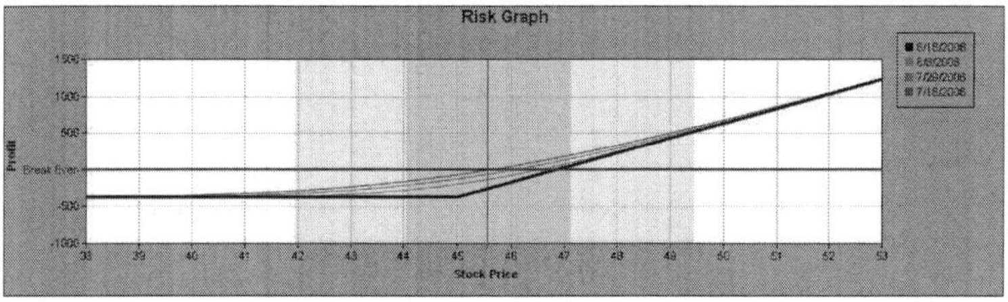

Summary

Cost of Trade	370	Max Reward	1,230	Delta	115.3
Current Value	360	Probable Reward	-123	Theta	-$4.91
Profit/Loss	-10	Risk/Max Reward	332.4%	Gamma	20.7
Max Risk	-370	Risk/Prb Reward	-33.3%	Vega	$10.39

Trade Details

Type	Qty	CostBasis	CurrValue	Strike	Expiration	Total Cost	Profit	IV	Delta
call	2	1.8500	1.8000	45	Aug 2006	370	-10	28.5000	115.28

Break Evens

	Expiration	Aug 08	Jul 29	Today
Upper B/E	46.85	46.55	46.10	45.65
Lower B/E	46.85	46.55	46.10	45.65

Trade structure is long 2 August 45 strike calls @ 1.85 each. Cost of trade is $370, risk of trade is $370, max profit is unlimited.

August 18, 2006 – I have waited oh so patiently for TGT to bounce back to 48 and the days drug into weeks and then just when I am ready to convert the trade to a BearCall spread TGT moves from 46 to 48 in one day.

Normally I would close the trade once the target is hit, however this is an emotional move and they tend to have follow through. I placed a stop just below the last swing high and let the stock run to expiration of my August contracts.

Trade closed with a $570 profit on a $370 risk for a 154% ROR.

Symbol: tgt (49.8) **DT29 TGT long call** Date: 8/18/2006

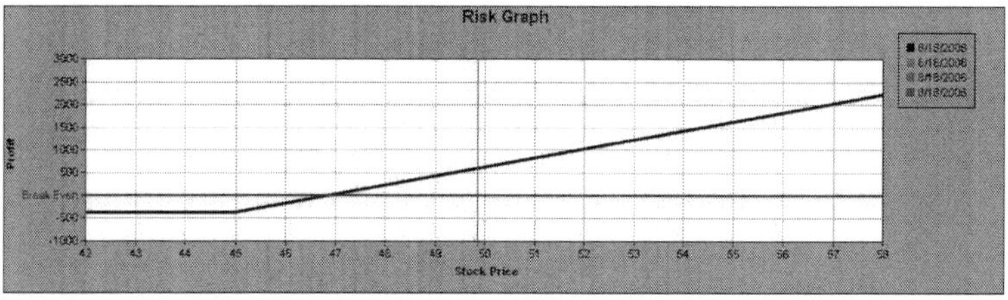

Summary

Cost of Trade	370	Max Reward	2,230	Delta	200.0
Current Value	940	Probable Reward	0	Theta	NaN
Profit/Loss	570	Risk/Max Reward	602.7%	Gamma	0.0
Max Risk	-370	Risk/Prb Reward	0%	Vega	$0.00

Trade Details

Type	Qty	CostBasis	CurrValue	Strike	Expiration	Total Cost	Profit	IV	Delta
call	2	1.8500	4.7000	45	Aug 2006	370	570	1.0000	200.00

Break Evens

	Expiration	Aug 18	Aug 18	Today
Upper B/E	46.85	46.85	46.85	46.85
Lower B/E	46.85	46.85	46.85	46.85

July 25, 2006 – LEG.

Here is yet another example of a stock trading in a narrow range (I am really getting tired of these, maybe I should learn how to aim the dart, but then I guess that would be cheating).

LEG is a stock that apparently likes to react to news and then go about its life. It appears that earnings were announced on July 21 and of course the reaction was violent... a $2 move...anyway history suggests that after an earnings report the stock tends to reverse the "earnings move" after a period of stagnation.

If this is the case the trade selection is simple... structure a trade to profit from a stagnant to mildly bullish move.

Strategy Selection: Call Calendar Spread.

Symbol: leg (22.85) **DT30 LEG call calendar** Date: 7/25/2006

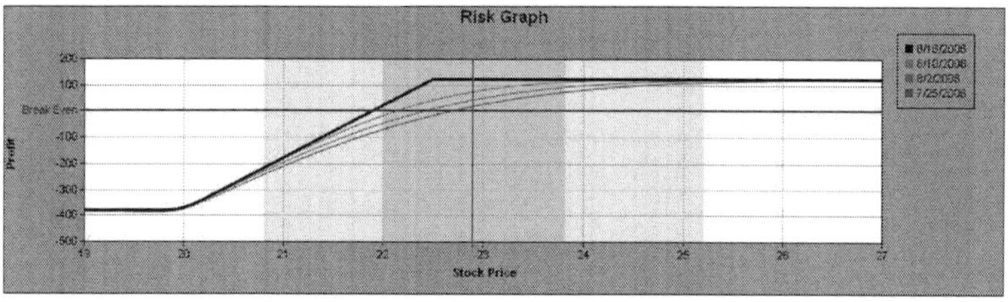

Summary

Cost of Trade	380	Max Reward	123	Delta	80.6
Current Value	380	Probable Reward	54	Theta	$2.82
Profit/Loss	0	Risk/Max Reward	32.4%	Gamma	-43.6
Max Risk	-380	Risk/Prb Reward	14.3%	Vega	-$4.54

Trade Details

Type	Qty	CostBasis	CurrValue	Strike	Expiration	Total Cost	Profit	IV	Delta
call	2	2.8000	2.8000	20	Sep 2006	560	0	1.0000	200.00
call	-2	0.9000	0.9000	22.5	Aug 2006	-180	0	30.3100	-119.43

Break Evens

	Expiration	Aug 10	Aug 02	Today
Upper B/E	21.90	22.15	22.45	22.70
Lower B/E	21.90	22.15	22.45	22.70

Trade structure is Long 2 September 20 strike calls @ 2.80 each and short 2 August 22.50 strike calls @ .90 each. Trade cost is $380. trade risk is $380, max gain is $123.

August 18, 2006 – LEG has performed exactly as expected... Earnings announcement = violent move. After announcement stagnation and price reversal.

Trade closed with a $40 profit on a $380 risk for a 10% ROR.

"I measure what's going on, and I adapt to it. I try to get my ego out of the way. The market is smarter than I am so I bend."

- Martin Zweig

PDE – Pride International			
Ratio Put Calendar Spread	+ $165.00	68%	303
TWX – Time Warner			
Long Put	- $225.00	(47%)	307
BMY – Bristol, Myers			
Call Calendar Spread	+ $285.00	71%	311
AIV – Apt. Investment			
Long Call	+$1040.00	208%	315
PTEN – Patterson Energy			
Long Call	- $270.00	(73%)	319

May Results – 3 Wins vs. 2 Losses

Net result $995.00 Profit.

Successful investing is anticipating the anticipations of others.

- John Maynard Keynes

August 1, 2006 – PDE.

I look at this chart and my immediate thought is bearish trending stock at the top of a wave about to head south… easy money.

Its 50 DMA is strong resistance. The 50 DMA has finally crossed below the 200 DMA my training says that move screams bearish. Simple outlook – mildly bearish trend.

Strategy Selection: Ratio Put Calendar Spread.

Symbol: PDE (29.67) **DT31 PDE** Date: 8/1/2006

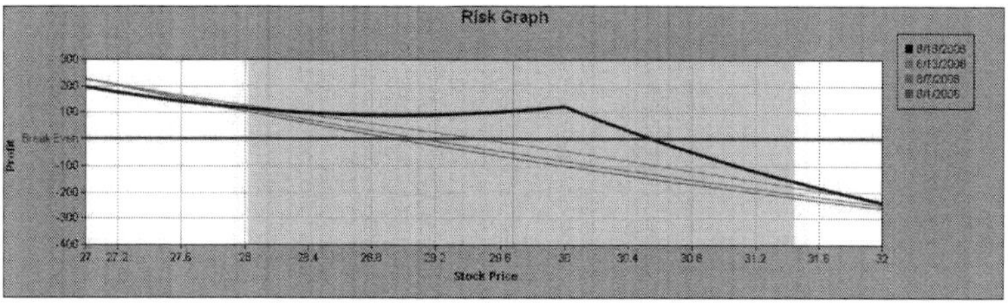

Summary

Cost of Trade	545	Max Reward	197	Delta	-94.9
Current Value	475	Probable Reward	31	Theta	$2.41
Profit/Loss	-70	Risk/Max Reward	81.7%	Gamma	11.1
Max Risk	-240	Risk/Prb Reward	12.9%	Vega	$13.12

Trade Details

Type	Qty	CostBasis	CurrValue	Strike	Expiration	Total Cost	Profit	IV	Delta
put	-3	1.3500	1.5000	30	Aug 2006	-405	-45	52.0500	154.56
put	5	1.9000	1.8500	30	Sep 2006	950	-25	40.7200	-249.45

Break Evens

	Expiration	Aug 13	Aug 07	Today
Upper B/E	30.56	29.50	29.14	28.98
Lower B/E	30.56	29.50	29.14	28.98

Trade structure is long 5 September 30 strike puts @ 1.90 each and short 3 August 30 strike puts @ 1.50 each. Trade cost is $545, trade risk is $240, max profit is $197.

August 18, 2006 – PDE is a beautiful bearishly trending stock. I love when a trade does exactly what it is supposed to do without any surprises.

Trade closed with a $165 profit on a $240 risk for a 68% ROR.

Symbol: PDE (26.35) **DT31 PDE** Date: 8/18/2006

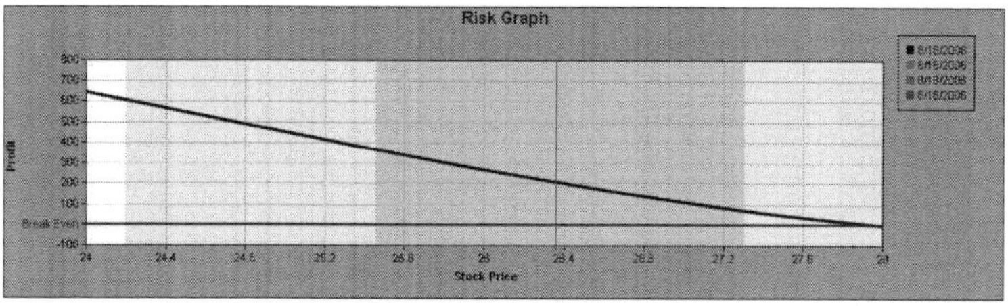

Summary

Cost of Trade	545	Max Reward	645	Delta	-163.0
Current Value	710	Probable Reward	213	Theta	NaN
Profit/Loss	165	Risk/Max Reward	24903.3%	Gamma	30.7
Max Risk	-3	Risk/Prb Reward	8213.1%	Vega	$5.12

Trade Details

Type	Qty	CostBasis	CurrValue	Strike	Expiration	Total Cost	Profit	IV	Delta
put	-3	1.3500	3.8000	30	Aug 2006	-405	-735	1.0000	300.00
put	5	1.9000	3.7000	30	Sep 2006	950	900	31.2600	-462.96

Break Evens

	Expiration	Aug 18	Aug 18	Today
Upper B/E	27.98	27.98	27.98	27.98
Lower B/E	27.98	27.98	27.98	27.98

August 8, 2006 – TWX.

I Couldn't Find The Chart Snapshot of TWX… Sorry.

Remember when AOL bought TWX, that still cracks me up… AOL (no earnings) buys TWX (operators are standing by)… funny.

Enough nostalgia, lets look at the chart. Hmmm… looks like a bearish trend with periods of stagnant rest, right up until July when TWX decides it is going to make a rally move and clear out all the short sellers… the gate opens and TWX rallies to the 50 DMA and the market says "NO"… go back to your trend.

I believe based on everything the chart says that TWX will sell off to support at 15.50ish and stagnate before ultimately moving lower… what is my goal? Throw Darts – Pick Stocks – Make Money (while minimizing risk). This is an easy one.

Strategy Selection: Long Put. Price Target $15.50

Symbol: TWX (16.19) **DT32 TWX long put** Date: 8/8/2006

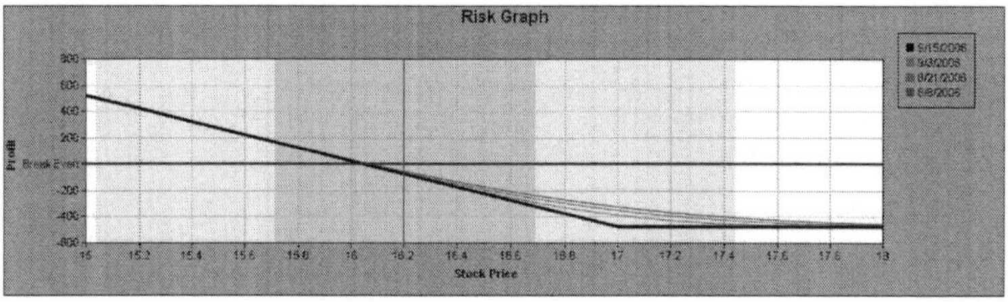

Summary

Cost of Trade	475	Max Reward	525	Delta	-423.5
Current Value	425	Probable Reward	-77	Theta	-$0.95
Profit/Loss	-50	Risk/Max Reward	110.5%	Gamma	159.8
Max Risk	-475	Risk/Prb Reward	-16.3%	Vega	$6.17

Trade Details

Type	Qty	CostBasis	CurrValue	Strike	Expiration	Total Cost	Profit	IV	Delta
put	5	0.9500	0.8500	17	Sep 2006	475	-50	14.1500	-423.48

Break Evens

	Expiration	Sep 03	Aug 21	Today
Upper B/E	16.05	16.05	16.06	16.08
Lower B/E	16.05	16.05	16.06	16.08

Trade structure is long 5 September 17 strike puts @ .95 each. Trade cost is $475, trade risk is $475, max profit is unlimited.

Symbol: TWX (16.58) **DT32 TWX long put** Date: 8/22/2006

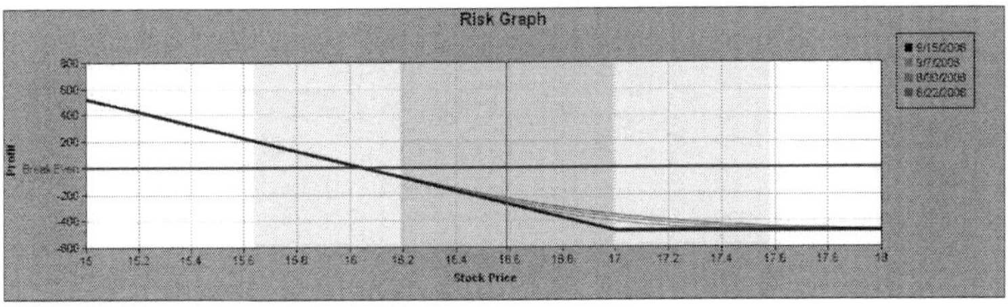

Summary

Cost of Trade	475	Max Reward	525	Delta	-371.7
Current Value	250	Probable Reward	-225	Theta	-$1.84
Profit/Loss	-225	Risk/Max Reward	110.5%	Gamma	268.0
Max Risk	-475	Risk/Prb Reward	-47.4%	Vega	$6.85

Trade Details

Type	Qty	CostBasis	CurrValue	Strike	Expiration	Total Cost	Profit	IV	Delta
put	5	0.9500	0.5000	17	Sep 2006	475	-225	14.1300	-371.72

Break Evens

	Expiration	Sep 07	Aug 30	Today
Upper B/E	16.05	16.05	16.05	16.06
Lower B/E	16.05	16.05	16.05	16.06

August 22, 2006 – TWX has decided to reverse and move higher, it is now approaching its 50 DMA... logic says, cut your losses and live to fight another day.

Trade closed with a $225 loss on a risk of $475 for a 47% loss on risk.

"An investment in knowledge pays the best interest."

- Benjamin Franklin

August 15, 2006 – BMY.

Ohhhh, how I love a massive emotional move, I really love them before they happen (if I have the stock straddled), however after the move can be profitable as well.

On an emotional move like this 2 things come to mind... 1. Throw technical analysis out the window and 2. Remember to RESPOND when others REACT.

The reaction was a massive sell off from 26 to 20, a 30% move. Historically a move like this can't be sustained. Logic (a response to a reaction) would suggest that BMY will bounce (think dead cat) or stagnate as it finds its direction.
Strategy Selection: Call Calendar Spread. This provides profit if it bounces or stagnates and provides minimal risk exposure if BMY continues to sell off.

Symbol: BMY (20.79) **DT33 BMY call calendar** Date: 8/15/2006

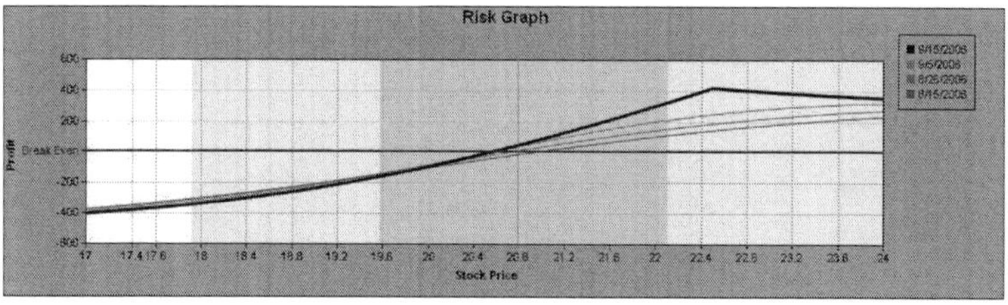

Summary

Cost of Trade	465	Max Reward	418	Delta	105.4
Current Value	450	Probable Reward	41	Theta	$2.28
Profit/Loss	-15	Risk/Max Reward	104.1%	Gamma	-9.4
Max Risk	-401	Risk/Prb Reward	10.2%	Vega	$7.55

Trade Details

Type	Qty	CostBasis	CurrValue	Strike	Expiration	Total Cost	Profit	IV	Delta
call	3	2.0000	1.9000	20	Dec 2006	600	-30	30.5200	188.42
call	-3	0.4500	0.4500	22.5	Sep 2006	-135	15	41.1000	-82.99

Break Evens

	Expiration	Sep 05	Aug 26	Today
Upper B/E	20.56	20.54	20.72	20.94
Lower B/E	20.56	20.54	20.72	20.94

Trade structure is Long 3 December 20 strike calls @ 2.00 each and short 3 September 22.50 strike calls @ .45 each for a trade cost of $465. Trade risk is $400 and max profit is $418.

September 15, 2006 – Not only did the dead cat bounce, I think it came back to life. My trade worked beautifully as BMY rallied back to 25. My only regret is that I am in a limited gain trade… oh well, better to be safe and profitable than exposed and broke.

Trade closed with a $285 profit on a $400 risk for a 71% ROR.

Symbol: BMY (24.92) **DT33 BMY call calendar** Date: 9/15/2006

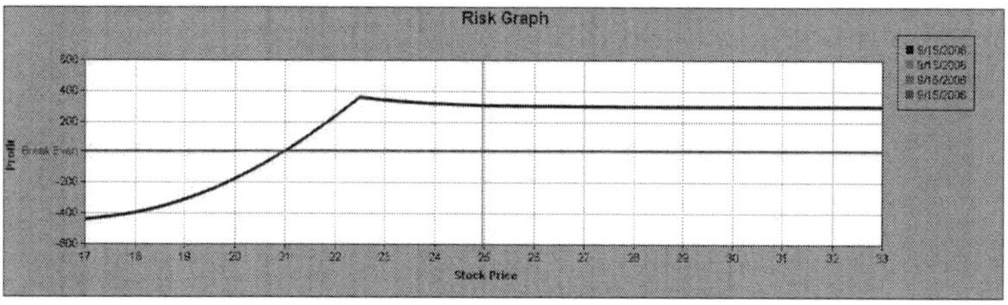

Summary

Cost of Trade	465	Max Reward	360	Delta	-7.8
Current Value	750	Probable Reward	0	Theta	NaN
Profit/Loss	285	Risk/Max Reward	82.1%	Gamma	6.2
Max Risk	-439	Risk/Prb Reward	0%	Vega	$2.26

Trade Details

Type	Qty	CostBasis	CurrValue	Strike	Expiration	Total Cost	Profit	IV	Delta
call	3	2.0000	5.0000	20	Dec 2006	600	900	23.6500	292.19
call	-3	0.4500	2.5000	22.5	Sep 2006	-135	-615	1.0000	-300.00

Break Evens

	Expiration	Sep 15	Sep 15	Today
Upper B/E	21.00	21.00	21.00	21.00
Lower B/E	21.00	21.00	21.00	21.00

August 22, 2006 – AIV.

"I love a trending stock" (sung to the tune of "I love a rainy night" by Eddie Rabbit 1980). I really do love a trending stock and I don't really care if the trend is bullish, bearish or stagnant.

This is a no brainer (for me) trade. Profit from trend while minimizing risk.

Strategy Selection: Long Call. Price Target… Go Baby Go.

Symbol: AIV (50.92) **DT34 AIV long call** Date: 8/22/2006

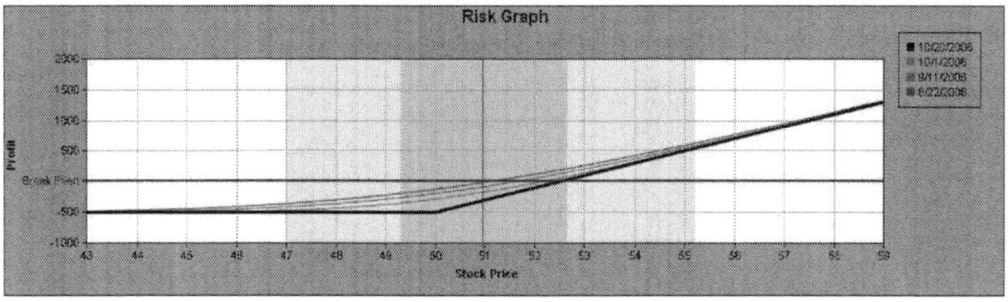

Summary

Cost of Trade	500	Max Reward	1,300	Delta	120.6
Current Value	480	Probable Reward	-189	Theta	-$3.23
Profit/Loss	-20	Risk/Max Reward	260%	Gamma	16.4
Max Risk	-500	Risk/Prb Reward	-37.8%	Vega	$15.79

Trade Details

Type	Qty	CostBasis	CurrValue	Strike	Expiration	Total Cost	Profit	IV	Delta
call	2	2.5000	2.4000	50	Oct 2006	500	-20	22.9700	120.60

Break Evens

	Expiration	Oct 01	Sep 11	Today
Upper B/E	52.50	52.15	51.65	51.10
Lower B/E	52.50	52.15	51.65	51.10

Trade structure is long 2 October 50 strike calls @ 2.50 each. Trade cost is $500, trade risk is $500, Max profit is unlimited.

October 20, 2006 – "Well, I love a trending stock. It's such a beautiful sight…" (sorry Eddie). Oh, how sweet it is. A long call was the absolute best trade to be in for this move.

Trade closed $1,040 profit on a risk of $500 for a 208% ROR.

Symbol: AIV (57.9)	**DT34 AIV long call**	Date: 10/20/2006

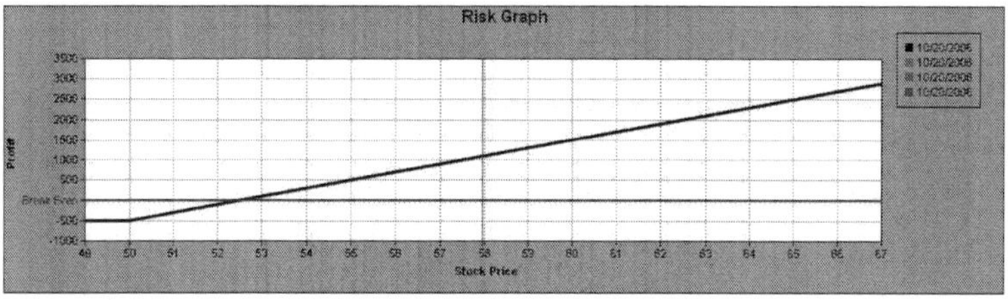

Summary

Cost of Trade	500	Max Reward	2,900	Delta	200.0
Current Value	1,540	Probable Reward	0	Theta	NaN
Profit/Loss	1,040	Risk/Max Reward	580%	Gamma	0.0
Max Risk	-500	Risk/Prb Reward	0%	Vega	$0.00

Trade Details

Type	Qty	CostBasis	CurrValue	Strike	Expiration	Total Cost	Profit	IV	Delta
call	2	2.5000	7.7000	50	Oct 2006	500	1,040	1.0000	200.00

Break Evens

	Expiration	Oct 20	Oct 20	Today
Upper B/E	52.50	52.50	52.50	52.50
Lower B/E	52.50	52.50	52.50	52.50

August 29, 2006 – PTEN.

My immediate outlook is stagnant to mildly bullish. However, as I dig deeper I see some things that give me a slightly more bullish outlook.

1. MACD is above its signal line and just recently crossed above the zero line indicating that PTEN is entering a new bullish trend.
2. PTEN has crossed above its 50 DMA and it now looks to be support.
3. Bollinger Bands are contracting which indicates a breakout is imminent.
4. All would suggest the break out will be to the upside.

Strategy Selection: Long Call. Price Target $30 and potentially higher.

Symbol: PTEN (27.73) **DT35 PTEN long call** Date: 8/29/2006

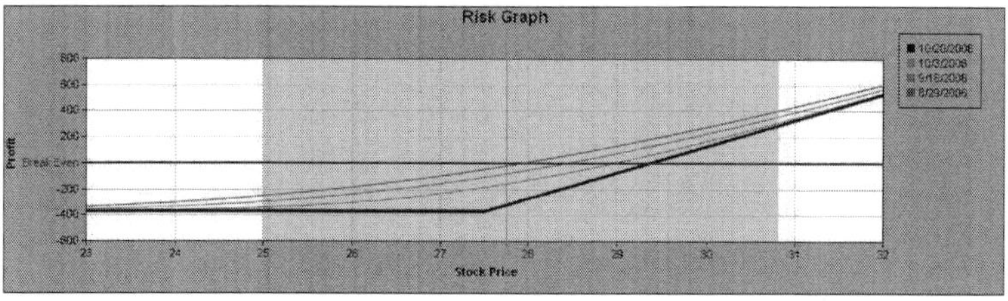

Summary

Cost of Trade	370	Max Reward	530	Delta	111.1
Current Value	350	Probable Reward	-121	Theta	-$3.16
Profit/Loss	-20	Risk/Max Reward	143.2%	Gamma	19.4
Max Risk	-370	Risk/Prb Reward	-32.7%	Vega	$8.27

Trade Details

Type	Qty	CostBasis	CurrValue	Strike	Expiration	Total Cost	Profit	IV	Delta
call	2	1.8500	1.7500	27.5	Oct 2006	370	-20	38.8200	111.12

Break Evens

	Expiration	Oct 03	Sep 16	Today
Upper B/E	29.35	28.95	28.45	27.95
Lower B/E	29.35	28.95	28.45	27.95

Trade structure is long 2 October 27.50 strike calls @ 1.85 each. Trade cost is $370, trade risk is 370, max profit is unlimited.

September 8, 2006 – Well I was right about one thing there was a break out, unfortunately it was to the downside. My mental stop was hit, it is time to close the trade and fight another day.

Trade closed with a $270 loss on a risk of $370 for a 73% loss on risk.

"What we do in life echoes in eternity."

- Maximus Decimus Meridius

September 2006

WMB – Williams Co.			
Call Calendar Spread	+ $300.00	62%	325
SEPR – Sepracor			
Condor	+ $160.00	47%	329
SLM – SLM Corp			
Condor	- $130.00	(30%)	333
GOOG – Google, Inc.			
Call Ratio BackSpread	+$2070.00	115%	337

May Results – 3 Wins vs. 1 Loss

Net result $2,400.00 Profit.

"You don't learn to hold your own in the world by standing on guard, but by attacking and getting well hammered yourself."

- George Bernard Shaw

September 5, 2006 – WMB.

Once again my dart has smashed into another slow trending (and narrow range) stock. WMB (as opposed to W.M.D.) is in a very tight bullish trading range.

On a trend like this I basically just want to buy a LEAPS option and let it run. However the challenge is to make money quickly with randomly selected stocks.

Strategy Selection: Call Calendar Spread.

Symbol: WMB (24.97) **DT36 WMB call calendar** Date: 9/5/2006

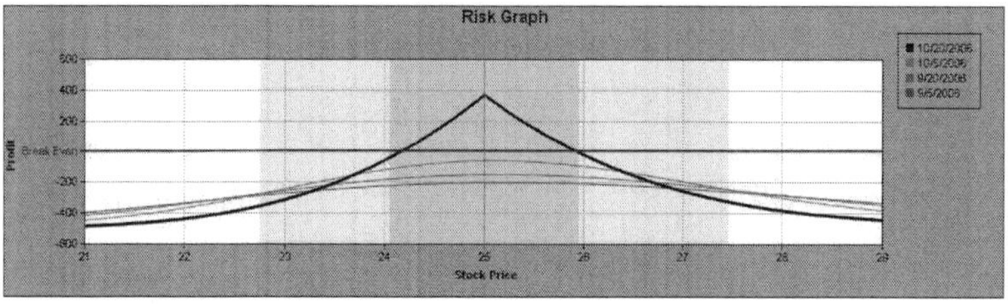

Summary

Cost of Trade	500	Max Reward	371	Delta	8.0
Current Value	300	Probable Reward	-23	Theta	$2.70
Profit/Loss	-200	Risk/Max Reward	76.7%	Gamma	-30.4
Max Risk	-483	Risk/Prb Reward	-4.8%	Vega	$9.50

Trade Details

Type	Qty	CostBasis	CurrValue	Strike	Expiration	Total Cost	Profit	IV	Delta
call	-10	1.0000	1.1000	25	Oct 2006	-1,000	-100	31.4500	-522.13
call	10	1.5000	1.4000	25	Nov 2006	1,500	-100	31.2400	530.12

Break Evens

	Expiration	Oct 05	Sep 20	Today
Upper B/E	25.95	0.00	0.00	0.00
Lower B/E	24.20	0.00	0.00	0.00

Trade structure is long 10 November 25 strike calls @ 1.50 each and short 10 October
25 strike calls @ 1.00 each. Trade cost is $500, trade risk is $483 and trade max profit is $371.

October 20, 2006 – Another beautiful trade when left to run its course.

Trade closed with a $300 profit on a $480 risk for a 62% ROR.

Symbol: WMB (24.54) **DT36 WMB call calendar** Date: 10/20/2006

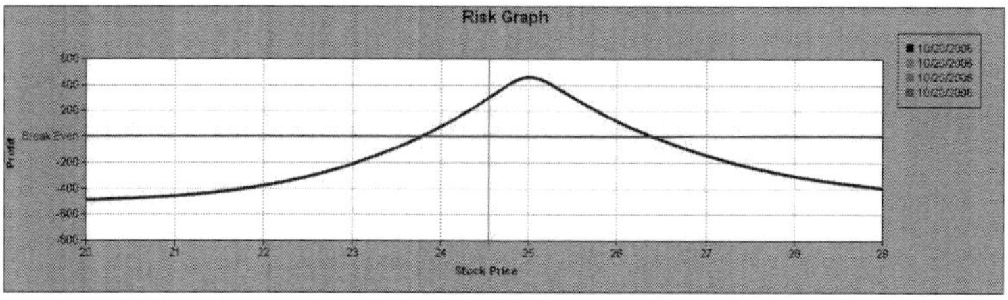

Summary

Cost of Trade	500	Max Reward	460	Delta	450.7
Current Value	800	Probable Reward	0	Theta	NaN
Profit/Loss	300	Risk/Max Reward	94.2%	Gamma	158.5
Max Risk	-488	Risk/Prb Reward	0%	Vega	$26.91

Trade Details

Type	Qty	CostBasis	CurrValue	Strike	Expiration	Total Cost	Profit	IV	Delta
call	-10	1.0000	0.0001	25	Oct 2006	-1,000	1,000	2031.2500	0.00
call	10	1.5000	0.8000	25	Nov 2006	1,500	-700	36.7500	450.66

Break Evens

	Expiration	Oct 20	Oct 20	Today
Upper B/E	26.45	26.45	26.45	26.45
Lower B/E	23.80	23.80	23.80	23.80

September 12, 2006 – SEPR.

Finally my dart has hit the jackpot on the type of stock I would "prefer" to trade. What is so great about this stock? Massive Volatility Inside A well Defined Range.

There are so many ways to trade a stock like this because of the volatility there is juice in the options, because of the well defined range there is expectation that resistance and support will hold.

Trade evaluation: Support at 40 – Resistance at 60. Make it tighter: Support at 45 – Resistance at 55.

Trade Selection: Condor. Sell premium in its range.

Symbol: SEPR (48.74) **DT37 SEPR condor** Date: 9/12/2006

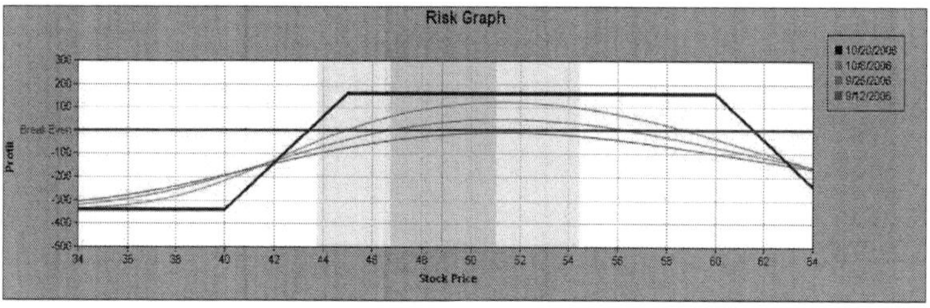

Summary

Cost of Trade	-160	Max Reward	160	Delta	8.5
Current Value	-180	Probable Reward	145	Theta	$3.85
Profit/Loss	-20	Risk/Max Reward	47.1%	Gamma	-3.4
Max Risk	-340	Risk/Prb Reward	42.6%	Vega	-$4.99

Trade Details

Type	Qty	CostBasis	CurrValue	Strike	Expiration	Total Cost	Profit	IV	Delta
call	-1	0.7000	0.7000	60	Oct 2006	-70	0	58.3900	-15.78
call	1	0.2500	0.1500	65	Oct 2006	25	-10	50.8800	4.79
put	-1	1.6000	1.6000	45	Oct 2006	-160	0	52.1000	28.60
put	1	0.4500	0.3500	40	Oct 2006	45	-10	49.1000	-9.12

Break Evens

	Expiration	Oct 08	Sep 25	Today
Upper B/E	61.60	58.90	56.50	0.00
Lower B/E	43.40	44.90	46.70	0.00

Trade Structure is long 1 October 65 strike call @ .25 each and short 1 October 60 strike call @ .70 each.

Long 1 October 40 strike put @ .45 each and short 1 October 45 strike put @ 1.60 each.

Trade cost is $160, trade risk is $340, max profit is $160 with a profit range between 43.50 and 61.50 well inside its current range.

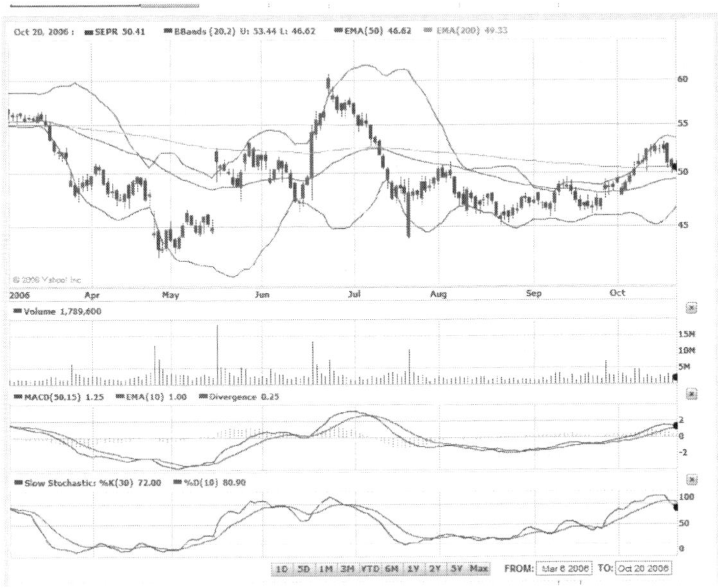

October 20, 2006 – I have said many times before… I love volatility inside a well defined range. This stock performed on script.

Trade closed with a $160 profit on a $340 risk for a 47% ROR.

Symbol: SEPR (50.41) **DT37 SEPR condor** Date: 10/20/2006

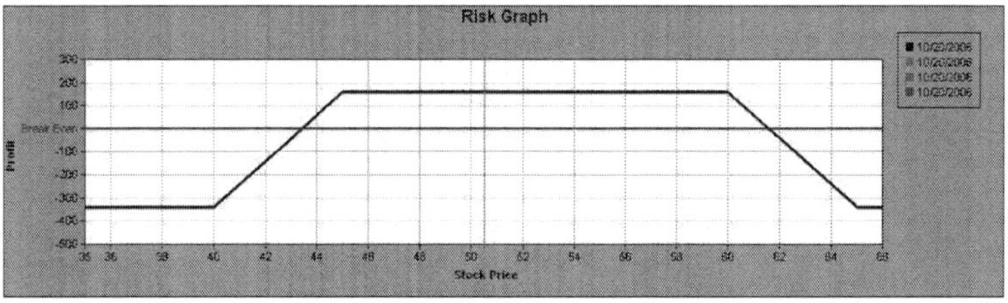

Summary

Cost of Trade	-160	Max Reward	160	Delta	0.0
Current Value	0	Probable Reward	0	Theta	$0.00
Profit/Loss	160	Risk/Max Reward	47.1%	Gamma	0.0
Max Risk	-340	Risk/Prb Reward	0%	Vega	$0.00

Trade Details

Type	Qty	CostBasis	CurrValue	Strike	Expiration	Total Cost	Profit	IV	Delta
call	-1	0.7000	0.0001	60	Oct 2006	-70	70	0.0000	0.00
call	1	0.2500	0.0001	65	Oct 2006	25	-25	0.0000	0.00
put	-1	1.6000	0.0001	45	Oct 2006	-160	160	0.0000	0.00
put	1	0.4500	0.0001	40	Oct 2006	45	-45	0.0000	0.00

Break Evens

	Expiration	Oct 20	Oct 20	Today
Upper B/E	61.60	61.60	61.60	61.60
Lower B/E	43.40	43.40	43.40	43.40

September 19, 2006 – SLM.

Just like last week we have a volatile stock inside a range. Other than the emotional roller coaster move the last 4 weeks this is a stock that has a defined range between 50 and 55.

SLM has moved back into its normal price range and has some volatility around its options because of the price swing in August – September. If the range holds a condor would be a profitable low risk trade.

Strategy Selection: Condor.

Symbol: SLM (51.62) **DT38 SLM condor** Date: 9/19/2006

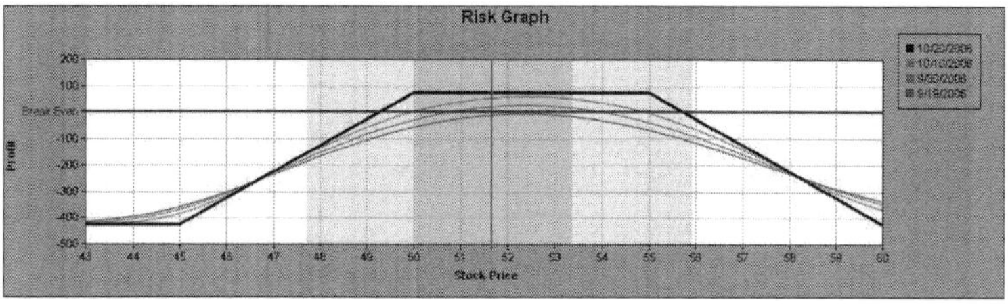

Summary

Cost of Trade	-75	Max Reward	75	Delta	13.2
Current Value	-85	Probable Reward	28	Theta	$2.95
Profit/Loss	-10	Risk/Max Reward	17.6%	Gamma	-18.3
Max Risk	-425	Risk/Prb Reward	6.6%	Vega	-$8.73

Trade Details

Type	Qty	CostBasis	CurrValue	Strike	Expiration	Total Cost	Profit	IV	Delta
call	-1	0.2500	0.2500	55	Oct 2006	-25	0	20.7200	-15.72
call	1	0.0500	0.0001	60	Oct 2006	5	-5	14.6500	0.02
put	-1	0.6000	0.6000	50	Oct 2006	-60	0	21.3500	28.87
put	1	0.0500	0.0001	45	Oct 2006	5	-5	13.4300	-0.02

Break Evens

	Expiration	Oct 10	Sep 30	Today
Upper B/E	55.75	55.00	54.10	0.00
Lower B/E	49.25	49.95	50.75	0.00

Trade structure is:

Long 1 October 60 strike call @ .05 each and short 1 October 55 strike call @ .25 each.
Long 1 October 45 strike put @ .05 each and short 1 October 50 strike put @ .60 each.
Trade Cost is $75, trade risk is $425 and max profit is $75.

October 13, 2006 – SLM has made a strong downward move down and broken below 50 with less than a week until expiration it is best to close the trade with a known loss than to lose the entire trade if it continues to drop.

Trade closed with a $130 loss on $425 risk for a 30% loss on risk.

Symbol: SLM (48.4) **DT38 SLM condor** Date: 10/13/2006

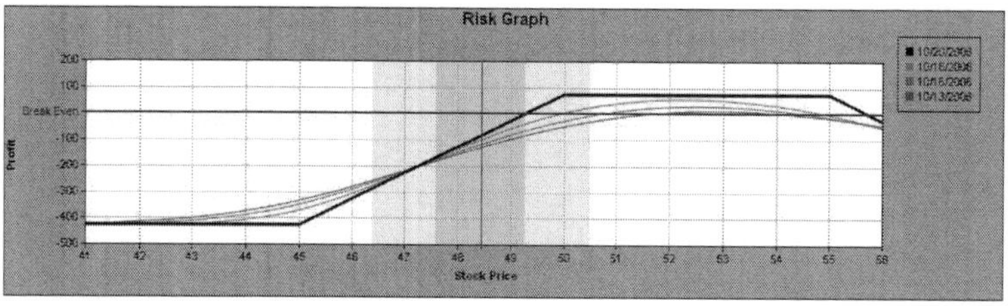

Summary

Cost of Trade	-75	Max Reward	75	Delta	59.8
Current Value	-205	Probable Reward	-88	Theta	$4.19
Profit/Loss	-130	Risk/Max Reward	17.6%	Gamma	-7.4
Max Risk	-425	Risk/Prb Reward	-20.6%	Vega	-$1.48

Trade Details

Type	Qty	CostBasis	CurrValue	Strike	Expiration	Total Cost	Profit	IV	Delta
call	-1	0.2500	0.0500	55	Oct 2006	-25	20	50.8100	-3.76
call	1	0.0500	0.0001	60	Oct 2006	5	0	77.7400	2.62
put	-1	0.6000	2.1500	50	Oct 2006	-60	-155	43.7700	69.25
put	1	0.0500	0.1000	45	Oct 2006	5	5	38.7600	-8.27

Break Evens

	Expiration	Oct 18	Oct 16	Today
Upper B/E	55.75	55.00	54.65	54.30
Lower B/E	49.25	49.95	50.70	51.55

September 25, 2006 – GOOG.

Bulls-eye. My dart has found GOOG. I could spend a week evaluating Google, however I will get right to the point.

GOOG is in a trading range between 360 and 420. It is currently sitting at roughly 405 with a recently turned bullish MACD. I say lets go buy a short term call and let goog run back up to 420 and make some easy money. The only problem is that the short term calls are $18.60 each and even buying one would put $1860 at risk and that violates my Dart-Throw Trader rules.

The only solution is to sell "premium" in order to buy "premium".

Strategy Selection: Call Ratio Backspread. Use the markets money to place the trade, minimize risk and give myself unlimited upside profit potential.

Symbol: GOOG (406.87)	**DT39 Goog crb**	Date: 9/26/2006

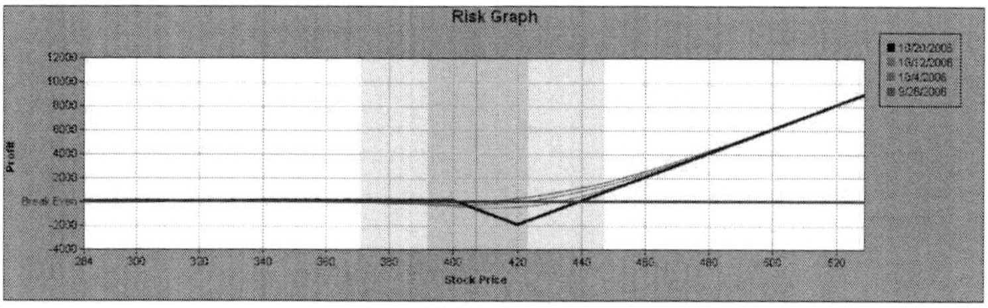

Summary

Cost of Trade	-120	Max Reward	9,020	Delta	15.4
Current Value	-140	Probable Reward	-343	Theta	-$24.99
Profit/Loss	-20	Risk/Max Reward	480.7%	Gamma	1.1
Max Risk	-1,876	Risk/Prb Reward	-18.3%	Vega	$38.62

Trade Details

Type	Qty	CostBasis	CurrValue	Strike	Expiration	Total Cost	Profit	IV	Delta
call	-1	18.6000	18.6000	400	Oct 2006	-1,860	0	35.7900	-59.43
call	2	8.7000	8.6000	420	Oct 2006	1,740	-20	33.3700	74.85

Break Evens

	Expiration	Oct 12	Oct 04	Today
Upper B/E	439.00	433.00	421.00	409.00
Lower B/E	402.00	378.00	367.00	360.00

Trade structure is:

Short 1 October 400 strike call @ 18.60 each and Long 2 October 420 Strike calls @ 8.60 each. Trade Cost is a $120 CREDIT (get paid to trade). Trade risk is $1800 if Goog closes at $420 on the 3rd Friday of October and Max profit is unlimited.

October 19, 2006 – God must be a trader and he must love me. It is the day before expiration and GOOG closes at $426.06. This trade is almost a complete bust. There is nothing I can do. I am going to lose at least $1,000.00 in this trade, maybe more.

October 19, 2006 – After hours GOOG thinks it will be a great idea to announce their quarterly earnings. News is good. GOOG will emotionally react tomorrow.

October 20, 2006 – Traders react to GOOG's earnings and the stock gaps up to $460. What was a horribly losing trade 24 hours ago is now an amazing winner.

Trade closed with a $2,070 profit on a risk of $1,800 for a 115% ROR.

Symbol: GOOG (459.67)	**DT39 Goog crb**	Date: 10/20/2006

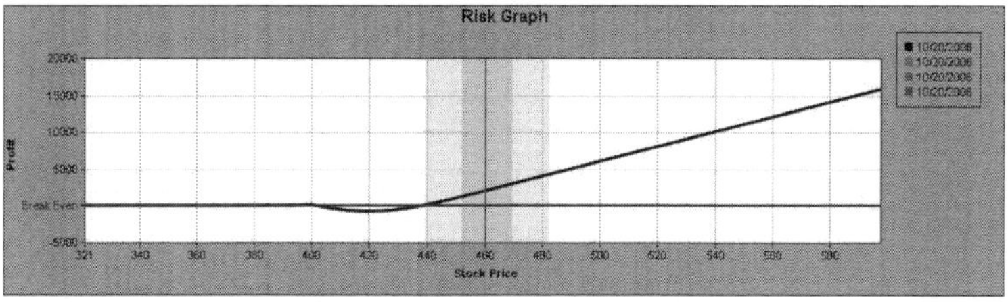

Summary

Cost of Trade	-120	Max Reward	15,920	Delta	100.0
Current Value	1,950	Probable Reward	2,188	Theta	NaN
Profit/Loss	2,070	Risk/Max Reward	2349.7%	Gamma	0.0
Max Risk	-678	Risk/Prb Reward	322.9%	Vega	$0.00

Trade Details

Type	Qty	CostBasis	CurrValue	Strike	Expiration	Total Cost	Profit	IV	Delta
call	-1	18.6000	59.9000	400	Oct 2006	-1,860	-4,130	1.0000	-100.00
call	2	8.7000	39.7000	420	Oct 2006	1,740	6,200	11347.6600	200.00

Break Evens

	Expiration	Oct 20	Oct 20	Today
Upper B/E	437.00	437.00	437.00	437.00
Lower B/E	404.00	404.00	404.00	404.00

October 2006

PFE – Pfizer, Inc. Call Calendar Spread	+ $100.00	45%	343
GPS – Gap, Inc. Call Calendar Spread	+ $150.00	33%	347
BOL – Bausch & Lomb Call Calendar Spread	- $300.00	(79%)	351
SYY – Sysco, Corp Call Calendar Spread	+ $200.00	50%	353

May Results – 3 Wins vs. 1 Loss

Net result $150.00 Profit.

"I will tell you how to become rich. Close the doors. Be fearful when others are greedy. Be greedy when others are fearful."

- Warren Buffett

October 3, 2006 – PFE.

Sometimes being an intuitive trader annoys me. Have you ever just looked a chart and you can just "see" the future behavior? This happens to me everytime I look at a chart. I am not always right and that is the most frustrating part about it. This is why I must enter LOGICAL trades expecting EMOTIONAL reactions.

Too explain what I mean about seeing the future behavior. When I look at the MACD indicator do you see how it is just curving over? That is what I see the price of PFE doing in the short term.

How to profit from a slow "curve" down in price? Put Calendar Spread.
Strategy Selection: Call Calendar Spread. The Risk/Reward was better in the Call Calendar Spread than in the Put Calendar Spread.

Symbol: PFE (28.41) **DT40 PFE call calendar** Date: 10/3/2006

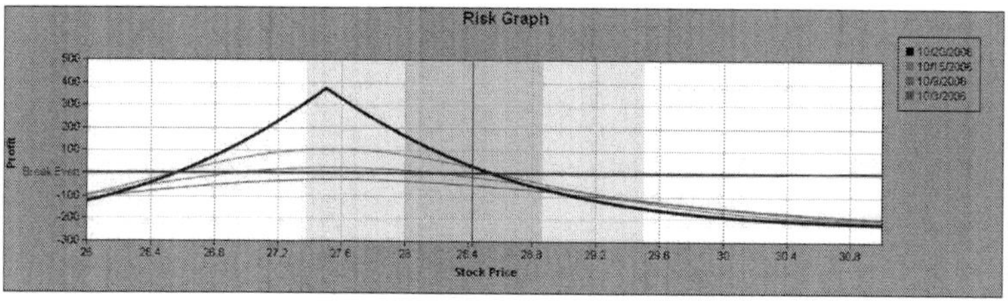

Summary

Cost of Trade	250	Max Reward	373	Delta	-51.8
Current Value	200	Probable Reward	53	Theta	$5.97
Profit/Loss	-50	Risk/Max Reward	169.6%	Gamma	-44.5
Max Risk	-220	Risk/Prb Reward	24.2%	Vega	$15.32

Trade Details

Type	Qty	CostBasis	CurrValue	Strike	Expiration	Total Cost	Profit	IV	Delta
call	-10	1.1500	1.2000	27.5	Oct 2006	-1,150	0	23.8800	-747.45
call	10	1.4000	1.3500	27.5	Nov 2006	1,400	-50	20.1900	695.70

Break Evens

	Expiration	Oct 15	Oct 09	Today
Upper B/E	28.56	28.60	28.26	0.00
Lower B/E	26.56	26.56	26.92	0.00

Trade structure is long 10 November 27.50 strike calls @ 1.40 each and short 10 October 27.50 strike calls @ 1.15 each. Trade cost is $250, trade risk is $220, max profit is $373.

October 20, 2006 – Ok, I admit the "roll over" was a little faster than I thought however the result is the same.

Trade closed with a $100 profit on a $220 risk for a 45% ROR.

Symbol: PFE (27.68) **DT40 PFE call calendar** Date: 10/20/2006

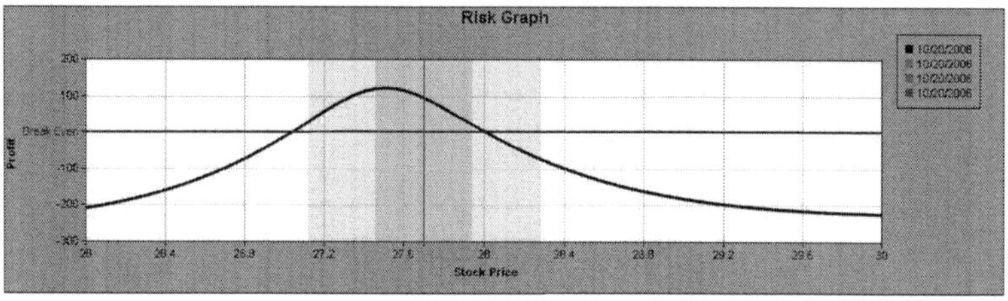

Summary

Cost of Trade	250	Max Reward	122	Delta	-420.2
Current Value	350	Probable Reward	53	Theta	NaN
Profit/Loss	100	Risk/Max Reward	54.6%	Gamma	351.3
Max Risk	-223	Risk/Prb Reward	23.6%	Vega	$29.97

Trade Details

Type	Qty	CostBasis	CurrValue	Strike	Expiration	Total Cost	Profit	IV	Delta
call	-10	1.1500	0.2000	27.5	Oct 2006	-1,150	950	2294.9200	-1,000.00
call	10	1.4000	0.5500	27.5	Nov 2006	1,400	-850	14.5200	579.83

Break Evens

	Expiration	Oct 20	Oct 20	Today
Upper B/E	28.02	28.02	28.02	28.02
Lower B/E	27.04	27.04	27.04	27.04

October 10, 2006 – GPS.

Wow. GPS again. It is abundantly apparent that I need to adjust the board or where I stand when I throw the dart. This is the 3rd time I have hit GPS, once for a profit and once for a loss, lets see what the third trade holds.

This stock just made a \$3 run in 30 days. Last time it made a \$3 run it took 4 months. History would suggest that this move is too far to fast. A couple of points of interest that I see. MACD is in a bullish trend, however it is showing weakness. Stochastics is overbought and GPS is hovering around 20 which should prove to be an intermediate level of resistance dating back to July of 2005.
My outlook tight trading range for the short term.

Strategy Selection: Call Calendar Spread.

Symbol: GPS (19.62) **DT41 GPS call calendar** Date: 10/10/2006

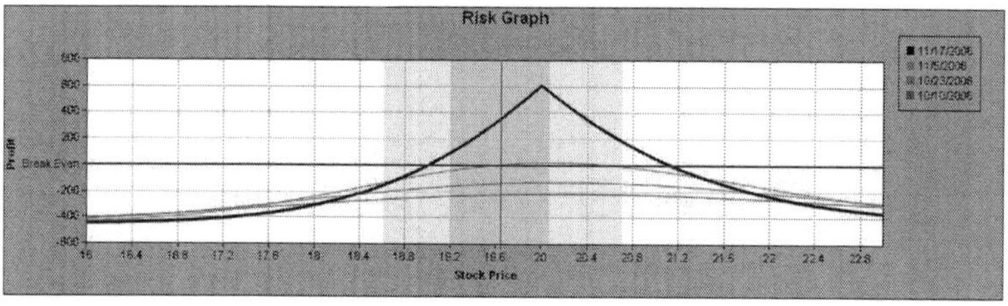

Summary

Cost of Trade	450	Max Reward	610	Delta	21.6
Current Value	225	Probable Reward	247	Theta	$5.92
Profit/Loss	-225	Risk/Max Reward	136.8%	Gamma	-35.0
Max Risk	-446	Risk/Prb Reward	55.4%	Vega	$12.13

Trade Details

Type	Qty	CostBasis	CurrValue	Strike	Expiration	Total Cost	Profit	IV	Delta
call	-15	0.7000	0.7500	20	Nov 2006	-1,050	-75	36.0600	-691.59
call	15	1.0000	0.9000	20	Dec 2006	1,500	-150	31.6900	713.19

Break Evens

	Expiration	Nov 05	Oct 23	Today
Upper B/E	21.16	20.66	0.00	0.00
Lower B/E	19.02	19.56	0.00	0.00

Trade structure is long 15 December 20 strike calls @ 1.00 each and short 15 November 20 strike calls @ .70 each. Trade cost is $450, trade risk is $450, max profit is $610

November 17, 2006 – Well GPS tried to throw a scare at me by running up to $21 which was the very top of the BE range for my trade however it just couldn't hold that level and sold back down to the $20 price range which of course was perfect for this trade.

Trade closed with a $150 profit on a $450 risk for a 33% ROR.

Symbol: GPS (19.81) **DT41 GPS call calendar** Date: 11/17/2006

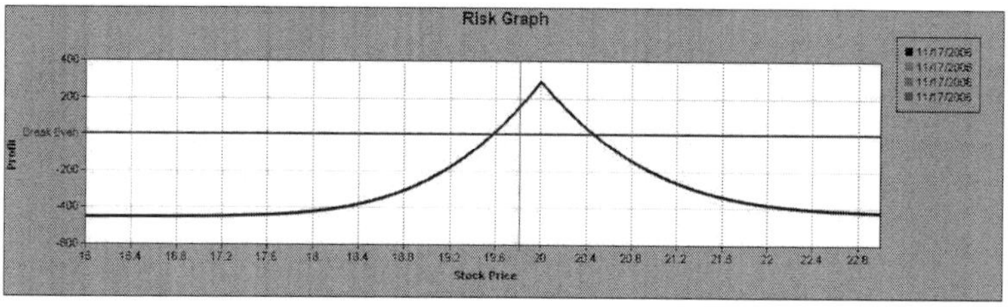

Summary

Cost of Trade	450	Max Reward	289	Delta	681.9
Current Value	600	Probable Reward	0	Theta	-$13.14
Profit/Loss	150	Risk/Max Reward	64.1%	Gamma	493.8
Max Risk	-450	Risk/Prb Reward	0%	Vega	$32.62

Trade Details

Type	Qty	CostBasis	CurrValue	Strike	Expiration	Total Cost	Profit	IV	Delta
call	-15	0.7000	0.0000	20	Nov 2006	-1,050	1,050	0.0000	0.00
call	15	1.0000	0.4000	20	Dec 2006	1,500	-900	21.9400	681.90

Break Evens

	Expiration	Nov 17	Nov 17	Today
Upper B/E	20.48	20.48	20.48	20.48
Lower B/E	19.58	19.58	19.58	19.58

October 17, 2006 – BOL.

This is the result of a trade I did on Bausch & Lomb Incorporated before they were take private by Warburg Pincus. Since it is now a privately owned company I can't show a chart of the stock.

Strategy Selection: Call Calendar Spread.

Symbol: BOL (51.51) **DT42 BOL call calendar** Date: 10/17/2006

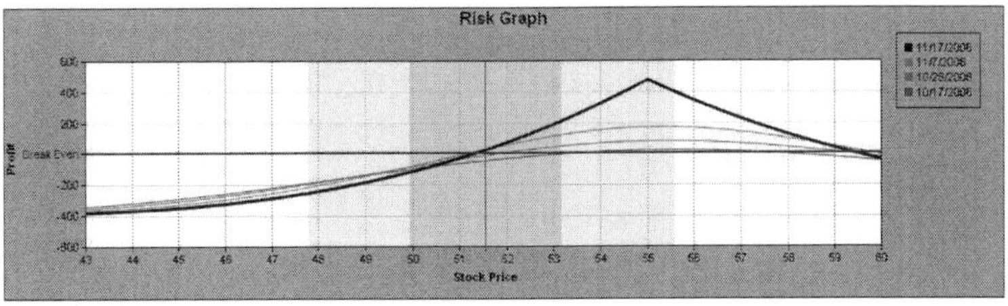

Summary

Cost of Trade	405	Max Reward	476	Delta	32.2
Current Value	360	Probable Reward	47	Theta	$3.04
Profit/Loss	-45	Risk/Max Reward	125%	Gamma	-5.9
Max Risk	-381	Risk/Prb Reward	12.4%	Vega	$14.90

Trade Details

Type	Qty	CostBasis	CurrValue	Strike	Expiration	Total Cost	Profit	IV	Delta
call	-3	0.8000	0.9000	55	Nov 2006	-240	0	33.7100	-81.33
call	3	2.1500	2.0000	55	Jan 2007	645	-45	31.7700	113.49

Break Evens

	Expiration	Nov 07	Oct 28	Today
Upper B/E	59.50	59.90	59.40	58.00
Lower B/E	51.30	51.15	51.80	53.25

Trade structure is long 3 January 2007 55 strike calls @ 2.15 each and short 3 November 55 strike calls @ .80 each. Trade cost $405, trade risk is $381, max profit is $476.

November 17, 2006 - Trade closed with a $300 loss on a $381 risk for a 79% loss on risk.

Symbol: BOL (48.61) **DT42 BOL call calendar** Date: 11/17/2006

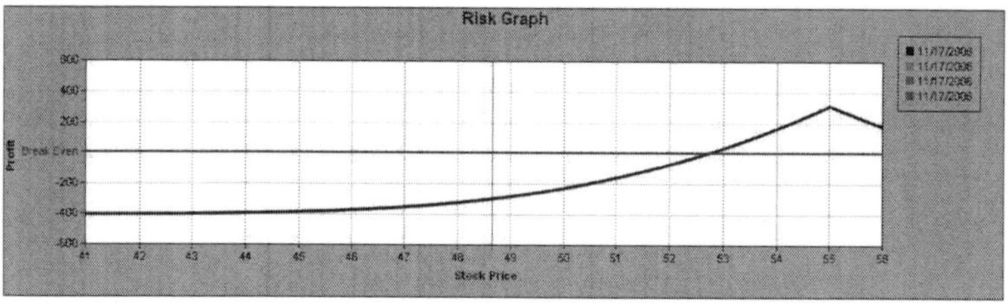

Summary

Cost of Trade	405	Max Reward	312	Delta	41.6
Current Value	105	Probable Reward	0	Theta	-$2.79
Profit/Loss	-300	Risk/Max Reward	77.3%	Gamma	12.8
Max Risk	-404	Risk/Prb Reward	0%	Vega	$13.40

Trade Details

Type	Qty	CostBasis	CurrValue	Strike	Expiration	Total Cost	Profit	IV	Delta
call	-3	0.8000	0.0000	55	Nov 2006	-240	240	0.0000	0.00
call	3	2.1500	0.3500	55	Jan 2007	645	-540	25.7300	41.62

Break Evens

	Expiration	Nov 17	Nov 17	Today
Upper B/E	52.70	52.70	52.70	52.70
Lower B/E	52.70	52.70	52.70	52.70

October 24, 2006 – SYY.

SYY is an interesting stock to read. I like the move-reverse-stagnate behavior it has exhibited in the past. The stock is in a bullish trend and MACD suggests it is going to stall and catch its breath before its next move. Stochastics is giving an early buy signal, however I am not convinced that we are going to see a strong directional move here.

Strategy Selection: Call Calendar Spread.

Symbol: SYY (34.04) **DT43 SYY call calendar** Date: 10/24/2006

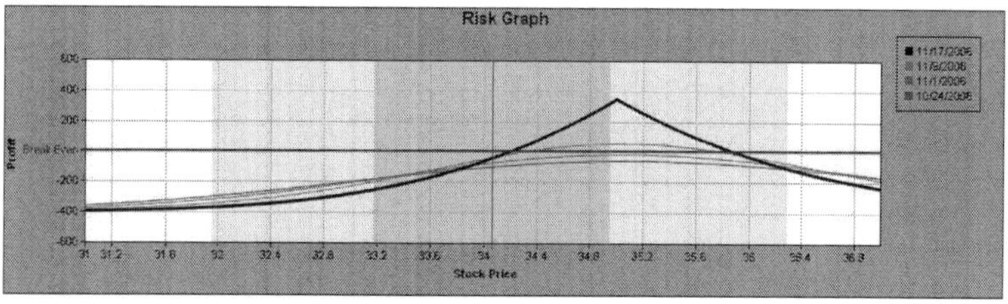

Summary

Cost of Trade	400	Max Reward	349	Delta	74.6
Current Value	300	Probable Reward	-63	Theta	$2.90
Profit/Loss	-100	Risk/Max Reward	88.7%	Gamma	-55.4
Max Risk	-393	Risk/Prb Reward	- 16.1%	Vega	$18.38

Trade Details

Type	Qty	CostBasis	CurrValue	Strike	Expiration	Total Cost	Profit	IV	Delta
call	-10	0.3000	0.4000	35	Nov 2006	-300	0	18.8700	- 295.67
call	10	0.7000	0.6000	35	Dec 2006	700	-100	19.0500	370.31

Break Evens

	Expiration	Nov 09	Nov 01	Today
Upper B/E	35.90	35.84	0.00	0.00
Lower B/E	34.20	34.30	0.00	0.00

Trade structure is long 10 December 35 strike calls @.70 each and short 10 November 35 strike calls @ .30 each. Trade cost is $400, trade risk is $400, Max profit is $350.

November 17, 2006 – Ok I can admit when I am wrong. I was wrong about the "strong directional move", a $3 dollar move on a $30 stock is strong especially in 30 days. The good news is I chose a good trade for the behavior. A long call would have been so much better, but I will take the profit here.

Trade closed with a $200 profit on a $400 risk for a 50% ROR.

Symbol: SYY (35.18) **DT43 SYY call calendar** Date: 11/17/2006

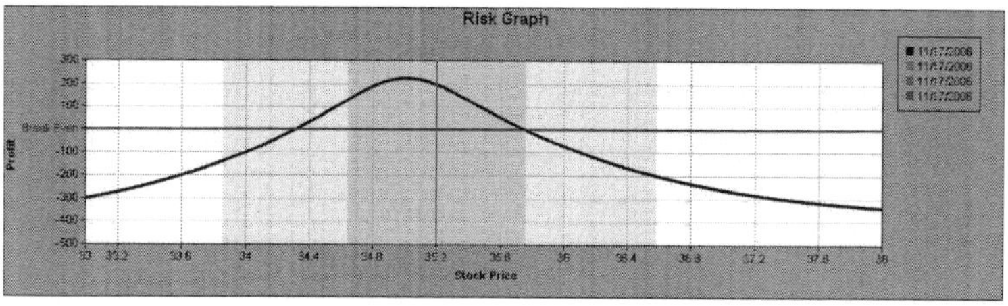

Summary

Cost of Trade	400	Max Reward	224	Delta	-442.8
Current Value	600	Probable Reward	38	Theta	NaN
Profit/Loss	200	Risk/Max Reward	66.1%	Gamma	227.0
Max Risk	-339	Risk/Prb Reward	11.3%	Vega	$38.47

Trade Details

Type	Qty	CostBasis	CurrValue	Strike	Expiration	Total Cost	Profit	IV	Delta
call	-10	0.3000	0.2000	35	Nov 2006	-300	100	1801.7600	-1,000.00
call	10	0.7000	0.8000	35	Dec 2006	700	100	17.8500	557.25

Break Evens

	Expiration	Nov 17	Nov 17	Today
Upper B/E	35.78	35.78	35.78	35.78
Lower B/E	34.32	34.32	34.32	34.32

November 2006

UTX – United Tech.			
Long Call	- $190.00	(46%)	359
SCHW – Charles Schwab			
Ratio Bull Call Spread	+ $ 60.00	13%	363
ZMH – Zimmer Holdings			
Long Call	- $250.00	(44%)	367
RMBS – Rambus, Inc.			
Long Call	+ $ 0.00	0%	371
OXY – Occidental Petrol.			
Call Calendar Spread	+ $ 0.00	0%	375

November Results – 1 Wins vs. 2 Losses & 2 Break Even

Net result - $380.00 Loss.

"I am not so much concerned with return on principal as I am on return of principle."

- Will Rogers

October 31, 2006 – UTX.

These are the kinds of stocks every investor/trader looks for. Here is a stock that is in an established trend (bullish) it is a weak trend but a trend none-the-less and it has definite "swings" inside the trend.

UTX is currently coming off of a downward swing and looks to want to retest 67ish before moving higher in its trend. Best trade under the circumstances…

Strategy Selection. Long Call. Price Target 67 and higher.

Symbol: UTX (65.72) **DT44 UTX long call** Date: 10/31/2006

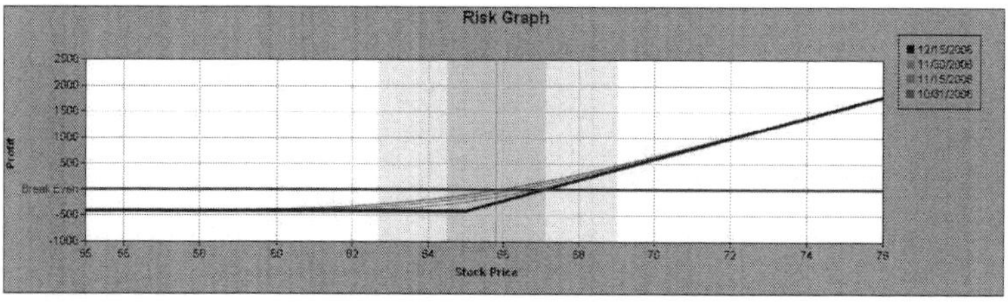

Summary

Cost of Trade	410	Max Reward	1,790	Delta	118.9
Current Value	390	Probable Reward	-166	Theta	-$3.50
Profit/Loss	-20	Risk/Max Reward	436.6%	Gamma	20.3
Max Risk	-410	Risk/Prb Reward	-40.5%	Vega	$17.89

Trade Details

Type	Qty	CostBasis	CurrValue	Strike	Expiration	Total Cost	Profit	IV	Delta
call	2	2.0500	1.9500	65	Dec 2006	410	-20	16.5700	118.93

Break Evens

	Expiration	Nov 30	Nov 15	Today
Upper B/E	67.10	66.80	66.40	65.90
Lower B/E	67.10	66.80	66.40	65.90

Trade structure is long 2 December 65 strike calls @ 2.05 each. Trade cost is $410, trade risk is $410 and max profit is unlimited.

November 1, 2006 – Hey Dart-Throw Trader. Yes? How do you feel about risk? I hate it, why? Because risk management is your number one priority. Did you check the news on this stock before you placed your trade? Yes, earnings came out on October 17, the news was already factored in. Then why did it drop on 11/1? Negative comments from the company about future earnings. Oh.

Trade closed (mental stop hit) with a $190 loss on a $410 risk for a 46% loss on risk.

Symbol: UTX (64.25) **DT44 UTX long call** Date: 11/1/2006

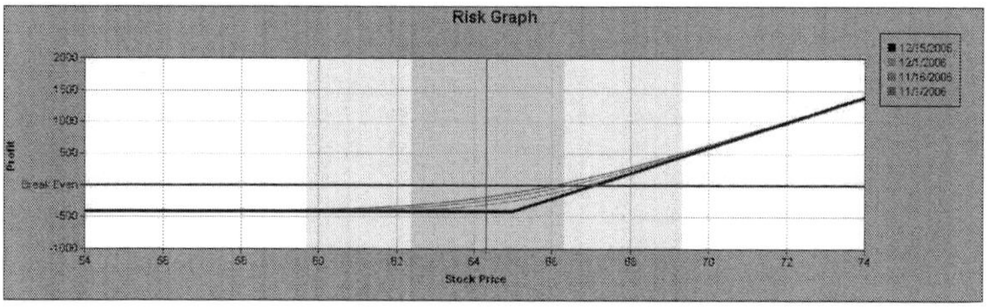

Summary

Cost of Trade	410	Max Reward	1,390	Delta	87.1
Current Value	220	Probable Reward	-235	Theta	-$3.29
Profit/Loss	-190	Risk/Max Reward	339%	Gamma	22.4
Max Risk	-410	Risk/Prb Reward	-57.3%	Vega	$17.57

Trade Details

Type	Qty	CostBasis	CurrValue	Strike	Expiration	Total Cost	Profit	IV	Delta
call	2	2.0500	1.1000	65	Dec 2006	410	-190	15.7700	87.08

Break Evens

	Expiration	Dec 01	Nov 16	Today
Upper B/E	67.10	66.90	66.50	66.10
Lower B/E	67.10	66.90	66.50	66.10

November 7 2006 – SCHW.

I am currently doing the happy Dart-Throw Trader dance. I really love what I see on this chart.

MACD is bullish (since August) MACD just crossed above its signal line while still above the zero line (strong bullish). SCHW just broke above resistance @ 18.50ish which was established in May and tested in October. SCHW broke through this resistance on a strong price move on above average volume (commitment).

Strategy Selection: Ratio Bull Call Spread.

Symbol: SCHW (18.92) **DT45 SCHW ratio bull call** Date: 11/7/2006

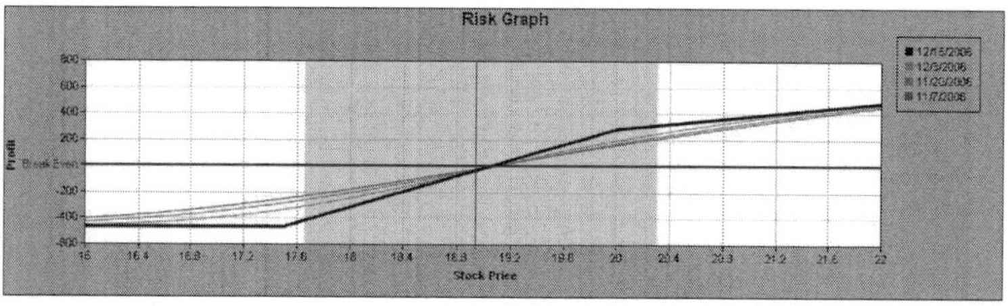

Summary

Cost of Trade	465	Max Reward	485	Delta	174.0
Current Value	440	Probable Reward	-40	Theta	-$0.69
Profit/Loss	-25	Risk/Max Reward	104.3%	Gamma	5.5
Max Risk	-465	Risk/Prb Reward	-8.6%	Vega	$1.05

Trade Details

Type	Qty	CostBasis	CurrValue	Strike	Expiration	Total Cost	Profit	IV	Delta
call	3	1.7500	1.7000	17.5	Dec 2006	525	-15	33.2600	235.59
call	-2	0.3000	0.3500	20	Dec 2006	-60	-10	30.6100	-61.56

Break Evens

	Expiration	Dec 03	Nov 20	Today
Upper B/E	19.06	19.10	19.10	19.08
Lower B/E	19.06	19.10	19.10	19.08

Trade structure is Long 3 December 17.50 strike calls @ 1.75 each and short 2 December 20 strike calls @ .30 each. Trade cost $465, trade risk is $465 and max profit is $485.

December 15, 2006 – After breaking through resistance on a strong move and increased volume.. SCHW just died. Hindsight says that a call calendar spread would have been a better trade. Oh well, I will take the profit anyway.

Trade closed with a $60 profit on a $465 risk for a 13% ROR.

Symbol: SCHW (19.33) **DT45 SCHW ratio bull call** Date: 12/15/2006

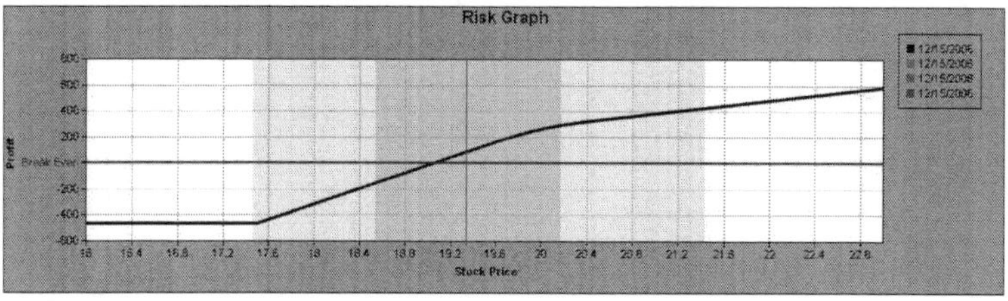

Summary

Cost of Trade	465	Max Reward	585	Delta	300.0
Current Value	525	Probable Reward	55	Theta	NaN
Profit/Loss	60	Risk/Max Reward	125.8%	Gamma	0.0
Max Risk	-465	Risk/Prb Reward	11.8%	Vega	$0.00

Trade Details

Type	Qty	CostBasis	CurrValue	Strike	Expiration	Total Cost	Profit	IV	Delta
call	3	1.7500	1.7500	17.5	Dec 2006	525	0	1.0000	300.00
call	-2	0.3000	0.0001	20	Dec 2006	-60	60	3750.0000	0.00

Break Evens

	Expiration	Dec 15	Dec 15	Today
Upper B/E	19.06	19.06	19.06	19.06
Lower B/E	19.06	19.06	19.06	19.06

November 14, 2006 – ZMH.

Ok, I got a little excited over TWX last week because of the trend it was in and the breakout that had just occurred. Maybe trading karma was trying to keep me in check... Then I look at this stock and its trend and I begin to do the Dart-Throw Trader dance all over again.

Strategy Selection: Long Call. (simply because of the cost of trade)

Symbol: ZMH (74.38) **DT46 ZMH long call** Date: 11/14/2006

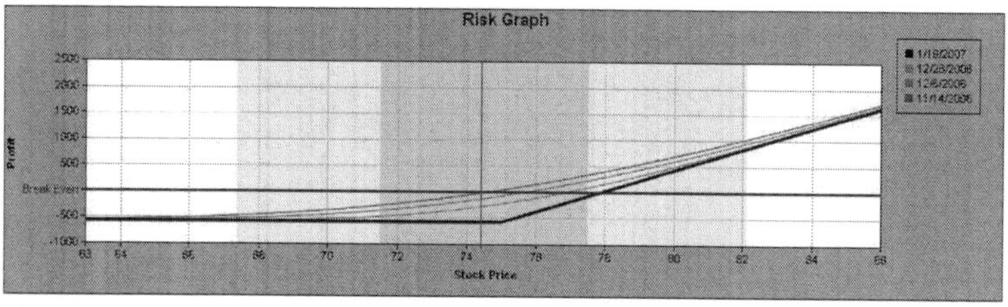

Summary

Cost of Trade	570	Max Reward	1,630	Delta	98.8
Current Value	550	Probable Reward	-268	Theta	-$4.70
Profit/Loss	-20	Risk/Max Reward	286%	Gamma	10.7
Max Risk	-570	Risk/Prb Reward	- 47.1%	Vega	$25.23

Trade Details

Type	Qty	CostBasis	CurrValue	Strike	Expiration	Total Cost	Profit	IV	Delta
call	2	2.8500	2.7500	75	Jan 2007	570	-20	23.6000	98.84

Break Evens

	Expiration	Dec 28	Dec 06	Today
Upper B/E	77.90	76.90	75.70	74.60
Lower B/E	77.90	76.90	75.70	74.60

Trade structure is long 2 January 75 strike calls @ 2.85 each.

November 24, 2006 – Apparently doing the Dart-Throw Trader dance does NOT bring good trade karma, therefore effective today all dancing will cease.

ZMH just turned. Blame on the overall market, blame it on exhaustion, blame it on the rain… doesn't matter. ZMH has turned and broken its bullish channel and hit my mental stop.

Trade closed with a loss of $250 on a risk of $570 for a 44% loss on risk.

Symbol: ZMH (72.7) **DT46 ZMH long call** Date: 11/24/2006

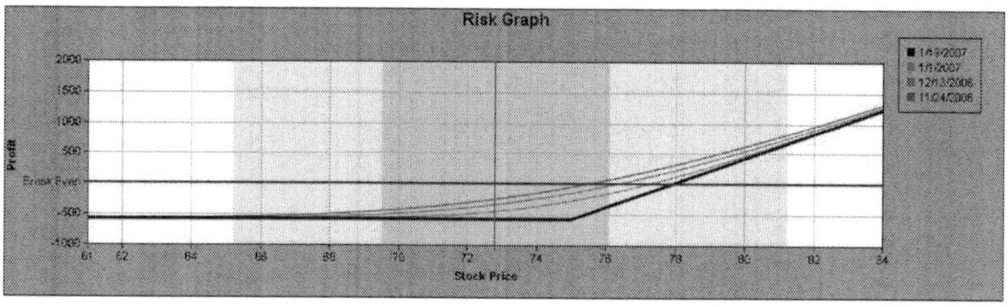

Summary

Cost of Trade	570	Max Reward	1,230	Delta	76.5
Current Value	320	Probable Reward	-372	Theta	-$4.43
Profit/Loss	-250	Risk/Max Reward	215.8%	Gamma	12.1
Max Risk	-570	Risk/Prb Reward	-65.3%	Vega	$21.73

Trade Details

Type	Qty	CostBasis	CurrValue	Strike	Expiration	Total Cost	Profit	IV	Delta
call	2	2.8500	1.6000	75	Jan 2007	570	-250	22.0800	76.48

Break Evens

	Expiration	Jan 01	Dec 13	Today
Upper B/E	77.90	77.20	76.30	75.40
Lower B/E	77.90	77.20	76.30	75.40

November 21, 2006 – RMBS.

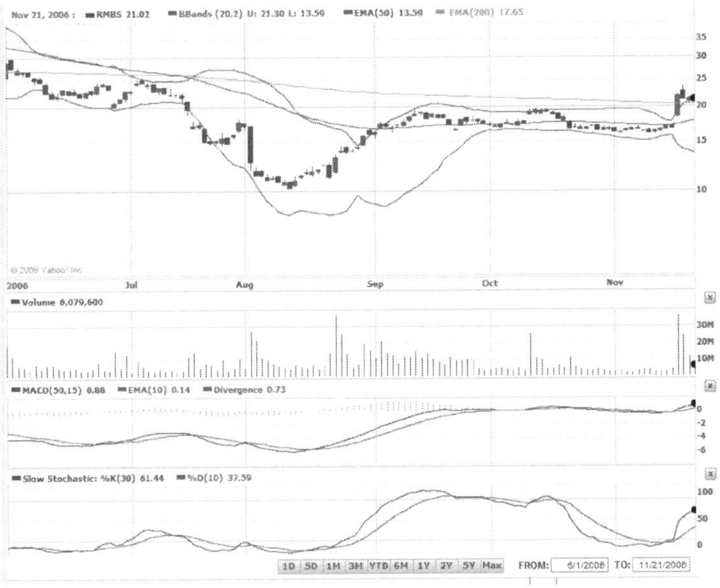

After a series of analyst downgrades and earning woes, RMBS drifted down to the $ $10 price level in August. After hitting that low RMBS began to show signs of life as many believed the stock was tremendously oversold and undervalued.

After slowly climbing back up into the $15 - $20 price range RMBS settled into a period of range bound stagnation until November 16 when a price surge based on earnings surprises caused RMBS to break above its 200 DM and for its MACD to cross the zero line on amazing volume, clearly indicating the beginning of a technical bullish trend.

Am I convinced the march back to old highs is imminent? No. However, I am never opposed to profiting from emotional moves.

Strategy Selection: Long Call.

Symbol: RMBS (21.02) **DT47 RMBS long call** Date: 11/21/2006

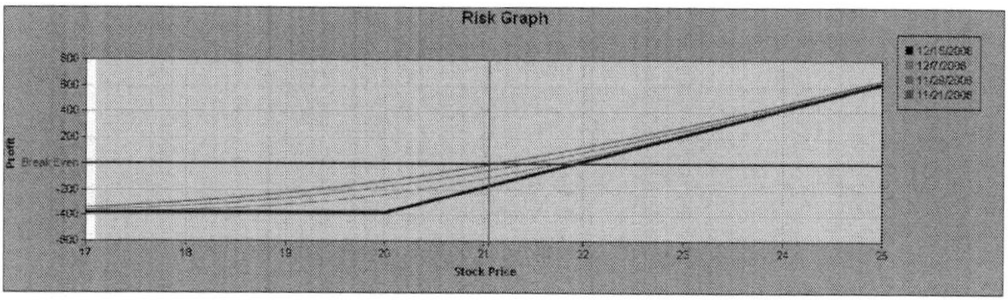

Summary

Cost of Trade	380	Max Reward	620	Delta	131.3
Current Value	370	Probable Reward	-47	Theta	-$5.06
Profit/Loss	-10	Risk/Max Reward	163.2%	Gamma	22.6
Max Risk	-380	Risk/Prb Reward	-12.4%	Vega	$3.97

Trade Details

Type	Qty	CostBasis	CurrValue	Strike	Expiration	Total Cost	Profit	IV	Delta
call	2	1.9000	1.8500	20	Dec 2006	380	-10	60.4800	131.27

Break Evens

	Expiration	Dec 07	Nov 29	Today
Upper B/E	21.90	21.75	21.45	21.10
Lower B/E	21.90	21.75	21.45	21.10

Trade structure is long 2 December 20 strike calls @ 1.90 each. Trade cost is $380, trade risk is $380, max profit is unlimited.

December 1, 2006 – With the formation of a "Three Crows" candlestick pattern, the fact that RMBS has lost its emotional push higher and the reality that there is not a viable adjustment to make in the trade. I am pulling the trigger on this one today.

Trade closed for $0 on $380 risk for a 0% ROR.

Symbol: RMBS (21.51) **DT47 RMBS long call** Date: 12/1/2006

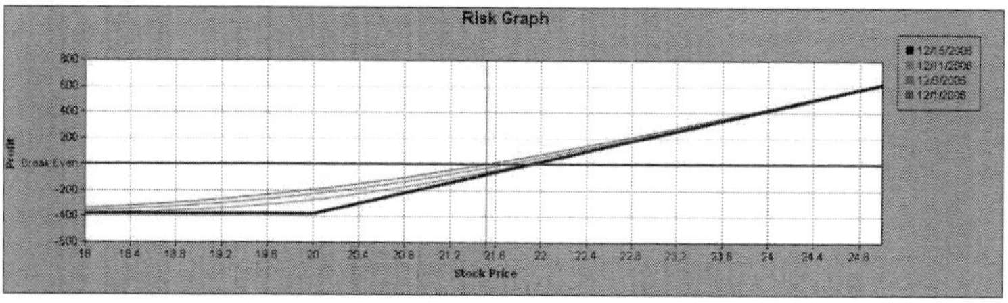

Summary

Cost of Trade	380	Max Reward	620	Delta	151.1
Current Value	380	Probable Reward	-23	Theta	-$5.66
Profit/Loss	0	Risk/Max Reward	163.2%	Gamma	25.3
Max Risk	-380	Risk/Prb Reward	-6%	Vega	$2.65

Trade Details

Type	Qty	CostBasis	CurrValue	Strike	Expiration	Total Cost	Profit	IV	Delta
call	2	1.9000	1.9000	20	Dec 2006	380	0	58.9900	151.05

Break Evens

	Expiration	Dec 11	Dec 06	Today
Upper B/E	21.90	21.84	21.70	21.52
Lower B/E	21.90	21.84	21.70	21.52

November 28, 2006 – OXY.

I have to catch myself sometimes before I start writing in this journal... I want to write how this is a beautiful, tight range, trending stock that is destined to make any trader money. That is what I want to write. So I will.

OXY is all of those things. My only hesitation with this stock is the earnings report which is due to be released in the next 30-45 days, what kind of an impact will it have on the stock. Will it react like it did in May and September or will "efficient market" theory take over?

Its too early to do a straddle/strangle, personally I want to sit back and wait a week or so and position myself to take advantage of earnings but in this challenge I don't have that luxury. Therefore I must trade its current behavior... mildly bullish.

Strategy Selection: Call Calendar Spread.

Symbol: OXY (48.17) **DT48 OXY call calendar** Date: 11/28/2006

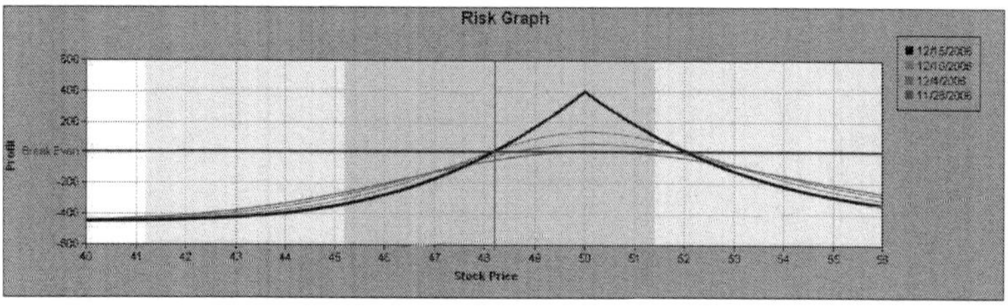

Summary

Cost of Trade	450	Max Reward	401	Delta	55.7
Current Value	400	Probable Reward	-108	Theta	$4.44
Profit/Loss	-50	Risk/Max Reward	89.5%	Gamma	-21.0
Max Risk	-448	Risk/Prb Reward	-24.2%	Vega	$17.46

Trade Details

Type	Qty	CostBasis	CurrValue	Strike	Expiration	Total Cost	Profit	IV	Delta
call	-5	0.4500	0.5500	50	Dec 2006	-225	0	26.7800	-135.76
call	5	1.3500	1.2500	50	Jan 2007	675	-50	27.2000	191.44

Break Evens

	Expiration	Dec 10	Dec 04	Today
Upper B/E	52.10	52.25	51.90	51.00
Lower B/E	48.15	48.10	48.50	49.45

Trade structure is long 5 January 50 strike calls @ 1.35 each and short 5 December 50 strike calls @ .45 each. Trade cost is $450, trade risk is $450, max profit is $400.

December 15, 2006 – Once again I believe I have become a victim of the "urban legend" of Max Pain. OXY was performing as it should on 12/13 it was trading at $50 which was the absolutely best place the stock could be for this trade to make max gain.

On 12/14 the day before expiration OXY makes a $2 price move to $52 and effectively blows my trade out. Remember... MAX PAIN.

Trade closed with a $0 profit on a risk of $450 for a 0% ROR.

Symbol: OXY (51.92) **DT48 OXY call calendar** Date: 12/15/2006

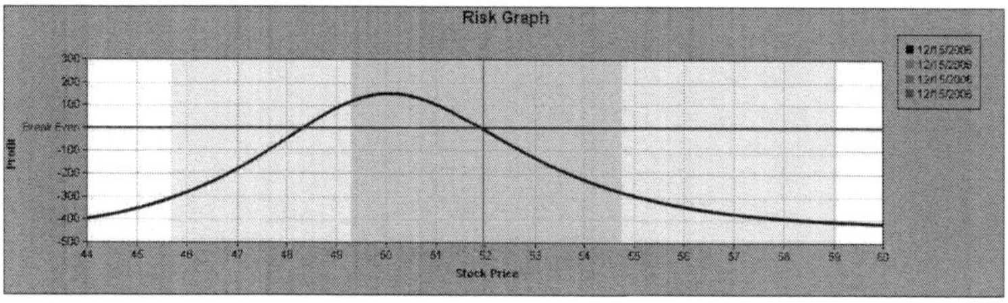

Summary

Cost of Trade	450	Max Reward	151	Delta	-153.1
Current Value	450	Probable Reward	-114	Theta	NaN
Profit/Loss	0	Risk/Max Reward	36.5%	Gamma	40.7
Max Risk	-415	Risk/Prb Reward	-27.5%	Vega	$28.20

Trade Details

Type	Qty	CostBasis	CurrValue	Strike	Expiration	Total Cost	Profit	IV	Delta
call	-5	0.4500	1.9500	50	Dec 2006	-225	-750	7558.5900	-500.00
call	5	1.3500	2.8500	50	Jan 2007	675	750	26.8100	346.94

Break Evens

	Expiration	Dec 15	Dec 15	Today
Upper B/E	51.95	51.95	51.95	51.95
Lower B/E	48.35	48.35	48.35	48.35

December 2006

PH – Parker Hannifin			
Condor	+ $120.00	31%	381
DE – Deere & Co.			
Call Calendar Spread	+ $360.00	95%	385
ED – Consolidated Edison			
Call Calendar Spread	+ $ 70.00	15%	389
MMM – 3M Co.			
Bear Put Spread	+ $130.00	35%	393

May Results – 4 Wins vs. 0 Losses

Net result $680.00 Profit.

"Whenever you see a successful business, someone once made a courageous decision."

- Peter Drucker

December 5, 2006 – PH.

- Prices reflect a 3/2 Split

Now here is a stock that has run out of bullish steam and has begun its trek into the world of stagnation. I am of the opinion that every stock must "rest" after a move of significance (in relation to itself).

During PH's bullish move it managed to trade in a 2-4 range as it climbed in price, not that it has come to a period of rest that 2-4 range should remain intact only now on a more sideways move.

Strategy Selection: Condor.

Symbol: PH (83.67) **DT49 PH condor** Date: 12/5/2006

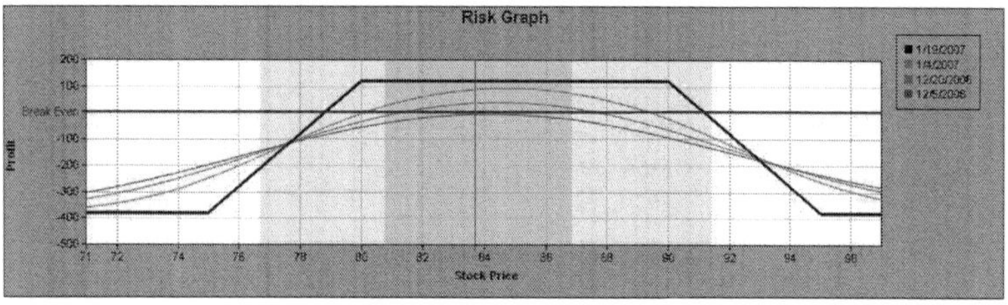

Summary

Cost of Trade	-120	Max Reward	120	Delta	3.0
Current Value	-125	Probable Reward	60	Theta	$2.51
Profit/Loss	-5	Risk/Max Reward	31.6%	Gamma	-6.0
Max Risk	-380	Risk/Prb Reward	15.8%	Vega	-$10.90

Trade Details

Type	Qty	CostBasis	CurrValue	Strike	Expiration	Total Cost	Profit	IV	Delta
call	-1	0.6000	0.7000	90	Jan 2007	-60	5	20.8500	-17.29
call	1	0.1000	0.0500	95	Jan 2007	10	-5	18.0500	2.55
put	-1	1.0000	1.2000	80	Jan 2007	-100	0	21.2600	25.63
put	1	0.3000	0.2500	75	Jan 2007	30	-5	22.9900	-7.92

Break Evens

	Expiration	Jan 04	Dec 20	Today
Upper B/E	91.20	89.50	87.80	0.00
Lower B/E	78.80	80.10	81.30	0.00

Trade structure is:

Long 1 January 95 strike call @ .10 each and short 1 January 90 strike call @ .60 each
Long 1 January 75 strike put @ .30 each and short 1 January 80 strike put @ 1.00 each

Trade cost is $120, trade risk is $380, max profit is $120.

January 19, 2007 – PH held its range. Trade closed with a $120 profit on a $380 risk for a 31% ROR.

Symbol: PH (81.85)	**DT49 PH condor**	Date: 1/19/2007

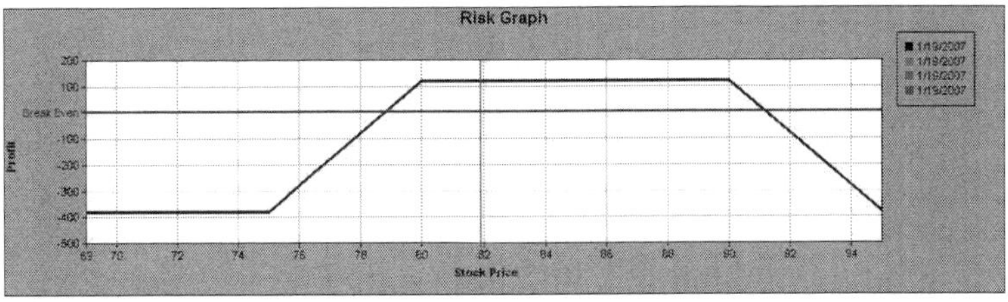

Summary

Cost of Trade	-120	Max Reward	120	Delta	0.0
Current Value	0	Probable Reward	0	Theta	$0.00
Profit/Loss	120	Risk/Max Reward	31.6%	Gamma	0.0
Max Risk	-380	Risk/Prb Reward	0%	Vega	$0.00

Trade Details

Type	Qty	CostBasis	CurrValue	Strike	Expiration	Total Cost	Profit	IV	Delta
call	-1	0.6000	0.0000	90	Jan 2007	-60	60	0.0000	0.00
call	1	0.1000	0.0000	95	Jan 2007	10	-10	0.0000	0.00
put	-1	1.0000	0.0000	80	Jan 2007	-100	100	0.0000	0.00
put	1	0.3000	0.0000	75	Jan 2007	30	-30	0.0000	0.00

Break Evens

	Expiration	Jan 19	Jan 19	Today
Upper B/E	91.20	91.20	91.20	91.20
Lower B/E	78.80	78.80	78.80	78.80

"Wide diversification is only required when investors do not understand what they are doing."

- Warren Buffett

December 12, 2006 – DE.

* Reflects 2/1 Stock Split

Being from Arkansas this is a stock I understand, in fact I would go so far as to say that DE is the nemesis of Mr. Bubble. DE makes getting dirty fun.

DE is currently in a well established slow moving bullish trend and all indications suggest it will continue. The trend is too slow for a straight call purchase or Bull Call Spread so we have to stick with the tried and true Call Calendar Spread.

Strategy Selection: Call Calendar Spread.

Symbol: DE (94.49) **DT50 DE call calendar** Date: 12/12/2006

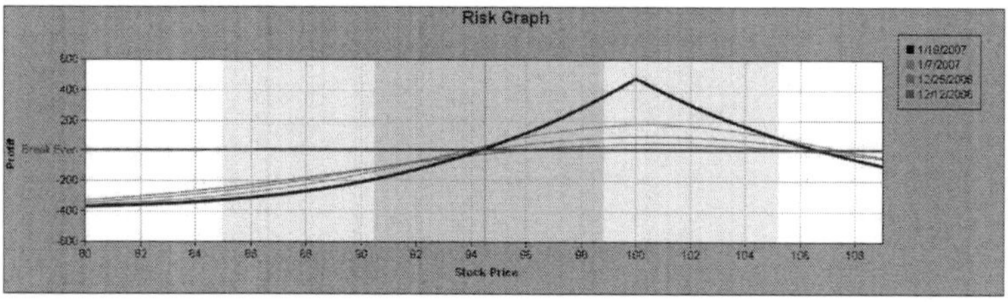

Summary

Cost of Trade	380	Max Reward	480	Delta	20.0
Current Value	360	Probable Reward	19	Theta	$1.82
Profit/Loss	-20	Risk/Max Reward	130.7%	Gamma	-2.4
Max Risk	-367	Risk/Prb Reward	5.3%	Vega	$16.03

Trade Details

Type	Qty	CostBasis	CurrValue	Strike	Expiration	Total Cost	Profit	IV	Delta
call	-2	1.3000	1.3000	100	Jan 2007	-260	0	26.6100	-54.52
call	2	3.2000	3.1000	100	Mar 2007	640	-20	27.0800	74.52

Break Evens

	Expiration	Jan 07	Dec 25	Today
Upper B/E	106.80	107.80	107.40	106.30
Lower B/E	94.30	93.80	94.30	95.60

Trade structure is long 2 March 100 strike calls @ 3.20 each and short 2 January 100 strike calls @ 1.30 each. Trade cost is $380, trade risk is $367, max profit is $480.

January 19, 2007 – DE performed right on script. I love a predictable pattern; I get to see these way too rarely.

Trade closed with a $360 profit on a $380 risk for a 95% ROR.

Symbol: DE (98.7) **DT50 DE call calendar** Date: 1/19/2007

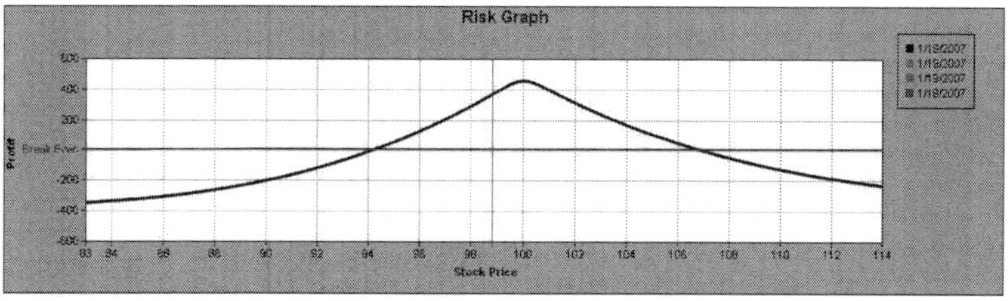

Summary

Cost of Trade	380	Max Reward	457	Delta	95.7
Current Value	740	Probable Reward	0	Theta	NaN
Profit/Loss	360	Risk/Max Reward	132.1%	Gamma	7.5
Max Risk	-346	Risk/Prb Reward	0%	Vega	$30.80

Trade Details

Type	Qty	CostBasis	CurrValue	Strike	Expiration	Total Cost	Profit	IV	Delta
call	-2	1.3000	0.0001	100	Jan 2007	-260	260	1328.1300	0.00
call	2	3.2000	3.7000	100	Mar 2007	640	100	27.4000	95.70

Break Evens

	Expiration	Jan 19	Jan 19	Today
Upper B/E	107.00	107.00	107.00	107.00
Lower B/E	94.20	94.20	94.20	94.20

December 19, 2006 – ED.

Another well established slow bullish trending stock. The only downside to this is that it has only moved $5 in 6 months. Too slow for a straight call and too slow for a BullCall spread... Only one strategy can take full advantage of this trade... Call Calendar Spread.

Strategy Selection: Call Calendar Spread.

Symbol: ED (48.38) **DT51 ED call calendar** Date: 12/19/2006

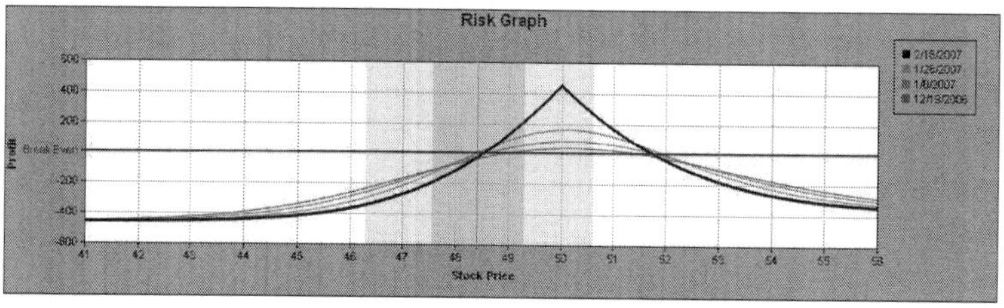

Summary

Cost of Trade	455	Max Reward	452		Delta		79.1
Current Value	420	Probable Reward	-2		Theta		$0.89
Profit/Loss	-35	Risk/Max Reward	99.4%		Gamma		-30.9
Max Risk	-455	Risk/Prb Reward	-0.5%		Vega		$38.01

Trade Details

Type	Qty	CostBasis	CurrValue	Strike	Expiration	Total Cost	Profit	IV	Delta
call	-7	0.3500	0.3500	50	Feb 2007	-245	0	11.7000	-182.26
call	7	1.0000	0.9500	50	May 2007	700	-35	12.4000	261.37

Break Evens

	Expiration	Jan 28	Jan 08	Today
Upper B/E	51.80	52.00	51.90	51.60
Lower B/E	48.55	48.40	48.55	48.90

Trade structure is long 7 May 2007, 50 strike calls @ 1.00 each and short 7 February 2007, 50 strike calls @ .35 each. Trade cost is $455, trade risk is $455, max profit is $452.

February 16, 2006 – As a trader with over 20 years of experience in the financial industry I have seen some amazing and bizarre things. This trade is one of those things.

When this trade was entered on 12/19/2006 ED closed @ $48.38. Since that date ED has risen as high as $49.28 and fallen as low as $47.07 which is obviously a vary narrow $2 trading range.

What is remarkable is that almost 2 months after this trade was entered I find my self at expiration of the February contracts and ED is trading @ $48.51... $ 0.13 from its price at entry. So basically in two months... This Stock Did Not Move.

Trade Closed with a profit of $70 on a risk of $455 for a 15% ROR.

Symbol: ED (48.38) **DT51 ED call calendar** Date: 02/16/2007

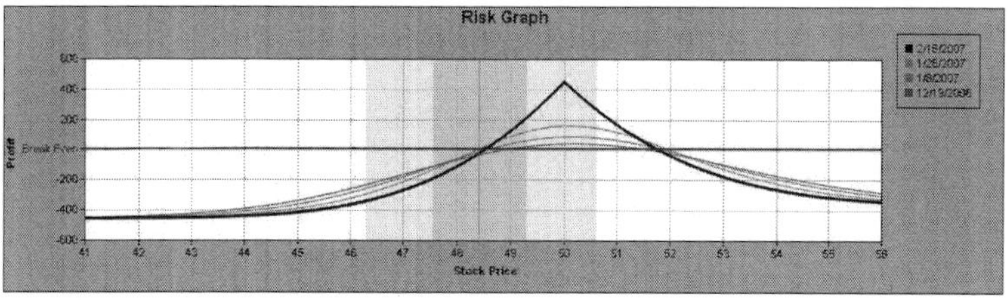

Summary

Cost of Trade	455	Max Reward	452	Delta	79.1
Current Value	420	Probable Reward	-2	Theta	$0.89
Profit/Loss	70	Risk/Max Reward	99.4%	Gamma	-30.9
Max Risk	-455	Risk/Prb Reward	-0.5%	Vega	$38.01

Trade Details

Type	Qty	CostBasis	CurrValue	Strike	Expiration	Total Cost	Profit	IV	Delta
call	-7	0.3500	0.0000	50	Feb 2007	-245	0	11.7000	000.00
call	7	1.0000	0.7500	50	May 2007	700	-175	12.4000	134.05

December 26, 2006 – MMM.

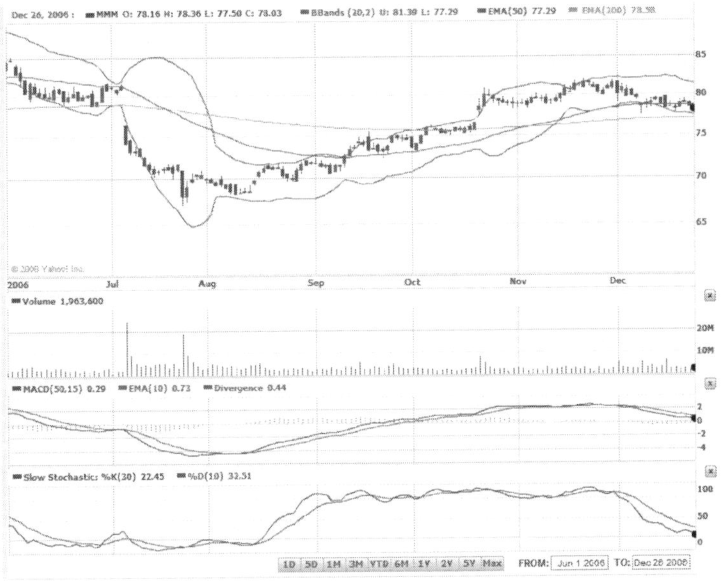

The last trade of the year and the last trade of the challenge. MMM is one of the most predictable (for me) stocks I have ever traded. It consistently does what I expect it to do, I can only hope that for the last trade of the challenge MMM holds to my expectations at least one last time.

Obviously MMM has been in a slow bullish trend, however, it would appear that MMM is gearing up to exhibit past behavior. As the bullish trend rolls into a bearish trend MMM is doing what it normally does heading into January, it is selling off as the end of year profit takers and fund managers re-adjust their portfolios for the new year.

Strategy Selection: Bear Put Spread.

Symbol: MMM (78.03) **DT52 MMM bear call** Date: 12/26/2006

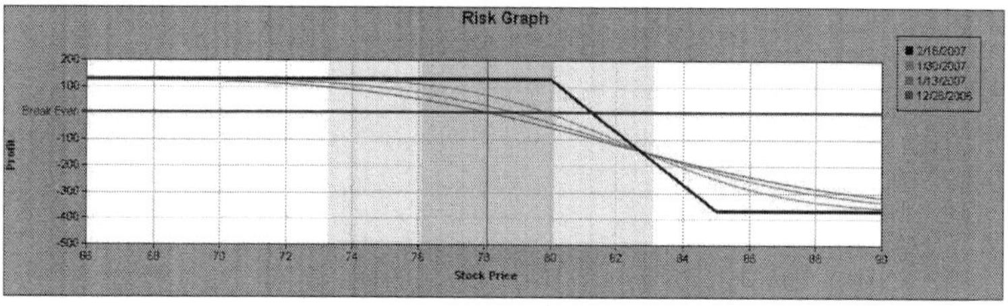

Summary

Cost of Trade	-130	Max Reward	130	Delta	-27.4
Current Value	-125	Probable Reward	82	Theta	$1.20
Profit/Loss	5	Risk/Max Reward	35.1%	Gamma	-2.9
Max Risk	-370	Risk/Prb Reward	22.2%	Vega	-$5.51

Trade Details

Type	Qty	CostBasis	CurrValue	Strike	Expiration	Total Cost	Profit	IV	Delta
call	-1	1.6000	1.5500	80	Feb 2007	-160	5	19.8800	-39.14
call	1	0.3000	0.3000	85	Feb 2007	30	0	18.2300	11.74

Break Evens

	Expiration	Jan 30	Jan 13	Today
Upper B/E	81.30	80.00	79.10	78.30
Lower B/E	81.30	80.00	79.10	78.30

Trade structure is long 1 February 85 strike put @ .30 each and short 1 February 80 strike put @ 1.60 each. Trade cost is $130 credit, trade risk is $370, max profit is $130.

February 16, 2006 – The MMM January sell off occurred as expected, only this time it was far more abrupt and short-lived than history would have suggested. In fact MMM looked to want to rally back and blow me out of my trade... alas, it did not occur.

Trade closed with a $130 profit on a risk of $370 for a 35% ROR.

Symbol: MMM (76.84) **DT52 MMM bear call** Date: 2/16/2007

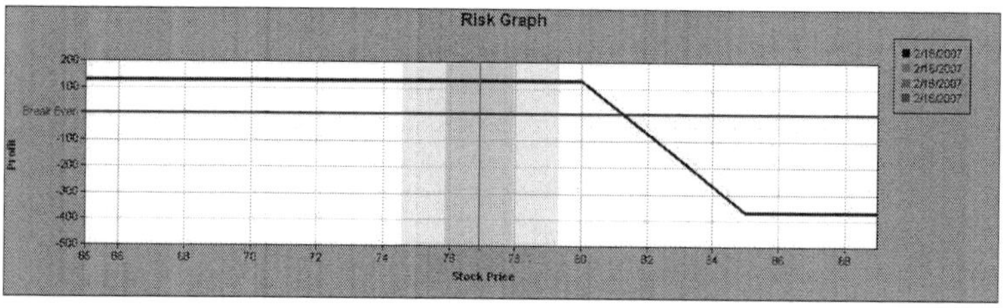

Summary

Cost of Trade	-130	Max Reward	130	Delta	0.0
Current Value	0	Probable Reward	129	Theta	$0.00
Profit/Loss	130	Risk/Max Reward	35.1%	Gamma	0.0
Max Risk	-370	Risk/Prb Reward	34.9%	Vega	$0.00

Trade Details

Type	Qty	CostBasis	CurrValue	Strike	Expiration	Total Cost	Profit	IV	Delta
call	-1	1.6000	0.0000	80	Feb 2007	-160	160	0.0000	0.00
call	1	0.3000	0.0000	85	Feb 2007	30	-30	0.0000	0.00

Break Evens

	Expiration	Feb 16	Feb 16	Today
Upper B/E	81.30	81.30	81.30	81.30
Lower B/E	81.30	81.30	81.30	81.30

	Starting amount	$5,000.00

Trade	Gain/Loss	Balance	Trade	Gain/Loss	Balance
#1 USB	-$140.00	$4,860.00	#27 PG	$690.00	$11,475.00
#2 CDWC	$80.00	$4,940.00	#28 PMI	$210.00	$11,685.00
#3 SYMC	-$30.00	$4,910.00	#29 TGT	$570.00	$12,255.00
#4 GPS	$280.00	$5,190.00	#30 LEG	$40.00	$12,295.00
#5 CSCO	$1,320.00	$6,510.00	#31 PDE	$165.00	$12,460.00
#6 DD	$420.00	$6,930.00	#32 TWX	-$225.00	$12,235.00
#7 ROH	$725.00	$7,655.00	#33 BMY	$285.00	$12,520.00
#8 LLTC	$180.00	$7,835.00	#34 AIV	$1,040.00	$13,560.00
#9 DUK	$180.00	$8,015.00	#35 PTEN	-$270.00	$13,290.00
#10 CCI	-$80.00	$7,935.00	#36 WMB	$300.00	$13,590.00
#11 KBH	$460.00	$8,395.00	#37 SEPR	$160.00	$13,750.00
#12 CNP	$250.00	$8,645.00	#38 SLM	-$130.00	$13,620.00
#13 JNPR	$0.00	$8,645.00	#39 GOOG	$2,070.00	$15,690.00
#14 SWK	$460.00	$9,105.00	#40 PFE	$100.00	$15,790.00
#15 KMB	-$20.00	$9,085.00	#41 GPS	$150.00	$15,940.00
#16 GPS	-$70.00	$9,015.00	#42 BOL	-$300.00	$15,640.00
#17 FRX	$320.00	$9,335.00	#43 SYY	$200.00	$15,840.00
#18 RYL	$460.00	$9,795.00	#44 UTX	-$190.00	$15,650.00
#19 OCR	-$125.00	$9,670.00	#45 SCHW	$60.00	$15,710.00
#20 XTO	-$130.00	$9,540.00	#46 ZMH	-$250.00	$15,460.00
#21 UST	$315.00	$9,855.00	#47 RMBS	$0.00	$15,460.00
#22 EBAY	-$50.00	$9,805.00	#48 OXY	$0.00	$15,460.00
#23 IBM	-$220.00	$9,585.00	#49 PH	$120.00	$15,580.00
#24 KIM	$450.00	$10,035.00	#50 DE	$360.00	$15,940.00
#25 DOV	$720.00	$10,755.00	#51 ED	$70.00	$16,010.00
#26 DUK	$30.00	$10,785.00	#52 MMM	$130.00	$16,140.00

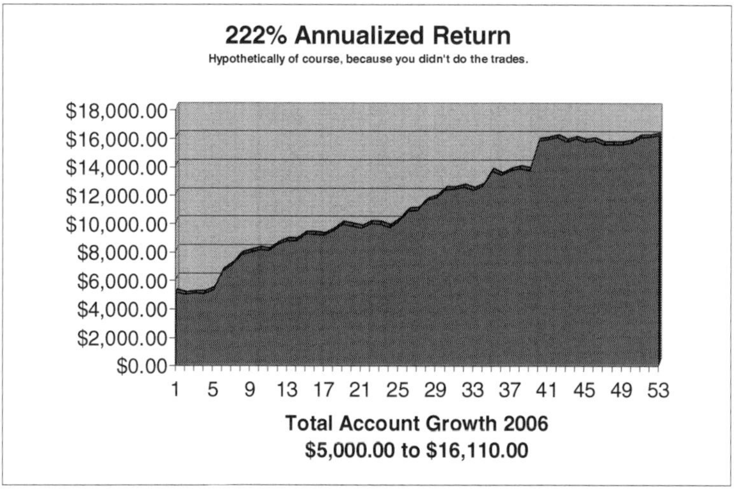

NO REPRESENTATION IS BEING MADE THAT ANY ACCOUNT WILL OR IS LIKELY TO ACHIEVE PROFIT OR LOSSES SIMILAR TO THOSE SHOWN.

Section 5 – What Does The Future Hold For Dart-Throw Trading?

The Dart-Throw Traders Final Thoughts...

"If you don't profit from your investment mistakes, someone else will."

- Yale Hirsch

The Dart-Throw Traders Final Thoughts...

I am often asked... "Jimmy, is there a future in dart-throw trading?" and my response is... "I don't know".

When it comes to the financial markets, I am confident about many things; one is that the markets are constantly in a state of change and evolution, and another is that the vast majority of investors who put their money at risk do not continue their education at the same pace the markets evolve.

Fortunately, for all of us, the basics will always remain true. In other words, regardless of what stock you choose to invest in, how much you choose to invest, the time frame you choose to stay in your position, or any of a hundred other factors to evaluate, one thing remains true...

The asset you choose is going to go up in value, down in value, or stay the same. It can't do anything else. Because of that fact, it is important that we always remember to manage our risk.

"If you do not effectively manage your risk you will effectively have no risk to manage"

- Jimmy Slagle

Do I believe that the average educated investor could literally throw darts – pick stocks – make money? Yes, and I believe that this book has proven that to an extent.

I also believe that the vast majority of investors will not purposely immerse themselves in the education necessary to do so. However, if you believe that you are one of the few who has the desire, motivation, and self-control to reach a new level of training, I would invite you to join me as I once again challenge my self to throw darts, pick stocks, and make money.

Beginning in the first quarter of 2012 I am going to issue another challenge to myself. It will follow the same basic rules as described in earlier chapters, only this time I am going to allow others to follow along. This time around, I have three specific outcomes I will attempt to obtain.

1. **My first goal is to teach others how to Throw Darts – Pick Stocks – Make Money.**
2. **My second goal is to (once again) keep a journal of this adventure, only this time it will be online for the Dart-Throw Insiders to join in with.**
3. **I will attempt to raise $100,000 for various charities by Throwing Darts – Picking Stocks – Making Money.**

I am confident that one of two outcomes will occur.

1. **I will reach my 3 stated objectives thereby once again proving that I can Throw Darts – Pick Stocks – Make Money...**
2. **Or I will Crash and Burn under the public eye.**

Either way, this next round of throwing darts will be the most fun for me, because I now have a better understanding of what is possible and what is probable.

I now know that I am more capable of responding when others react because of the speed of information that is available and the tools that investors/traders can use.

If you are reading this book during the 2012 $100,000 Charity Challenge, then I would invite you to visit www.dartthrowtrading.com and see how you can participate.

If you are reading this after the challenge has completed, I would invite you to stop by www.dartthrowtrading.com and see how I did... I either reached my goals or crashed and burned. Either way, I am sure it was a wonderful ride.

Thanks for choosing to explore the world of the Dart-Throw Trader. I hope you leave with more than you brought.

Jimmy Slagle
The Dart-Throw Trader
November 2011

"If you know what you are doing you can simply place the stock page on a wall, throw a dart, randomly pick a stock and make money."

- Jimmy Slagle, The Dart-Throw Trader

8841147R00228

Made in the USA
San Bernardino, CA
25 February 2014